YOU MEAN

New Help for

I DON'T *HAVE*

Depression, Anxiety,

TO FEEL

and Addiction

THIS WAY?

With a Foreword by Harrison G. Pope, Jr., M.D.,
and James I. Hudson, M.D.

Colette Dowling

BANTAM BOOKS

NEW YORK · TORONTO · LONDON · SYDNEY · AUCKLAND

YOU MEAN I DON'T *HAVE* TO FEEL THIS WAY?

A Bantam Book / published by arrangement with Macmillan Publishing Co. Inc.

PUBLISHING HISTORY
Scribner's edition published 1991
Bantam edition / June 1993

Library of Congress Cataloging-in-Publication Data
Dowling, Colette.
   You mean I don't have to feel this way? : new help for depression, anxiety, and addiction / Colette Dowling ; with a foreword by Harrison G. Pope, Jr., and James I. Hudson.
      p.   cm.
   Originally published: New York : Scribner, 1991.
   Includes bibliographical references and index.
   ISBN 0-553-37169-X
   1. Depression, Mental—Chemotherapy. 2. Anxiety—Chemotherapy.
3. Compulsive behavior—Chemotherapy. 4. Manic-depressive psychoses—Chemotherapy. 5. Affective disorders—Popular works.
I. Title.
RC537.D68   1993
616.85'27061—dc20   92-46657
                                                           CIP

Published simultaneously in the United States and Canada

Bantam Books are published by Bantam Books, a division of Bantam Doubleday Dell Publishing Group, Inc. Its trademark, consisting of the words "Bantam Books" and the portrayal of a rooster, is Registered in U.S. Patent and Trademark Office and in other countries. Marca Registrada. Bantam Books, 1540 Broadway, New York, New York 10036.

PRINTED IN THE UNITED STATES OF AMERICA

FFG   0   9   8   7   6   5

To Gabrielle, with love and gratitude

Psychiatry has labored too long under the delusion that every emotional malfunction requires an endless talking out of everything the patient ever experienced.

Nathan Kline

Contents

···

Foreword

by Harrison G. Pope, Jr., M.D.
Associate Professor of Psychiatry, Harvard Medical School, and
Staff Psychiatrist, McLean Hospital, Belmont, Massachusetts

and James I. Hudson, M.D.
Associate Professor of Psychiatry, Harvard Medical School, and
Staff Psychiatrist, McLean Hospital, Belmont, Massachusetts

Millions, if not tens of millions, of Americans suffer from serious mood and anxiety disorders at some time in their lives. Unfortunately many are not aware that they may be experiencing a biological illness caused by a chemical imbalance in the brain. They attribute their mood swings, their anxieties, and related symptoms such as compulsive eating and drug-taking behaviors to defects in their own personalities, problems with their social relationships, or to other external factors. Often they are reinforced in such beliefs by popular literature and by messages in the media that obscure the fact that these are medically treatable conditions. Women with bulimia are told that their problems are due to society's oppression of the female sex or to flawed relationships in their families. Men and women with substance abuse problems are told that they are "addicts"—and the possibility of an underlying psychiatric illness may never be considered. And many men, women, and children with depressive or anxiety syndromes may suffer for years, unrecognized and undiagnosed.

Mood and anxiety disorders can appear in many forms. Major depression, one of the most common forms, can rob the individual of his or her interest in life, and profoundly impair sleep, appetite, attention, memory, and the ability to perform routine tasks. Manic-depressive illness (bipolar disorder) can produce "highs"—weeks or months of unnatural euphoria, extreme agitation, irritability, racing thoughts, sleeplessness, and reckless behavior—alternating with protracted "lows" of major depression.

Closely related illnesses include anxiety syndromes such as panic disorder (the syndrome of sudden panic attacks) and agoraphobia (the fear of going out in public places). Obsessive-compulsive disorder, another anxiety syndrome, can cause crippling compulsive behaviors in which the sufferer may spend hours each day in senseless rituals: constantly washing hands or endlessly checking to see that the door is locked. Research has suggested that the family of mood and anxiety disorders also includes bulimia nervosa, the syndrome of compulsive eating binges and self-induced vomiting that afflicts a significant percentage of young American women. Another serious cause of suffering among women, premenstrual syndrome, also appears to be related biologically to mood disorders. And addictive behaviors, including alcohol, marijuana, and cocaine dependence, may often develop because an individual has unknowingly been trying to "self-treat" an underlying mood or anxiety syndrome.

Remarkably, for years now, doctors have been able to treat these conditions effectively with safe, nonaddictive medications, including antidepressants, lithium, and a number of new agents. Yet it is estimated that only a small fraction—perhaps fewer than 10 percent—of individuals with mood disorders are correctly treated. Why?

In most cases, the problem is simply a lack of knowledge on the part of both those who suffer and those who treat. First, victims of these disorders are often not aware that they have a readily treatable condition, and so they fail to seek the help of a professional. Second, even when they consult a professional—a counselor, a psychotherapist, a family doctor, or a psychiatrist—studies have shown that the majority of such patients receive inappropriate or inadequate treatment. We have known for thirty years, for example, that the syndrome of panic attacks usually responds dramatically to even modest doses of antidepressant medications. These medications are not habit-forming and do no long-term harm to the body. Yet a majority of sufferers from panic disorder spend needless months or years in psychotherapy, where they are inappropriately told that antidepressants are a "crutch" to be avoided. Patients with major depression are similarly often misdiagnosed or denied a trial of antidepressants while they receive other therapies of unproven efficacy. And when such patients are treated with antidepressants, they often receive inadequate doses, or suffer needless side effects, because many general physicians and even psychiatrists are simply not sufficiently familiar with the proper use of these drugs.

Similarly, women with bulimia nervosa are often treated with ineffective psychological treatments. Sometimes, for example, the patient is told that her disorder must be the consequence of unremembered childhood sexual abuse—despite the fact that there is no acceptable scientific evidence that sexual abuse is any more common in the histories of bulimic women than in the general population. On the other hand, there is rigorous scientific evidence that antidepressant medications can arrest or greatly reduce bulimic patients' urge to binge and their constant preoccupation with food. Yet, only a minority of women with bulimia ever get a trial of antidepressants, and when such a trial is performed, too often it is performed incompetently.

In short, the family of mood, anxiety, and related disorders may account for more unnecessary suffering than any condition in medicine. What is to be done?

The key is education. People need to learn that these mental conditions are, in fact, traceable to biological imbalances in the brain and readily treatable with widely used and safe medications. Only when the myths and misunderstandings surrounding mood and anxiety disorders are dispelled will sufferers know that effective treatment exists, that they deserve such treatment, and that they should not be satisfied until they have obtained such treatment from a professional who can administer it competently.

In the following pages, Colette Dowling provides invaluable information for the millions of people who suffer from mood and anxiety disorders. Perhaps more than any previous work of its kind, the book integrates insights from both the human and the scientific sides of biopsychiatry. The chapters are filled with personal accounts, including some from the author's own experiences and those of her family, that illustrate the nature of these disorders and the toll they may take. These stories will quickly be recognized by readers who themselves have suffered from such conditions or who have witnessed them in friends or loved ones.

On the scientific side, the book provides a carefully researched synthesis of the most recent medical discoveries regarding mood and anxiety disorders. Ms. Dowling deftly exposes many of the misconceptions often shared by both patients and therapists—particularly the belief that the patient is somehow responsible for his or her symptoms and can be relieved of them only through hard work. In the chapter on how to obtain good treatment, the author provides scientifically accurate, practical information on the available treatments for mood and anxiety disorders, and tells her readers how to obtain such treatment. This information will be invaluable to those who have long suffered from depression and other mood disorders and who can at last profit from the latest advances in biological psychiatry.

ACKNOWLEDGMENTS

The first person I talked with, in the spring of 1990, was Michael Lowry, M.D., a psychiatrist at Wasatch Canyon Hospital in Salt Lake City, Utah. From him I learned that the National Institute of Mental Health, concerned about the widespread prevalence of depression and other mood disorders in the United States, had launched the D'ART (Depression Awareness, Recognition, and Treatment) program—a major campaign to teach physicians and mental health workers how to identify and treat these illnesses. Lowry and his colleagues had worked up an intensive three-day workshop for the D'ART program, which they present to clinicians around the country.

After reading the material for Lowry's workshop, I recognized that so much had changed in the scientific understanding of depression, anxiety, and addiction disorders that a team effort would be required to put the story together. First, there was a new field—biopsychiatry—whose researchers have developed a different way of thinking about these disorders. I wanted to talk to the researchers to find out what the new treatments consisted of, as well as the theories underlying them. I also wanted to talk to clinicians and therapists who were offering these treatments and to people who had gotten help. I asked my brother, Dr. William H. Hoppmann III, if he could help with the interviewing. Bill is a psychotherapist who supervises an outpatient mental health clinic that is part of Northern Southwest Community Mental Health, in Pittsburgh. He contributed a great deal to this book, both through the clinicians he interviewed and through his own long experience with people suffering from mood disorders.

Among the people Bill spoke with at length was Karen Gainer, A.C.S.W., L.S.W., a family and child therapist working with the Allegheny East MH-MR system in Pittsburgh who shared her extensive knowledge about depression in children.

The psychiatric treatment of children suffering from addictions and mood disorders is a new area. Dr. Oscar Bukstein, of Western Psychiatric Institute, discussed at length with Bill the special problems of "dual diagnosis" adolescents and new ways to help them get better.

Dr. Moshe Torem, director of psychiatry at the Akron Medical Center in Akron, Ohio, met with Bill and me to talk about the importance of divising well-rounded treatment strategies. Torem believes that while biopsychiatry has made an important contribution to our understanding of the biology of mood disorders, these illnesses are not simply a question of quirks in brain chemistry. The whole person needs to be recognized—and treated. Dr. Torem's views, which came early in the research stage of this book, provided us with an important, balancing perspective. When something as exciting as biopsychiatry comes along to help with illnesses that in the past have destroyed lives, it can be tempting—and misguided—to turn away from everything else that has been learned so laboriously about the human condition. I am grateful for Dr. Torem's guidance in this regard.

Jeffrey Jonas, M.D., a specialist in the biopsychiatry of eating disorders, at Fair Oaks Hospital in Summit, New Jersey, had a number of enlightening conversations with my daughter, Gabrielle Dowling, who worked closely with me on all phases of this book. Jonas has done research on the brain chemistry of both eating disorders and substance abuse, and has made novel observations about the overlap between the two. He thinks that bulimia and alcohol addiction, which often coexist, may share the same abnormality in the pathophysiology of the brain.

Eric Peselow, M.D., medical director of the Foundation for Depression and Manic Depression, in New York, was generous in meeting several times with Gabrielle and me to talk about his research in depression. One of Dr. Peselow's recent studies is of particular interest, because it reveals that major depressive episodes produce fewer long-term cognitive distortions (negativity and self-esteem problems, for example) than the milder but more chronic types of depression. One important implication of Peselow's work is that depression should be treated as soon as possible, because the longer it goes on, the more lasting are its effects on the personality. Dr. Peselow also put us in touch with patients who were willing to talk about their experiences with mood disorders.

Our understanding of the new research on the connection between addiction and mood disorders was greatly enhanced by talks with Jack Mendelson, M.D., and Roger D. Weiss, M.D., at McLean Hospital, in Belmont, Massachusetts. McLean has the largest psychiatric research laboratory in the country. Mendelson heads up addiction research, and Weiss is in charge of McLean's drug abuse treatment program.

Myra Schwartz, a school guidance counselor in Kingston, New York, interviewed spouses and parents of people with mood disorders. All felt that clinicians don't do enough to educate patients' families, so there is much groping in the dark as people try to figure out, on their own, what has caused the illness in their loved ones, what to expect, how to help, and what the future holds. Robert Hausman, M.S.W., a therapist who specializes in helping families understand and cope with mood disorders, offered his valuable perspective on the family as part of the patient treatment team.

A new understanding of compulsive eating is emerging from the laboratories of biologists and neuroscientists. Cell biologist and nutritionist Judith Wurtman, M.D., met with me at her office at M.I.T. to talk about the advances in this area. Particularly interesting is her own work in helping people who compulsively overeat understand that what is happening to them is biochemical—and can be changed by altering brain chemistry.

Many people would lose out on the new treatments science has made available were it not for those experienced psychotherapists who have gained an understanding of the important biological component of mood disorders. Rima Greenberg, C.S.W., in Manhattan, explained how therapists can work hand in hand with psychopharmacologists to provide the most comprehensive treatment for those patients for whom therapy alone is not enough.

Extremely important to us have been our ongoing conversations with Harrison Pope and Jim Hudson, professors of psychiatry at Harvard Medical School and staff psychiatrists at McLean Hospital. Hudson and Pope have done research in all the areas we cover in this book but perhaps are most noted for discovering that antidepressant medication is a highly effective treatment for bulimia. It is due, in part, to Hudson and Pope's far-ranging work that what we now think of when we use the word "depression" will probably be quite different in five or ten years. Gabrielle and I have had several meetings and considerable correspondence with these two scientists, who helped us understand the meaning of some of the new research being done in biopsychiatry. Moreover, they were willing to examine the final manuscript meticulously, to make sure the medical and scientific material is correct. It can be difficult, in writing about science and medicine, to interpret the most recent original research. One needs help from scientists who care about informing the public. Harrison Pope and Jim Hudson are two such scientists, and I am grateful to them for their ongoing interest and encouragement.

In any project of this size, there are always people who have worked tirelessly and intelligently to help make the final manuscript what it is. I wish to thank my publisher, Barbara Grossman, for her unflagging enthusiasm and general smartness. Generous, too, in his willingness to look carefully at the manuscript, paying special attention to the chapter on women, was Ivan Strausz, M.D., a New York gynecologist and good friend. And for transcribing tapes and providing computer services that allowed me to work faster than I ever have before on a project based on an enormous amount of research, I thank friend and fellow writer Rebecca Daniels.

A final note about my work with my daughter. Gabrielle's acuity in intepreting psychiatric research has informed this book from its beginning to its end. Her main contributions have been to chapter 5, "Compulsive Eating: A Disturbance in the Brain," and chapter 8, "Getting Help," which covers new treatments and medications.

You Mean I Don't Have to Feel This Way? has been a tremendous project for both of us. Gabrielle was diagnosed with major depression in the spring of 1989. Her experience has formed the emotional core of this book and her intelligence has helped to shape both its content and tone. Learning together what depression and addiction are all about has been one of those experiences that changes a life. We have been introduced to an area of science that is transforming—utterly—old ideas about mental illness. In so doing, my daughter and I have shared a remarkable adventure.

YOU MEAN

I DON'T *HAVE*

TO FEEL

THIS WAY?

"I Wish There Were a Pill"

In the late sixties, my husband, Ed, and I and our three small children were living on the Upper West Side of Manhattan. The neighborhood we lived in attracted writers, actors, and musicians. As a community, we prided ourselves on political consciousness, on *caring* about those less privileged than ourselves. We worried that our own lives were in some way overly indulgent, even though none of us had an extra dime. I worked as a free-lance writer, taking care of our children during the day and writing at night. Ed was a staff writer on a magazine. We had been married seven years when he made what I would think of, ever after, as "that fateful trip to Puerto Rico."

It was only for a week, to visit friends, his first vacation in several years. I had urged him to go without us, since we hadn't the money for a family trip. When he returned, it was clear immediately that something was wrong. Ed was cheerful, very cheerful. But he was also restless and agitated. The first night home, Ed didn't sleep well. The second night, he slept hardly at all. I'd get up from time to time to find him pacing in the living room, lights on all over and his electric typewriter whirring. He was feverishly creative, bursting with ideas, wordplay, puns, chuckling with self-delight.

On his second day back at the office, his managing editor called to say he was worried. Ed had torn up the galleys intended for the printer, saying they were "graven images." Even though I was terrified for him, I smiled as I heard of his rebellion against the magazine whose editorial policies he had always thought to

1

be tainted by advertising interests. "We tried to get him to go to a doctor, but he became insulted and stalked out," the managing editor said. What he was telling me confirmed devastatingly my suspicion that something was terribly wrong. But what?

Late that afternoon, Ed telephoned to announce that he was at Big Wilt Chamberlain's, a popular bar in Harlem. He wanted me to know he'd be walking home soon, "by way of Grant's Tomb," he added grandly, as if mere proximity to the general's resting place would confirm his princely state. I begged him to come immediately. He arrived home a short while later, sweating from the exertion of his long, fast walk and smiling fiercely. I had worried that he'd be drunk. He wasn't drunk, but he was high, very high, elated beyond all reason. Yet he seemed completely unaware that he was not his normal self. His behavior was baffling. It was also frightening.

That evening, I consulted the psychiatrist who had run the therapy group Ed and I had attended earlier. Although the doctor knew Ed fairly well, his response, after hearing of the events of the previous forty-eight hours, was "Anyone can wig out on lack of sleep." Those were his exact words. He never questioned what might have caused the lack of sleep, but wrote up a prescription for Thorazine, a powerful antipsychotic. The drug apparently did its work, putting Ed to sleep for over twenty-four hours. When he awoke, he was himself again, although fragile and shaken.

We were relieved, but confused and anxious about what had happened. Another two years were to pass before we learned that what Ed had suffered was a manic episode, the upward swing of a form of mood illness called *bipolar disorder*. Related to the more common *unipolar* type of depression, it is marked by volatile shifts between grandiose elation and utter despair.

It was strange and terrifying to see the man I had known and loved for seven years slip from one week to the next into a kind of hell. What was going on here, I yearned to know. What *was* this? Only recently he had been healthy and in his prime. What did this illness mean for the remainder of Ed's life, and what did it mean for our children? These were the questions that haunted me. I'm sure they haunted Ed as well. He had left a normal, if troubled, existence and, for reasons that were beyond us, had entered the fathomless stretch of a wildly altered state.

There were drugs, of course, though at the time they seemed primitive. Lithium brought the mania under control. In addition to lithium, Ed was given Thorazine to make him less agitated while waiting for the lithium to take effect. The Thorazine made his face stiff and masklike; the lithium caused his hands to shake. At night, these images of Ed, and of his innocence in the face of what was happening to him, would come into my mind, and I would cry.

By 1971, Ed and I had separated. During the periods when his mood was stable, he continued to visit the children, and he and I kept in touch, sometimes meeting for coffee in a neighborhood luncheonette. As time went by, I began to wonder if it had been our separation that had worsened his illness. In those days, the psychological interpretation of manic depression held sway, and I knew that loss was considered a significant factor. Had the end of our marriage caused the feelings connected with some earlier loss to resurface, destroying Ed's peace of mind?

Eventually, I would learn that though stress can trigger the onset of a manic episode, it doesn't cause it. Nevertheless, for a long time I felt implicated. It's easy to feel responsible. If only I had done things differently, been more sensitive, been more alert to his needs! We assume responsibility in part because it's less frightening than the alternative, which is recognizing that *no* one makes such illnesses happen. No one is in control.

As is characteristic of those with bipolar disorder, Ed was not able to recognize the early signs of his mood problem. Mostly he was very up, very optimistic, very keenly energized. Today this mood state would be called "hypomanic." While apparently feeling better than the rest of us, someone who is hypomanic is actually anxious and agitated and often has difficulty in relationships. The hypomanic gets worked up over every little thing and is overly sensitive to rejection. Physicians and therapists often miss the signs of this particular form of depressive illness.

Scientists have learned in the past decade or so that there are many different types of depression, each with its own cluster of symptoms, each with its own type of treatment. The types lie across a spectrum of severity. Of them all, bipolar disorder, or "manic depression," is the most severe.

In the Family

When someone in a family is very sick, it is natural enough to hope that the illness will come to rest with that person. Rarely does this turn out to be the case. More likely the illness will ripple out, touching the lives of everyone. The effects of their father's bipolar disorder reverberate in the lives of my children to this day. Growing up, they knew that he was ill. Eventually, because he couldn't work anymore, he had to accept welfare benefits. Still, he remained the children's doting father, visiting them frequently, taking them on excursions around the city, buying small presents for them on birthdays and holidays. Although they didn't speak of it until they were older, they worried about this illness in the family and what it might mean for them.

I worried, too. Research had begun to show that people are genetically predisposed to what then was called manic-depressive disease. When my children reached adolescence, the time the illness often makes its first appearance, I began looking at them for signs of mania—the inability to sleep, the jumble of brilliant thoughts, the grandiose plans. But while my kids were bright and intellectually expansive, their thoughts were not jumbled. They seemed, for the most part, happy, well organized, optimistic.

Yet as they grew out of adolescence and entered their early twenties, it began to be apparent that my oldest child was not as happy as she once had been. At first, the signs in Gabrielle were slight: a certain gravity, or somberness, which can be seen today in snapshots taken in her late teens and early twenties; a subtle diminution in her intellectual curiosity. In fact, she had returned home from college in her freshman year. I had always thought that being seventeen and leaving our little farm town to enter the competitive whirl of Harvard had been too much for her. When she was older, she'd go back, I thought; if not to Harvard, then somewhere else. But returning to school was not to be a part of Gabrielle's agenda. She worked at a few part-time restaurant jobs and went out with her friends at night. The friends, the going out, seemed at that point the only part of life that really interested her.

When I took an apartment in New York, Gabrielle came to the city too, got a job, and moved into her own apartment. Somehow, though, her life seemed flatter. After work, she'd come home and watch television. On weekends, she spent time with friends, but she often complained of being tired. When visiting with me at my house in the country, she'd sleep until noon. At family gatherings, she never seemed, really, well . . . happy. When I look now at snapshots from those holiday occasions, it's clear from Gabrielle's face that something was wrong. But then I would think, How happy was *I* at that age? And, measuring her youthful mood against my own, I deduced not that my own unhappiness as a young woman had been unnatural but that my daughter's unhappiness was natural because it was like mine!

It's remarkable, actually, how difficult it can be to admit that we're not content—that though we might get by, our experience lacks pleasure, or zest. We begin to rationalize depression almost as soon as the symptoms appear. "This will pass," we say; or, "Who do I know that's really happy, anyway?" As my daughter grew darker and less animated, I actually began thinking, Soon she'll get married. She'll have babies. Then everything will even out. I thought that because it had been that way for me. Having babies made me happier for a while, and certainly it made me less self-involved.

It can happen, though, in a woman's life, that in responding to others' needs, she ignores a sense of emptiness that lies at the core of everything.

Discovering That a Daughter Is Ill

By the time Gabrielle was twenty-five, it was clear that something was happening to her that having babies wouldn't help. Her reliable behavior had slowly become less so. One day she missed a lunch date with me in the city. "Forgot," she said. Several times I called her office in late morning to find that she was not expected until even later. When, on these occasions, I asked her what had happened, she always reported some cold or flu or stomachache. Increasingly, she complained of fatigue.

Gabrielle had been bulimic for several years in her teens, and I wondered now if her gastrointestinal system had been affected by the binging and purging. I'd suggest she have a physical, but after a while the malaise would disappear, and the doctor would be forgotten. Then the aches and pains would reappear. Everything one might imagine came to mind. I thought of drugs, I thought of alcohol, I thought perhaps she was still bulimic. Sometimes I'd comment that she seemed depressed. "Maybe I *have* been depressed and just haven't been aware of it," she mused, once. Our discussions never progressed beyond that. Somehow I thought it was up to her to figure out what was wrong. That's the way we've been taught to think about problems we assume are psychological.

Nevertheless, I was worried. It seemed to me that my daughter's face had lost some of its mobility. She didn't smile very often. Increasingly, her responses were brief, perfunctory. Unbeknownst to all of us, Gabrielle was on the huge parabola of a mood shift that was taking months to accomplish.

Confusing, too, was her apparent ability to function in the world. She had a demanding job as assistant to the president of a small public relations firm. Since moving out on her own, she had never asked for financial help. Now I thought she needed help of another kind, but I wavered on what sort and whether or not I could provide it.

My analyst encouraged me to stop feeling responsible. "She's not a child anymore," he remarked. "She knows what therapy is. If she wants it, she'll get it." This actually is a wrong idea when it comes to mood disorders, though it is a conviction many therapists hold. People who are depressed need others to acknowledge their symptoms and may also need help in getting help. The symptoms worsen gradually, insidiously, so that it's hard to recognize what's happening. *Thinking* is affected, so that one ends up blaming oneself for one's own ineffectualness. A vicious cycle ensues in which one cannot move because one is depressed, and one is increasingly depressed because one cannot move!

Like so many who continue trying to cope while inwardly becoming more desperate, Gabrielle kept on working, hoping that whatever was making it so difficult for her to *do* her work would disappear. Finally, she couldn't get herself to the office in the morning. It took another few weeks before she was able to tell me that she was in a bad way and needed help. Seriously frightened and having no idea what was wrong, Gaby was staying alone in her apartment and ignoring phone calls. To pay her bills, she was running up her credit-card balance.

I had been in Europe on a business trip and was calling and leaving messages for her from Amsterdam, Frankfurt, and Milan. For months her answering machine had been playing a message that was urban hip on the surface but hauntingly distant beneath. Hearing it day after day from another continent, I found the words ominous. "It was a regular kind of day in New York City," she crooned. "Gab was just doin' the hang, she was sittin' pretty. But then a knock came at the door, a knock she could not ignore, and so she went out into the zone of the unknown, but we think she'll come home, so please leave a message at the tone."

After this, there would be the predictable "beeeeeeep" and then nothing. I must have heard that plaintive message a dozen times. Finally, from Venice—it was two o'clock in the morning, my time—I pleaded outright, telling her that I loved her very much, and was terribly worried, and wouldn't she please pick up. She did then, at last, pick up, and she told me that things were very bad. She said, "I need to talk to someone." I asked if she wanted me to help her find a therapist. She said she did. "I don't think I have the energy," she added.

Four days later, I was back in New York.

A New Understanding

What I now understand is that Gaby was exhibiting symptoms of major depression, one of a whole spectrum of mood disorders that are highly prevalent in our population. In uncovering the biological nature of depression, scientists have made dramatic gains. What's happening in the field of biopsychiatry today is revolutionary. Minute disturbances in the balance of neurotransmitters, the chemical messengers that regulate mood, have been found to cause significant changes in behavior and thinking, and even in the immune system. This is why people who are depressed lose the ability to think straight and why energy, appetite, and libido fall off. Mood disorders don't simply affect mood. They are complex illnesses that affect us both physically and mentally.

It is fortunate that science is making such headway in understanding mood disorders, for they have become increasingly prevalent. *One in four women and one in ten men—or a total of*

13.7 million in the United States—can expect to experience at least one debilitating episode of mood disorder in the course of a lifetime.

In those born since World War II, the rate of depression is increasing. Many reasons for this have been suggested, including increased drug and alcohol use and decreased employment, although, in fact, no one really knows why depression is on the rise.

Depression used to be a disease of the elderly. That has changed. A new government study has found that the young are most likely to become depressed. They are also the most likely to commit suicide.

In part, it is the devastating prevalence of such illnesses that has prompted the boom in research. Dramatic advances have been made in the classification, diagnosis, and treatment of mood and anxiety disorders—and even of addictions. Yet a tremendous gap exists between what science knows about treating these illnesses and what clinicians know and use. Most doctors went to medical school years before the new research and its results became available, and many remain ignorant of them. Even psychiatrists often can't keep up with advances in new drugs. One National Institute of Mental Health (NIMH) study[1] showed that over half of depressed patients, including those with severe, protracted forms of the illness, are given the wrong drugs—when they're given anything at all! Tranquilizers are still the medications most commonly prescribed for depression, even though they don't touch the illness.

But of those who seek out treatment, only a third are prescribed the correct medication, the government studies say, and of those, only one in ten were given adequate doses. Lack of information among physicians and therapists prompted the NIMH to establish a multimillion-dollar program aimed at updating physicians and mental health workers. In 1988, teams of government-sponsored experts began fanning out across the country, giving intensive minicourses in how to identify—and treat—depression.

According to the NIMH, depression is an illness for which there is remarkably effective treatment, but most people who are depressed don't get treated. Either they don't seek help in the first place, believing mistakenly that depression is something they shouldn't "give in" to, or doctors don't provide adequate treatment. Actually, the amount of misdiagnosis or utter lack of diagnosis of depression in this country is staggering.

The government has discovered that *most* physicians miss the diagnosis entirely. They aren't up-to-date on the new information. They may not even know that depression is biologically based and that treatment with antidepressant medication is often required. The vast majority of physicians prescribe tranquilizers and antianxiety agents, which do nothing at all to treat depression. This shocking information was gathered in the NIMH's Epidemiological Catchment Area (ECA) study, conducted in the early eighties, the sum of whose information has recently been published in *Psychiatric Disorders in America.* "No data base can rival this one," say Lee N. Robins, Ben Z. Locke, and Darrel A. Regier. "It is the soundest fundamental information about the range and extent and variety of psychiatric disorders ever assembled."[2] Over 20,000 people in five parts of the United States were surveyed.

Such studies were much smaller in the past, and they covered those who had already been identified as ill—patients, in other words. This study uncovers for the first time how many people are suffering from various psychiatric disorders in the population at large. It reveals how many are sick without having had the illness identified or treated. The numbers are staggering. One out of three American adults have suffered from a psychiatric disorder at some time in their lives—36 percent of men as compared to 30 percent of women. In the 1980s, when the ECA study was being conducted, 20 percent of American adults were actively ill. Full-blown mood disorders are rather common, having occurred in 8 percent of the adult population. But according to Myrna Weissman, who was in charge of assembling and interpreting the ECA surveys of depression for *Psychiatric Disorders in America,* *"Severe and persistent affective symptoms are even more common, some of them occurring in close to a third of the adult population."*

The NIMH decided to mount its education campaign on mood disorders because they are among the most prevalent—and most treatable—of psychiatric problems. We now know that most people with mood disorders are not getting the help that could change their lives. Some suffer for months, even years, with smoldering forms of chronic depression that prevent them from having good relationships and doing gratifying work. Others have acute, episodic depressions whose symptoms are yet more severe and incapacitating. Actually, these "major" depressions are usually easier to treat than the milder, chronic forms, but the symptoms are so unsettling that most suffer from them in silence, trying to wait it out without seeking help.

Depression is episodic and even in its "chronic" form will eventually go into remission. In the meantime, though, people suffer psychic and physical pain that causes terrible difficulty in their lives. Also, when depression goes untreated, it often gets worse. Over 16,000 Americans a year commit suicide, usually as a result of depression. Many who are depressed become addicted to drugs or alcohol. The ECA study found that half of women alcoholics have a history of severe depression; in two thirds of them, the depression *precedes* the alcoholism.

There's no question that depression takes a very serious toll. One recent study shows that it is more debilitating and produces more days in bed than eight major chronic illnesses, including heart disease.[3] The question that remains is, why do people insist on accommodating themselves to this painful illness? Stigma undoubtedly plays a role. The NIMH has found tremendous resistance among the general public to seeking treatment for depression. Even worse, it has found similar resistance to diagnosing and treating depressive illnesses on the part of doctors! The cost to individuals, and to the economy, is enormous—estimated at $16.3 billion per year in the United States. And yet, although billions of dollars have gone into research that has resulted in major advances in the treatment of these illnesses, the public continues to remain uninformed. And to suffer.

People who are depressed tend to deny, or misidentify, their own symptoms. They attribute the physical symptoms of depression to "flu" and the mental symptoms to fatigue or improper diet. In a 1986 Roper poll, only 12 percent of those surveyed said they would take medication for depression if it were made available to them; 78 percent said they'd wait for the illness to pass.[4]

The denial of depression is due largely to stigma. No one wants to admit to being depressed. It's like admitting to a failure of will. Somehow we have gotten the idea that the courageous don't come down with depression. When people are depressed, even severely so, they tend to berate themselves for the lethargy they experience, the inability to "get moving." If we were better people we wouldn't be "giving in" this way.

What we end up disavowing is an illness that needs treatment as urgently as diabetes or heart disease.

Thousands of scientists are looking for better methods of treatment and prevention, and they are making dramatic progress. The advances of the last decade have changed the picture enormously. Today nine out of ten people suffering from mood disorders have every reason to expect successful treatment.

And, as has recently been discovered, so do others who suffer from illnesses that are biochemically related to depression.

The Spectrum Illnesses: A Radical Hypothesis

In 1990, a new and radical theory of mental illness emerged from the psychiatric research laboratory at McLean Hospital, outside of Boston. Its roots lay in an important medical discovery made at that same laboratory—and by the same scientists—a decade earlier.

In the early eighties, two of psychiatry's most noted researchers, James Hudson and Harrison Pope of Harvard Medical School, found that bulimia, an eating disorder that causes compulsive binging and purging, is caused by a chemical imbalance in the brain—perhaps by a deficit of a neurotransmitter called serotonin. When their serotonin level is boosted, most bulimic patients stop binging. This mysterious eating disorder, which had baffled therapists for years, at last made some sense. And, happily, it could be treated. (Medical treatment of various kinds of compulsive eating disorders is discussed at length in chapter 5.)

At the same time, other studies were beginning to show that bulimia is connected to major depression. *And* it is related to anxiety disorders and to alcohol and substance abuse. Most fascinating, though, was the discovery that all of these problems cluster among relatives of people with bulimia. Bulimics have parents who are eating disordered and/or depressed and/or phobic or panic disordered and/or alcoholic or drug abusing. A bulimic woman herself might be depressed *and* alcoholic *and* phobic.

11

While family studies had begun to show a relationship among depression, bulimia, and other disorders, psychopharmacologists were coming up with clinical data that buttressed the same relationship. Antidepressant medication, they found, works powerfully on many illnesses, not just depression. With the extremely impairing obsessive-compulsive disorder (OCD), for example, relief can be dramatic. Within weeks of being given an antidepressant, many with OCD are able to stop washing their hands, stop counting, stop "checking." Panic and phobia respond to antidepressants just as quickly. Bulimia responds, as Hudson and Pope discovered. So do some forms of the carbohydrate binge eating that leads to obesity.

As research on these antidepressant-responsive illnesses progressed, Hudson and Pope began to recognize that a syndrome exists, a network of illnesses that used to be thought entirely discrete, but which seem to be related. First, they were struck by the genetic picture. Looking into family histories, Hudson and Pope saw that the depressed have parents and uncles and cousins and grandparents who not only suffer from depression but from addiction, bulimia, panic attacks, or some debilitating combination of them.

Second, all of these illnesses respond to medication that increases the levels of serotonin and other neurotransmitters in the brain! For Hudson and Pope, this raised a fascinating question. Were these illnesses actually manifestations of a single organic disturbance? And, most provocatively, *might science eventually come up with a single treatment for them all?*

In a landmark paper published in 1990, the scientists presented for the first time their theory about the connection among all these illnesses, which they have labeled "affective spectrum disorder."[5]

More recently they have written, "The urge of the kleptomaniac to steal, the bulimic to binge eat, the obsessive-compulsive to carry out senseless rituals, the pathologic gambler to gamble, and the trichotillomanic to pull out hair might all involve abnormalities in central nervous system function similar to those hypothesized to occur in major mood disorder." This idea is supported by biochemical studies as well as by certain obvious similarities of the disorders.[6]

The more they pursue this "spectrum" hypothesis, the more convinced the scientists become that they are on to something.

"We predict that eventually a physiologic abnormality will be found in people who have all of the various disorders which we have listed under the affective spectrum umbrella," Harrison Pope told me in his office at McLean. "And assuming that we are right, that our hypothesis is confirmed, then this would prove to be perhaps the single most devastating disease of mankind. Collectively, various forms of affective disorder affect one third of the population of the world. And finding the abnormality, if indeed it does exist, would be a major breakthrough because it would then allow us to get to the source of many of these disorders rather than trying to look at them all individually."

The Second Stage: Finding the Connection

The first stage of the biopsychiatry revolution consisted of discovering drugs that affect mood and thinking. In the second stage, scientists are finding out why the drugs do what they do and how the illnesses they affect are actually interrelated. A major question to be answered by second-stage scientists is this: What is going on in the brains of those who are obsessive, who are anxiety ridden, who binge compulsively on food, who have phobias, who are abusing mood-altering substances? *What is the connection?* Are there certain brain dysfunctions that all of these people share? If so, are tiny metabolic flaws more likely to account for the family histories, risk factors, and potential prevention of the disorders than all the psychosocial theories combined?

With their new theory, Hudson and Pope suggest that the various forms of what they call the "affective spectrum disorder" respond to the same type of drug because similar brain processes are functioning abnormally in all of them. Certain mood-regulating neurotransmitters are not doing what they're supposed to be doing—in panic, just as in bulimia; in depression, just as in migraine. A central connection among these disorders is the brain hormone serotonin. What antidepressants *do* in all of these people is boost serotonin. Thus, the spectrum illnesses are in some way related to depletion of serotonin and other neurotransmitters—

and the propensity for that depletion, Hudson and Pope believe, is inherited.

A great many psychiatric disturbances once thought to be entirely "in the mind" are coming to be regarded as more biochemical than psychological in origin. The concept of neurosis itself is under siege. Medications that influence neurotransmitter production not only balance mood; they affect the way people think, create, and relate to others. Mood-regulating brain chemicals affect our total personalities.

The biochemical approach is having a dramatic effect on therapists (some of whom would like to minimize the importance of biopsychiatry's contributions) and on patients, who are able now to see their problems in a gentler light. Those with mood, anxiety, and addiction disorders can stop blaming themselves. They no longer need feel guilty about the jobs and relationships that have deteriorated because they were too ill to function. They can begin to focus, instead, on the task at hand—which is getting well. For many of the illnesses that were once thought purely "psychological," there *is* a pill. Medical treatment, of course, is not a simple one-step panacea. Still, the ramifications of the new theories and treatment strategies are extraordinary.

Drugs that boost serotonin and other neurotransmitters have been cast out over a troubled sea of mental illness, gathering up, like a giant, protective net, all kinds of chemical problems, including eating disorders, migraine, mood swings, and yes, even addictions. Addiction researchers have come to believe that substance abuse is often related to the spectrum illnesses.

Finding the Right Help

The strange thing, the thing I'm not quite sure of to this day, is how I ended up taking the particular helping course with Gabrielle that I did. Partly, it was the result of conversations I'd had with an old college roommate, a woman I hadn't seen in years, whose daughter had been treated chemically for depression. Eva's husband had also been manic-depressive and had finally committed suicide. Her daughter, Nikka, had been a college sophomore when her mood plunged so low she couldn't study for her exams and could barely get out of bed. Eva had said, "Get on a plane and come home tonight." Her daughter had said, "But it's the end of the semester; you'll lose the tuition." "Get on the plane," my friend said. "Money isn't the issue here." And while the first psychiatrist they went to said there was nothing wrong except that the girl was worried about her exams, Eva said, "Don't tell me there's nothing wrong when she's lying on her bed in a fetal position all day." Finally, another psychiatrist diagnosed Nikka as having cyclothymia, a less severe version of the bipolar illness her father had had. With lithium, the young woman was soon enormously improved, and before long she was off to London to study.

How could I not be struck by the parallels between this family history and my own? I became very excited, for it seemed that Gabrielle's depression, like Nikka's, might be biological in origin. If so, it could be treated with medication. I called her and said, "I think we should see a psychopharmacologist and get you evaluated for depression." She listened as I told her of Nikka's experience. There was a pause before Gabrielle said, "But what if I'm not depressed?"

Then she laughed, actually laughed.

Gabrielle's evaluation included a long diagnostic interview as well as a physical exam. At the end, the psychiatrist called me into his office and told me my daughter was suffering from major depression, an illness with recurrent episodes lasting six months or more. It was the *unipolar* form, he thought, not the manic type that her father had had. Depression doesn't necessarily get handed down to the next generation in the same form, he explained. The child of a bipolar parent is more likely to end up with unipolar depression. The doctor was certain Gaby could be helped with an antidepressant. She would be monitored weekly for side effects and for improvement.

At the end of the discussion, the doctor turned to me and asked, "Why hasn't she been evaluated before this?" It was a straightforward question. To him, Gabrielle's depression seemed achingly familiar. He wanted to know the details of her history, to add them to his compendium of families with this long-misunderstood—and often denied—illness. Still, I could hardly help but infer that had she been evaluated earlier, my daughter would have been spared several long episodes of illness, the first of which, we now understood, had occurred ten years earlier, when she was a senior in high school.

Fortunately for Gabrielle, her battle would soon be over. A month after she began treatment, the depression that had been putting her lower and lower, lifted. Actually, the medication's effect on her seemed almost magical. Renewed energy, renewed spirit, and a positive, confident attitude in her relations with others replaced her old feelings of anxious self-doubt. Remarkably, the turnabout occurred within several weeks—virtually as soon as the medication started working. She saw a therapist because she needed help in reorganizing her life. However, her negative, fearful attitudes fell away so immediately, so totally, it was clear that the drug was responsible. It had rebalanced the chemicals in her brain.

Before Gabrielle was evaluated, she had said to me at the end of one of her bad days, "I wish there were a pill." And then, with a little smile, she'd added, "Of course, I know that's a copout."

That was almost two years ago, in the summer of 1989. I'd thought not so much that it was a copout as "Who *wouldn't* want a pill?" The leadenness of her demeanor, the absolutely physical quality of the malaise, which had affected her speech, her face, her voice—so that she might have been in a torpor, infected by some tropical disease—was striking.

For three weeks she took her medication regularly and suffered from the light-headedness and muscular aches that were temporary side effects. She came to the country, and the rest of the family took turns giving her neck rubs and massages. A family friend who'd once worked in a psychiatric hospital said the side effects were an indication the medication was working. It's difficult to contend with physical side effects of medication when one is feeling low to begin with and is uncertain that any good will come of the effort. Our friend's reassurance helped Gabrielle put up with the side effects, and before too long they subsided.

Gabrielle knew that the medication had built to a therapeutic level when something bizarre happened. She was awakened in the middle of the night by an extraordinary dream—a series of huge, brilliantly colored abstract paintings. She was so excited by the dream pictures that she woke her sister in search of a pen. The shapes and colors of the dream paintings were so compelling that she wanted to describe them so as not to forget them.

Telling me about this the next morning, Gaby said it made her sad to think she had been so long without having had a creative experience. This sadness was not depression but normal grief over a real loss.

After her mood lifted, the first thing Gabrielle wanted to do was clean her apartment. Her therapist had said, "Isn't there a friend you can ask to help you?" Gabrielle had told her there wasn't. Not that she didn't have friends; she was too embarrassed by the state of things. I asked if I could help, and she said I could. A week later, the two of us started in together.

Cleaning a daughter's apartment is something I would never have considered—unless, of course, she was ill. Gabrielle was ill, and that she needed help with this overwhelming task seemed abundantly clear. The place was so disorganized it shocked me, but I thought it better to keep that to myself. What struck me most was the shower rod. Her closets were in such disarray that they had become unusable and she was hanging her clothes on the shower rod. Only a small passageway remained through which she could navigate her way to the tub.

This disorganization made me feel very sad. I wished I had understood earlier what desperate straits she'd been in. Still, working on that forlorn apartment, making it clean, and cheerful, and organized again, turned out to be a great bonding experience for both of us. It was in the dog days of August, and the air conditioner was on the fritz. We worked in our underwear, the sweat running down us in rivulets, while Gaby's three cats looked on. We laughed and ate frozen yogurt and drank gallons of Diet Pepsi. We listened to rock on the stereo as we scrubbed. When the scrubbing was done, we painted. Gabrielle kept running to the dime store to buy cleaning fluids and little containers for organizing everything. The whole job took a couple of weeks.

And then Gabrielle began to buy flowers. She bought them every day. "Would you believe, Mom, only three bucks?" she'd say, showing off an armful. There was a man on Sixth Avenue who sold them cheap—tulips and freesias and Dutch iris. One day I walked into her apartment and there were flowers all over the place—on the table, on the windowsill, high above the stereo cabinet. They were in the kitchen, in the bathroom, on the table by her bed. And her cats, those rambunctious guys I thought now might actually have saved her, were acting as if all this had been done for them, and they were in heaven.

Today science has clearly established the importance of brain biochemistry in most mood disorders and addictions, yet many find it difficult to take in the new information, to use it to modify old ideas. We still think we become depressed because we haven't "coped," because we haven't "confronted" spouse, sibling, or boss, because we haven't "separated" ourselves from our parents. Our list of reasons for why we are haunted by moods and addictions goes on and on. We haven't got "to the bottom" of things. We haven't learned to love ourselves. Like hamsters in a cage, we run a treadmill of endless self-examination. In the meantime, our moods worsen. But a new paradigm is emerging. The flat, affectless limbo of depression has come to be seen not as "mental," in the old sense, but biochemical. Eventually, biopsychiatry will help people understand that the cognitive distortions and negativity that accompany depression are not its cause but its effect. When this happens, perhaps the stigma associated with a cluster of illnesses from which millions suffer blamelessly—and from which most can be relieved—will begin to recede.

It saddens me to think that it may have been because he was one of the early, experimental cases in the use of lithium in this country that my husband was not successfully treated. For example, the doctor who prescribed his medication had not suggested psychotherapy. Without that support, people with bipolar disorder find it difficult to accept that they have a chronic illness. The periods of normal mood make it especially confusing. Many with bipolar disorder are tempted to give up on the medication, wishing to believe that they have gotten past it—that they won't become ill again. Ed was no different. But each time he stopped taking lithium he became manic in a matter of weeks. When the mania subsided, he'd become seriously depressed.

As the years passed, both the manic periods and the depressions worsened. Ed struggled, continuing to read, to listen to music, to attempt to write, but his capacity to earn an income deteriorated utterly. Then, one day, ten years after it had begun—it was the summer of 1979—he walked into the emergency ward of a large New York hospital, complained of stomach pains, and within two hours was dead. An intern, young and anxious, telephoned to give me the news. By now, the children and I were living out of the city, and Ed and I had been separated for eight years. Whatever had happened? I asked the intern. He could not tell me. Later, the autopsy report showed peritonitis, although this was not given as the explanation for Ed's death. The best the hospital could come up with was possible disturbance from an old and once healed ulcer.

To this day, the children and I do not know what killed their father, but I have never doubted that his death was related to his illness. We do know that he had stopped taking his medication. Several months before he died, he had joined AA and been vehemently encouraged to go off lithium. I tried persuading him that this was dangerous, but there was no brooking the influence of his group. Many in AA don't understand that medication for certain forms of depression is a necessity or that antidepressants, not being addictive, don't undermine sobriety. By the time Ed got himself to the emergency ward, he'd been off lithium—and severely manic—for weeks.

At the time Ed became ill it was not the practice for psychiatrists to spend much time educating patients and their families. Unfortunately, this is often still the case. Mood disorders and anxiety disorders and even addictions have been recognized as having an important biological component. An explosion of exciting and hopeful information has come out of this discovery; and yet, for the most part, the public remains in the dark.

Sadly, nearly 80 percent of those suffering from depression fail to recognize the illness and get the treatment that would help them. Much has been learned that can help. The creation of standardized diagnostic criteria has made it easier for therapists and physicians and various mental health professionals to recognize mood and anxiety disorders—at least when they learn to use them. The typing and subtyping of depression has made diagnosis more sophisticated. Treating the different types has become far more successful, because of new and more selective drugs.

If, along with the recently uncovered numbers of "purely depressed," we consider the "spectrum" disorders that sometimes coexist with depression, and which also are relieved by antidepressants—panic, phobia, PMS, addictions, bulimia, migraine, and even, some researchers have begun to suspect, chronic fatigue syndrome—we are speaking of a startlingly large segment of the population, all suffering because certain chemicals in their brains have gone out of balance.

Could it be, as scientists have begun to suggest, that such disorders, rather than "mental" in the old sense, are actually physical illnesses with cognitive consequences—mental distortions that recede once the chemical imbalance is treated? Do we inherit predispositions or vulnerabilities to these illnesses from our parents and grandparents, and will our children, in turn, inherit them from us? And is this gradually solidifying biological model for emotional illness in itself depressing beyond belief, or does it offer possibilities for treatment, and even prevention, that have never before been dreamed of?

These are the questions that lie, now, before the researchers and clinicians who are working on the frontiers of biopsychiatry. What they have uncovered, and *are* uncovering, virtually from one day to the next, is both fascinating and extremely hopeful. It is my goal in writing this book to relay the story of how and why psychiatry has shifted its theory of mood, anxiety and addiction disorders to a biomedical one and to describe new treatments that can relieve symptoms significantly, often totally. Taken together, these illnesses affect more people than has ever before been suspected—"possibly one third of the population of the world," as Harrison Pope says. And yet they go massively untreated. This is because we are still burdened by an almost medieval degree of stigma and ignorance.

Think how aggressive we are in treating illnesses we consider physical, and yet we avoid treating those disorders that distort our emotions and mental capabilities. Fear and suspiciousness abound. This is a hurdle that must be gotten over. Millions are affected by this newly defined "spectrum" of illnesses. Most are living lives that are limited, if not filled with pain. But once properly diagnosed and treated, we can move on surprisingly quickly to fuller lives—lives that are energetic, creative, and enhanced by the wonder of existence.

CHAPTER TWO

The Serotonin Connection

Pontificating is an old defense. When frustrated by someone's refusal to hear what I'm saying, I can easily become overbearing, summoning sources, citing data, lecturing as if my life depended on it. It happened recently at a dinner party. The subject of eating disorders came up. (It's quite amazing how frequently eating disorders are discussed at dinner parties.) Someone said, "What causes those things, anyway?" With the cryptic I-dare-you tone that creeps in when I expect disbelief, I replied, "It's probably chemical."

"*Chemical?*" someone said, as if on cue. All heads bobbed up from the dinner plates. "How do you mean, chemical?"

"Well, bulimia often occurs along with depression, and both respond to antidepressants. A couple of guys at Harvard are quite convinced eating disorders are inherited, like mood disorders."

There followed the kind of silence that descends when people fervently disagree but don't understand their reasons for doing so. Then, from a psychoanalyst, came the inevitable dissent. "I think these things are pretty much psychological," he said with the calm air of someone used to having the last word. That was it. The gloves were on the table.

I had spent the past year watching my daughter develop in her work and her personal life, had heard the smile in her voice when we spoke on the telephone, had seen the progress of her work and friendships. She was organized, curious, intellectually engaged in a way that she hadn't been for almost a decade, and it was due largely to the intervention of a drug called Nardil. Each morning, she places four red pills on the kitchen counter next to her vitamins. She counts out the full supply so that as the day progresses, she can easily determine how many she's already taken. This little ritual, she feels, is a small price to pay for the gift she's been given: She is free now to be herself.

By the time I met the psychoanalyst at the dinner party, both Gabrielle and I had been researching in the field of biopsychiatry for months. I knew the analyst's belief that mood disorders and illnesses like bulimia "are mostly psychological" was dated—a holdover from an earlier time.

The Brain's Effect on Behavior and Mood

Over the past two decades, biopsychiatry has gradually but steadily increased its influence. Today scientists view mood disorders as stemming from certain chemicals in the brain. These chemicals, known as "neurotransmitters," send electrical signals from one nerve cell to another. The chemical signaling sets in motion complex neural interactions that affect our behaviors, feelings—even our thoughts.

One of the most important of these neurotransmitters (though not by any means the only one presently being studied in depression) is *serotonin*.* Manufactured in the body from an amino acid called tryptophan, it seems to be involved in both sleep and mood regulation. When serotonin levels fall too low, mood drops. Once that chemical switch occurs, the drives for sleep, appetite, and libido diminish. Activity and speech slow, self-esteem evaporates, and a kind of negativity loop starts playing over and over in the mind: *I'm a mess and everyone knows it; it's not going to work; I'm going to lose everything.*

What is remarkable is that this tape loop can be brought to a halt by restoring to normal levels the depleted serotonin in the brain. Biopsychiatrists think the most potent way of doing this— although not the only way—is through direct chemical interven-

---

*Serotonin research has been prolific in recent years, but scientists think other neurotransmitters are also involved in brain functions affecting mood. These are under investigation and undoubtedly will lead to a more detailed picture of how the brain works. In this book serotonin is emphasized, both for its own importance and because it is a kind of metaphor for neurotransmitter action in general.

tion. Antidepressants work because they correct faulty brain metabolism, allowing the brain's own mood hormones to replenish themselves. There are other ways of doing this, exercise and exposure to light among them. But for mood disorders serious enough to impair work and social relationships, chemical intervention in the serotonin system is required. Exercise or light exposure alone usually won't do it.

Serotonin, it's turning out, is implicated in many other illnesses besides mood disorders. "It may be important in causing appetite disturbances and in the development of obsessions and compulsions," according to Dr. James M. Ellison, a professor of psychiatry at Harvard Medical School.[1] The suspicion that all these illnesses are biochemical disturbances treatable with drugs has prompted thousands of clinical and laboratory studies. "Every time a new drug is found, another disease disappears," psychiatrist Paul Wender told a newsmagazine in the spring of 1990. "What we're going to find out about the brain is mind boggling."[2]

What neuroscientists and biopsychiatrists are learning will alter fundamentally our way of thinking about mental illness. Beginning in the brain, mental illness is biological at its core. Moreover, it seems increasingly clear that it is genetic. Inheritability has long been suspected about schizophrenia but not about garden-variety depression, anxiety, and "silly" phobias. What science has found is that there are no garden-variety depressions, no silly fears and phobias. What people experience when they plummet to the depths or fear airplanes is not "neurotic." Scientific data indicate that these illnesses are no less "physical" than diabetes, no more "mental" than migraine.

The research leading up to the revolutionary changes of the late eighties has been going on for about three decades, but only recently has there been official endorsement of the new concepts of biopsychiatry. The biological model for depression, for example, was espoused five years ago at a conference sponsored by the NIMH. At that time, a consensus panel drawn from many fields[3] stated that antidepressant medication not only treats acute episodes of mood disorder, it increases the likelihood of preventing future episodes. The panel recommended that antidepressants be used "within the context of a supportive relationship among doctor, patient, and family."[4]

In the five years since that conference, many other illnesses have begun rolling off the analyst's couch as well. Panic and phobia, obsessive-compulsive disorders, and addictions are only some of them. There is tension in the ranks of therapists. In fact, rivalry between talk therapists and biopsychiatrists has become so adversarial that patients' welfare falls by the wayside. I have been surprised by the number of people whose therapists discouraged a trial of antidepressants even when mood problems persist for years. The single fact that antidepressants aren't addictive makes discouraging a trial in someone who is chronically depressed seem more withholding than sensible. What is there to lose in trying?

Resistance to a New Idea

"The quick, easy effortless solution will always be popular," says Michael Yapko, author of *When Living Hurts.* Yapko eschews the use of medication, professing that depression is not an illness but "a lifestyle," the result of the way a person interprets and responds to life, "a predictable way of interacting with the world."[5]

Therapists who share this view believe it is incumbent upon them to spend the therapeutic hours helping the patient find new ways of interacting with the world. When the mood problem persists, they spend more hours (or weeks, or months, or years) firmly resisting "the quick solution."

Other therapists resort to medication only *in extremis.* "If I'm faced with a choice between antidepressants and hospitalization, I'll use the medications," says Maryland psychiatrist Loren Mosher.[6] Only when patients suffer to the point of becoming suicidal, in other words, will doctors like Mosher offer medical relief, a heartless—and clearly dangerous—game.

Unfortunately, the stigma attached to chemical therapies is preventing many from getting the help they need and is at least in part perpetuated by therapists. Trained in psychologically oriented theories, they believe—and to some extent their careers hinge on the idea—that the "psyche," not the brain, is at the root of everything. To some, biopsychiatrists have become the enemy. "Many act as if the modern psychoanalyst should knuckle under to the new biology and trade in his couches for a new brain-imaging apparatus," huffed Dr. Theodore Shapiro, editor of the prestigious *Journal of the American Psychoanalytic Association*, in a 1989 editorial.[7] Therapists like Shapiro continue to insist that medication is only for the very ill. The implication is that, for anyone else, taking pills is the morally inferior course of action. Martin Seligman, a psychologist famous for his theory that depression is something we *learn*, epitomizes this misguided humanism when he writes in *Learned Optimism*, "The effectively drugged patient cannot credit himself for carving out his happiness and his ability to function with a semblance of normality; he must credit the pills."[8]

The depressed people I spoke with felt a tremendous sense of relief after their moods were restored. Who or what got the credit was not, for them, an issue. The idea of "carving out" one's happiness with talk therapy is, in any event, a moralistic notion, if not simply a therapist's notion. When medication can ameliorate the symptoms of a chemical imbalance, why should we be made to feel that taking it is somehow irresponsible? Do we condemn those with hypertension for their dependence on medications that lower blood pressure?

There's another important issue here, one that writers like Seligman often ignore. Many types of mood and anxiety disorders don't go away without medication. They may ameliorate slightly with talk therapy, but a residue of impaired mood remains.

There is a superior tone to such statements as "carving out one's happiness"—an implication that doing it cold turkey will make you if not a better person at least a stronger one. "Better," of course, is ridiculous. As for "stronger," there is no evidence at all that therapy without medication works a more effective cure. If anything, efficacy studies have shown the opposite: People whose mood disorders are not fully treated become worse over time. Early intervention—with medication when it's appropriate—affects both the severity and the frequency of future episodes, both of which play a big role in whether or not one ever achieves a sense of emotional "strength."

Family therapists have been among the most resistant to the use of medication. Psychiatrist Salvador Minuchin, one of the most respected practitioners in the field, says that in all the years he's practiced he's never found it necessary to medicate a patient. Fortunately, other family therapists have begun to loosen up.[9]

Carol Anderson has been a pioneer in the effort to get her colleagues to see the folly of withholding medication. "You wouldn't ask a diabetic not to take insulin and instead to work on changing her pancreas," she says. "We implicitly blame our clients when we assume that they are always responsible for their depression."[10]

"The entire emphasis of family therapy has been in the opposite direction from tracing a problem to a biochemical deficiency within an individual," writes Laura M. Markowitz in *The Family Therapist Networker*.[11] She cites a case from a family-therapy textbook in which Edith and Bob come in for therapy "because of Edith's depression, which has organized their marriage for the past 20 years. Bob has taken over the household tasks and looks after Edith, overfunctioning to her underfunctioning. He has not even let Edith take the dog for a walk by herself because of his fear that she might try to harm herself. As Edith responds to treatment and begins to show signs of improvement, Bob attempts suicide." The textbook says the focus of therapy in such a situation is to bring out the underlying reasons for the "symptom" of depression in the marriage, to ferret out the "function" it has served "not on the individual level, for Edith, but within their relationship."

Poor Edith. And, as Markowitz seems to imply, poor Bob.

In the spring of 1990, I attended the annual meeting of the American Psychoanalytic Association, held in the Grand Ballroom of the Waldorf-Astoria. I wanted to know what analysts were thinking about medication in the treatment of depression, and that very subject was the focus of an afternoon-long seminar. The room was packed with dark-suited psychoanalysts, mostly male. Several papers described successful outcomes of using drugs in conjunction with the analytic treatment of certain patients. The atmosphere in the ballroom was charged. Questions asked by analysts in the audience revolved around such issues as what "having to take medication" would do to patients' sense of autonomy, their dependency on and feelings about their analysts, and—significantly—whether relieving their symptoms would sabotage their motivation for continuing therapy.

The irony of this seemed lost on many. Symptoms are what keep people in treatment. Some of the analysts said they worried that if antidepressants were to significantly relieve depression, patients would drift off from therapy, leaving important, life-diminishing conflicts unresolved.

Psychiatrist Peter Kramer says another reason therapists resist offering medication is the fear that it will "threaten what we love to do: be empathic with people and help them reveal themselves." Spilling the beans, he adds, "There is also the economic situation. If medication makes clients feel better, they may not want to pay for therapy."[12]

Therapists are in a particularly strong position to influence vulnerable patients in whatever direction they choose. When patients would ask family therapist Frederick Brewster for an antidepressant, he would "show them the *Physician's Desk Reference* and make them read a description of the medication. I would say, 'This is what you are going to put into your body. Think about it.'" Recently, he has begun to change his position. "Now I am not so hard-line."[13]

What turns therapists around is seeing what can happen to a patient who manages to get the appropriate medication. Brewster recalls seeing a family a few years back that he describes as having been "off the wall." The kids were out of control, the marriage was in trouble, and the husband was depressed. "We worked for several months, and I came up with all kinds of interventions for them, but progress was sluggish. Then suddenly, almost as if by magic, there was no more pathology in the family—everyone was happy, calm, and well behaved." Soon after, Brewster found out that the husband had gone on antidepressant medication. This stopped Brewster in his tracks, he said. "I began to wonder if this meant that all some people might need is a drug to let them get on with their lives."[14]

The schism in the treatment of mood disorders results in suffering for many. Both the schism *and* the suffering are vividly revealed in the story of a doctor who, in spite of seriously deteriorating mood, was deliberately treated without medication.

On January 2, 1979, forty-two-year-old Dr. Rafael Osheroff was admitted to Chestnut Lodge, a prestigious private mental hospital in Maryland. An internist who was married and the father of three,[15] he'd suffered from brief periods of depression and

27

anxiety throughout his adult life. It was not for another decade that what ended up happening to Dr. Osheroff at Chestnut Lodge would appear in the news magazines. The more telling details came out in a 1990 article in the *American Journal of Psychiatry*.

"Dr. Osheroff had been suffering from anxious and depressive symptoms for approximately two years and had been treated as an outpatient with individual psychotherapy and tricyclic antidepressant medications," wrote Dr. Gerald Klerman, a psychiatrist noted for his research on depression. Klerman reported that according to notes kept by the physician who'd prescribed the medication, Dr. Osheroff had improved moderately but didn't stay on the recommended dose. His condition subsequently worsened to the point where he needed to be hospitalized.[16]

It was at Chestnut Lodge where the saga of Dr. Osheroff's treatment took a surprising turn. He stayed in the hospital, his medical practice and his family abandoned, for seven months. During that time he "was treated with individual psychotherapy four times a week," wrote Klerman. "He lost 40 pounds, experienced severe insomnia, and had marked psychomotor agitation. His agitation, manifested by incessant pacing, was so extreme that his feet became swollen and blistered, requiring medical attention."

Understandably, Dr. Osheroff's family was upset. They consulted an outside psychiatrist who spoke to the hospital on the patient's behalf. A clinical case conference was held to review Dr. Osheroff's treatment, but the hospital made a decision not to make any major changes—*and, specifically, not to institute medication.* Dr. Osheroff's clinical condition continued to deteriorate. After seven months, his family had him discharged from Chestnut Lodge and admitted to Silver Hill Foundation in Connecticut, where he was diagnosed as having a psychotic depressive reaction. The hospital put him on antidepressants immediately. Within weeks, Dr. Osheroff showed improvement. He was discharged from Silver Hill in three months.[17] Soon after, Dr. Osheroff returned to his medical practice. He received therapy and medication and, Dr. Klerman writes, "has not since been hospitalized or experienced any episodes of depressive symptoms severe enough to interfere with his professional or social functioning."

A Doctor Sues

Three years later, in 1982, Dr. Osheroff instituted a lawsuit against Chestnut Lodge. He claimed that as a result of not being given drug treatment, which would have quickly returned him to normal functioning, he lost a lucrative medical practice, his standing in the medical community, and custody of his children.

Eventually the hospital settled out of court. Given that in 1979 medication was a widely known treatment of severe depression, some might think the hospital's actions were reprehensible. The *Osheroff* v. *Chestnut Hill* lawsuit continues to have advocates on both sides, however.

In devising and carrying out its treatment scheme, Chestnut Lodge had followed the traditional psychoanalytic approach. Although the physician's depression was recognized and included in his diagnosis, hospital doctors had other ideas about Dr. Osheroff's condition. In testifying for the deposition, the hospital cited "narcissistic personality disorder" as the real bugbear. Depression, it said, was "secondary"—the result of a narcissistic wound the physician had suffered when his third wife left him. Chestnut Lodge had made the decision to home in on Dr. Osheroff's alleged narcissism and not to treat with medication, theorizing that the depression would resolve once the narcissism was treated.

In an article entitled "The Psychiatric Patient's Right to Effective Treatment," Dr. Klerman wrote, "It is difficult to justify the rationale used by the Chestnut Lodge staff in forming their treatment plan." There existed a body of scientific evidence from controlled trials "attesting to the value of medication and/or ECT for the type of severe depression that the institution diagnosed this patient as having." No scientific evidence existed for the value of intensive individual psychotherapy for either the patient's depression or for the part of his diagnosis described as personality disorder.

Klerman takes the position that patients have a right to be informed. They have the right to be told of alternative treatments and their relative efficacy and safety. But when it comes to psychotherapy, Klerman's is a rather provocative proposition. Therapists believe wholeheartedly in their own methods for approaching emotional problems. Unlike consulting a surgeon and asking, "What other methods exist for treating my spleen besides your own?" the consumer of psychotherapy probably cannot expect a therapist to lay out a panoply of alternative approaches that might be equally effective.

Efficacy is an important issue for Klerman, as it is for the U.S. government. Careful, controlled studies in psychopharmacology began to make headway after the passage in 1962 of the Kefauver-Harris Amendments to the Food, Drug, and Cosmetic Act, which required pharmaceutical companies to prove that the compounds worked.[18] You couldn't just *say* an antidepressant medicine relieved depression; you had to prove it to the satisfaction of the Food and Drug Administration before putting it in a vial and selling it.

By the 1970s, writes Harvard's Ellison, the two major factions of the American mental health community—the biological and the psychodynamic—were being pushed to become more integrated. In 1976, the American Psychiatric Association exhorted psychiatrists to "broaden their professional goals and de-emphasize a more rigid psychoanalytic approach."[19] President Carter's Commission on Mental Health challenged psychiatry as being based on speculations, with little basis in empirical data. To remedy this, increased federal funding was provided, laying the foundation for major advances in psychiatric research.

For years, analysts have minimized the notion of efficacy, claiming that the health of the inner person can't be measured in a laboratory. It's possible, of course, to use the efficacy issue as a bludgeon against a delicate and often helpful art, but it's also true that psychoanalysis is fast disappearing in its own theoretical ether. "Twenty years ago," says Klerman, "psychodynamic psychotherapy was the dominant paradigm in psychiatry in the United States, particularly in academic centers." But that is no longer the case, and as a result, he says, "psychoanalysis is on the scientific and professional defensive." No clinical trials have been reported "that support the claims for efficacy of psychoanalysis or intensive individual psychotherapy based on psychoanalytic theory *for any form of depression*" (italics mine).

Partly, this is a consequence of analysts' lack of interest in offering any evidence at all that what they do works.

*   *   *

For more than forty years Chestnut Lodge was a major center of theory and clinical practice, specializing in the kind of intensive individual psychotherapy it offered Dr. Osheroff. In the 1950s and 1960s, that began to change. Neuroscience started influencing psychiatric teaching, practice, and research. There emerged, as well, new therapies that were not based on psychoanalytic theory. Cognitive therapy: you could lift yourself from depression by changing the way you thought about things. Behavior therapy: you could "unlearn" a phobia by exposing yourself over and over again to the thing you feared. Family therapy: it wasn't the individual who was "sick" but the family that was dysfunctional. (Family therapists, until very recently, have been vigorously "anti" medication.[20]) Controversy heated up within the profession. How to evaluate the merits of psychoanalytic, behavioral, family, and group therapies? Which, in a word, worked? Or did one need to bounce around, getting a "hit" from all of them?

In 1979, when Dr. Osheroff was treated for psychotic depression, there was very good evidence for the efficacy of two dramatic treatments for clinical depression—electroconvulsive therapy (ECT) and antidepressants. Thirty years ago, a man with a depression as severe as Dr. Osheroff's would have to have been hospitalized for many months, regardless of what it did to his career and his marriage. But not in 1979. And not now. Yet even today there are many who only treat mood disorders analytically. The profession of psychiatry continues to be divided over whether depressions like Dr. Osheroff's originate chiefly in the "mind" or are due to chemical abnormalities within the brain.

The Arrival of the Pill

The modern era of pharmacotherapy began in 1949, when Australian psychiatrist John Cade serendipitously discovered a cure for mania. "What happened was one of those wild bounces that makes this kind of research both a fascinating and a humbling game," wrote the noted research psychiatrist Nathan Kline, tracing the early history of mood-altering drugs in *From Sad to Glad*.[21]

Cade didn't begin with grand expectations. He suspected that manic behavior might be the result of some toxic substance from the nervous system, and he wondered if excesses of it might turn up in the urine. To compare the urine of manic depressives with that of ordinary depressives, schizophrenics and normal controls, he relied on a method he knew was primitive. He injected guinea pigs with urine samples from the four types of subjects. Some animals barely reacted at all; others were seized with violent convulsions. One fact immediately became apparent: the urine from the manic depressives produced these seizures with doses three to four times *smaller* than urine from the other groups. Cade thought there must have been some catalyst in the urine of the manic depressives—possibly uric acid. He ran the tests again with an extra injection of uric acid, which he diluted in a solution using lithium salts, since they combine readily with the acid. When it turned out that the solution was indeed less toxic, he tried injecting lithium alone—and hit bingo. Lithium produced remarkably calming effects on the laboratory animals.

Cade tried his new idea on ten manic patients, with dramatic results. One of his patients was "a wizened little man of 51 who had been in a state of chronic manic excitement for five years." Restless, dirty, and interfering, he had been thought a nuisance on the back wards and "bid fair to remain there," said Cade, "for the rest of his life."[22] The treatment began on March 29, 1948. Five days later, it was obvious that the man was more settled, tidier, less disinhibited. "From then on, there was steady improvement, so that in three weeks he was enjoying the unaccustomed and quite unexpected amenities of a convalescent ward." In two months, Cade's "wizened little man," who had been hospitalized for years, was able to return home to a normal life.[23]

It took the careful work of others, in particular Mogens Schou of Denmark, to establish that lithium is reliable in the long-term maintenance of bipolar (manic-depressive) mood disorder. By the 1960s, lithium was successfully used in some forty countries—but not in the United States. Here it remained restricted to experimental use until 1971. "When we complained, we were informed that other countries lacked our high standards of safety," wrote Nathan Kline, a pioneer of drug therapy for mental illness in the United States.

In the early sixties, I had occasion to meet Kline. I was a very young writer and he was at the top of his profession. *Esquire* had decided that pharmacotherapy was on the cutting edge and had dispatched a colleague and me to interview him. It would be a long time before I'd have any personal reason to be interested in Dr. Kline's discoveries, but I found his work fascinating. He was attempting to treat the most complex-seeming distortions of mind and mood with a pill.

I remember the circumstances of our meeting more vividly than its content. Dr. Kline had allotted us an hour, at seven in the morning, in a coffee shop on Madison and Eighty-sixth Street. I had been up with anxiety all night. In the predawn dark, I got dressed for the interview, leaving my husband the job of giving breakfast to our babies. There was something soothing, I remember, about the empty streets my cab sped along, taking me to the meeting. When I arrived at the coffee shop, Kline already had a big breakfast sitting before him. He had waited for me before starting. I noticed the elegant cut of his suit as I fumbled with my tape recorder. From that point on, I forgot my anxieties as Kline launched ahead on the great passion of his life: the study of how and why certain medications are able to stabilize the mental distortions produced by metabolic defects in the brain.

That, as the editors of *Esquire* had intuited, was the beginning of the heyday of biological psychiatry. "In one great breakthrough year, our American team brought out the first MAO inhibitor, a Swiss team produced the first tricyclic, and a Danish psychiatrist unearthed the half-buried discovery of lithium," Kline himself would later write. "If some random circumstance had brought us together earlier, we would have been astounded to learn that we were all hot on the same trail."[24]

It was 1957 when Kline's research team discovered the powerful new MAO (monoamine oxidase) inhibitors. He had also been involved in developing the first discovered class of antidepressants, the tricyclics. MAOIs worked, and worked wonderfully, when tricyclics didn't. Thus, the two medications were soon seen to enable people who might previously have been consigned to mental institutions to live normal lives.

When tricyclics were discovered, it was found that they didn't touch schizophrenia but would help many who were depressed. The tricyclics, today, are the most commonly prescribed class of antidepressants. (Other classes are the monoamine oxidase inhibitors, such as Nardil and Parnate, described below, and a third class, discovered in the eighties, of which Prozac is representative. The three classes function biochemically in somewhat different ways.)

Though called antidepressants, tricyclics have been found to be useful in treating a number of disorders. "Of particular importance to psychotherapists," Ellison advises, "are the tricyclics' effectiveness in treating panic disorder, agoraphobia, obsessive-compulsive disorder, bulimic binging, narcolepsy, childhood enuresis (bedwetting), and attention deficit disorder or hyperactivity of childhood."[25]

Monoamine oxidase inhibitors (MAOIs) are as effective as tricyclics in treating some types of depression and may be more effective in treating other types. MAOIs and Prozac also appear to be effective in the disorders Ellison lists for tricyclics. (Different types of depression, anxiety, and panic disorders are discussed at length in the following chapter. Crucial dietary restrictions that accompany the use of MAOIs are discussed in chapter 8 and appendix D.)

How Mood-Control Messages Get Through

One reason it's hard to get a complete picture of how psychotropic medications do what they do is that, in the brain, everything happens on a minuscule scale. A typical three-pound brain is densely packed with about 10 billion nerve cells. "Each nerve cell operates as a kind of short-wave radio station, broadcasting and receiving coded messages," Kline explained.

How do the chemical messages get from cell to cell? At the top of each cell there's a bushy cluster of antennae consisting of dendrites, through which impulses arrive. From the other end of the cell trails the cell's transmission cable, the "axon." Tiny sacs are found in the nerve-cell axons. In these are stored *serotonin*, *norepinephrine*, and *dopamine*, chemical "messengers" whose action helps to push nerve signals along.

Nerve signals are transmitted in the form of electrochemical impulses. When dendrites pick up an incoming signal, they alter the sodium-to-potassium balance, triggering a discharge by the axon. This is how the signals are relayed from cell to cell throughout the entire system.

Discovering an Opiate in the Brain

By the early seventies, drug addiction had become such a nightmare for the American middle class that the government began putting some money into neuroscience in the hope of finding a cure. In 1973, Solomon Snyder and Candace Pert at Johns Hopkins were trying to figure out why the drug naloxone is capable of bringing people out of a heroin coma. In a landmark study that used radioactive tracers on morphine-soaked animal brains, Snyder and Pert made a tremendous leap. They found that the brain has its own receptors, or special binding sites,[26] for opiates. As we will see in chapter 7, this information would lead to a new understanding of how addiction works, as well as to new ways of treating it.

It was discovered that the place in the brain where antidepressants do their work is the *synapse*—the space between one nerve cell and the next. A chemical messenger—called a *neurotransmitter* because of the job it does—carries the signal across this space. The neurotransmitter flashes across the synapse and, by fitting into *receptors*, which are like little locks on the next cell, turns on that cell's electrical system. Then it returns to its station. The whole transaction takes about 1/1,000 of a second. Then another electrical impulse starts on down the line.

The Pert-Snyder work triggered an avalanche of new research. Certainly, scientists inferred, the brain had not evolved its own opiate receptors to accommodate street drugs. There must be natural, morphinelike substances in the body for relieving pain—not only physical pain, they suspected, but emotional pain as well.

Norepinephrine and serotonin were already being considered in depression research. Serotonin, investigated for its role in sleep disorders, was of particular interest, since sleep disorders accompany depression. Were serotonin and norepinephrine neurotransmitters? Did they play a role in alterations of mood? If so, there must be receptors for them.

The hypothesis would emerge as the seventies progressed that opiates must bind to specific sites, or receptors, in the brain. The binding, or tissue interaction, produces certain pharmacological responses to a drug—blocking pain, for example, or inducing euphoria. The receptor sites can be occupied only by molecules of a specific structure; thus, a "fit" takes place between a drug molecule and the receptor site. "This may explain the specific action of opiates: they bind to these sites and no other," writes Kenneth Blum.[27]

Eventually, it was found that the antidepressant imipramine attaches itself to neurotransmitter receptors in the brain. When taken in pill form, imipramine enters the blood, circulates to the brain, and snaps into a receptor in the part of the brain that regulates mood.

Morphine, too, affects the neurotransmitter system, raising the pain threshold in such a way that the user gets high. But this "high," it was soon seen, does not occur with imipramine, which works in a way that is both subtler and more specific than morphine.

Soon researchers discovered another receptor, this one for the neurotransmitter GABA (gamma-aminobutyric acid), which has a calming effect on the brain. They found that amphetamine produces its speediness by affecting dopamine and norepinephrine.

As these discoveries were taking place in laboratories hither and yon, Jon Franklin, a prize-winning journalist, saw that a major change was in the offing. He wrote, in *Molecules of the Mind*, "As the 1970s waned and the 1980s began, discovery followed discovery. The pattern, as it developed, underscored the dawning awareness that the mind was directed by chemical phenomena."[28]

To Franklin, the "new psychology," based on biology, was as important a development as the splitting of the atom or the breaking of the genetic code.

Depressed Rats

Enlightening animal models were being used to learn more about mood disorders. One group of studies lent considerable credence to the theory that enough stress can trigger the biological symptoms of depression. Rats were put in a cage with a metal floor and exposed to occasional but unpredictable shocks. If there was a ledge the rats could escape to, they were able to remain in the shock cage for long periods of time and still appear normal. But if escape was made impossible, the effect on the lab animals was dramatic. They developed sleep and eating disorders, stopped mating, and could no longer figure out how to get through a maze. Once stressed to this point, the rats continued to deteriorate. When put in cages where escape routes existed, they didn't try to use them, but seemed to give up. The picture, scientists thought, was startlingly like what happens to humans who are stressed heavily enough to become depressed.

A group of scientists led by Fritz Henn at the State University of New York at Stony Brook began analyzing rat brains for chemical changes at various stages of the stressing process. As the rats got depressed, predictable changes took place in their brain receptors, and the changes occurred at the same time their behavior changed. Thus, the scientists were able to see what was happening neurochemically when behavior changed. "I'm very excited about this," Franklin reports Henn as saying.[29]

However, the studies weren't providing any new information on what, other than environment, might contribute to depression. Apply enough stress and the rats, like humans, will experience a predictable mood dip. Research, at this point, seemed only to reinforce what psychologists had always believed—that environment is the chief cause of depression.

But when Henn tried repeating his procedures, something unexpected happened. Using a different strain of rats, he was unable to duplicate the results of his earlier studies, but doing more tests with the original strain, he got the same results. The conclusion? There must have been some genetic distinction between the two strains. Strain A, that is, seemed to have been predisposed to responding to stress with depression, whereas Strain B didn't buckle.

What a bombshell this innocuous-seeming research created. Henn's discovery of changes in rats' brains added important biological evidence to earlier twin and adoption studies indicating that mood disorders are genetic. The idea that mental illness was inherited would become one of the most volatile issues in modern biology.

The Beginning of the Nature/Nurture Debate

Early in the century, science documented the first example of a type of genetically caused insanity: Huntington's chorea. An illness that struck people in mid-life, drove them insane, and finally killed them, Huntington's chorea seemed clearly to be inherited. When one parent died of it, half of his or her children would die of it as well. Although insanity was a striking symptom, the illness was never considered "mental" because its early symptoms—disabling muscular spasms—were physical. Nevertheless, that Huntington's chorea was genetic *and* produced mental symptoms was worth noting. Could it be that there were other, more purely psychiatric disorders that were also inherited?

Schizophrenia is an illness marked by distorted perception of reality, by hallucinations and delusions, and by extreme apathy. Drugs can control the most flamboyant symptoms, but thus far there is no cure. Considered the most disabling of all mental disorders, schizophrenia today afflicts about 2.8 million Americans.

In 1916 the German scientist Ernst Rudin studied the victims of schizophrenia and their relatives and found that the illness runs in families. Although the odds—one in twenty—weren't flabbergasting, it was clear something was going on. Many, at this point, took the position that the illness was *not* genetic but environmental. The nature-nurture debate was off at a gallop. "Even as Rudin was calculating the excess risk to the sisters and brothers of schizophrenics," Franklin writes, "John B. Watson, already a looming giant in psychology, was staking out the claim that genes played no role at all in personality."

Watson was stunningly confident. "Give me a dozen healthy infants, well-formed, and my own specified world to bring them up in," he insisted, "and I'll guarantee to take anyone at random and train him to become any kind of specialist I might select—doctor, lawyer, artist, merchant-chief, and, yes, even beggar man and thief, regardless of the talents, penchants, tendencies, abilities, vocations and race of his ancestors."[30]

Equally autocratic were the "eugenicists," who were convinced "all human strengths and weaknesses, including psychological ones, were a product of breeding," says Franklin. The eugenicists, among them such prominent writers as H. G. Wells and George Bernard Shaw, were an influential bunch. From their camp emerged such dangerous ideas as the notion that criminals and others thought morally reprehensible ought to be sterilized.

Remarkably, during the first third of the century, eugenic thought swept America; eventually some sixty thousand Americans were sterilized and severe restrictions were imposed on nonwhite immigrants.

The eventual backlash against eugenics was stimulated in part by Hitler and a few scientists who'd come under his thumb. Rudin, for example, was one of the authors of the official Nazi book on sterilization regulations. Public opinion in America began to shift to the psychological left. From the 1940s through the 1960s, most research money went into the environment's effects on behavior. During those decades, the bulk of social-science research buttressed the notion that the personality is dramatically affected by such forces as economics and peer influence.

Science Ascends

The scientific work that would eventually produce a change in our understanding of mental illness began gathering momentum when small sums of money became available for genetic research, first on schizophrenia, then on manic-depressive illness. At about this time, pharmacologists were developing drugs that dramatically altered mood swings, delusions, and hallucinations. At first, how the drugs worked wasn't understood. Medical science has always been driven by the need to provide relief; often the whys and hows of a cure don't come until later.

Like all medicines, the new drugs for depression and anxiety produced side effects; much experimenting remained to be done. Still, these drugs would create revolutionary change. Undeveloped character, or "neurosis," would end up taking a backseat, and our own mood chemicals—the newly recognized "opiates of the brain"—would be perceived as playing a major role in the disorders that affect mood.

As pharmacology developed, so did the bright new field of psychogenetics. In London, two psychiatric geneticists completed a fascinating study of schizophrenics using genetically identical twins. They themselves didn't diagnose the twins, but gathered information from the patients and their brothers and sisters on tape. Independent psychiatrists made the diagnoses. The results, published in 1966, were startling: When one identical twin became schizophrenic, the odds were 58 percent that the other twin would, too. When borderline diagnoses were included, the concordance rate went up to 67 percent. Among nonidentical twins, the concordance rate was only 12 percent. In the general population, the odds were half a percent.[31]

Skeptics said, however, that having been raised with a schizophrenic might have been what produced the illness in the second twin. This objection was challenged by a study of the biological relatives of schizophrenics who had been adopted as children. Even when raised in separate families, *both* identical twins were likely to be schizophrenic, if the illness existed at all.

The debate that had gone on for decades as to whether schizophrenia is a psychological condition brought about by social factors or a disease caused by changes in the brain came to an end in March 1990. The *New England Journal of Medicine* published a study that, according to Lewis Judd, director of the NIMH, offered "irrefutable evidence that schizophrenia is a brain disorder."[32] Again, identical twins were used, but this time new technology had made it possible to "scan" their brains using magnetic resonance imaging (MRI). MRI depicts the brain's anatomy in precise detail. The brains of the schizophrenic twins were found to have wider spaces in the foldings at the surface of the cortex, "suggesting atrophy or failure of brain cells to develop," said Richard Suddah, the psychiatrist who headed the study. In addition, various parts of the schizophrenics' brains were smaller.

Though the mystery of schizophrenia still has not been penetrated, says Judd, "we're on the sharp ascending limb of discovery of its biological bases."[33]

Another Piece of the Puzzle: Predicting Suicide

When spinal fluid was studied in groups of depressed patients,[34] one group turned out to have very low levels of 5HIAA, a breakdown product of serotonin, while the other group didn't. The group with low 5HIAA had a much higher rate of serious suicide attempts.[35] Further research found that serotonin was related to suicidal behavior regardless of the psychiatric disorder.

In the 1980s, researchers studied the brains of people who had killed themselves. The brains were found to have fewer of the special "binding sites" that permit serotonin to be taken up and distributed. Within the next few years, new imaging techniques will make it possible to study brain tissue in *living* suicidal patients—those who have made attempts in the past. In the meantime, according to Dr. John Mann, the most probable explanation of suicide is low serotonin levels in the brain.

The question we are left with is, Why do some people's brains lack sufficient serotonin to begin with? Mann believes the most likely cause is an enzyme defect in the brain's ability to synthesize serotonin. "This could be genetic, or due to a developmental, perinatal or early environmental event." Stress, that is, can tip the balance when mood-regulating brain chemicals are genetically vulnerable in the first place. "Our goal," says Mann, "is to refine a set of biological and clinical predictors of suicidal behavior." They are working on this at his new Suicide Clinical Research Center at Western Psychiatric Institute—the first center for studying suicidal behavior in the United States.[36]

Studies suggest that aggressive behaviors—including homicide—may be related to brain chemical abnormalities like those that produce depression. Changes in serotonin may one day be used to predict the "likelihood that a person is going to act on a thought—either a suicidal thought or an aggressive thought."

Pharmacological research supports Mann's ideas. Lithium, which acts on the serotonin system, was given to violent prisoners in a California medical facility. In many, the drug substantially reduced angry, provocative behavior. Dr. Joseph Tupin, head of the University of California team that did the study, says lithium may be effective "in the long-term reduction of aggressive behavior."[37]

I mentioned this research to a friend who conducts therapy groups for men who are batterers. She had told me how poignant and frustrating are the men's attempts to refrain from lashing out and striking their wives and children. One man had arrived at a recent group meeting with the triumphant announcement, "I didn't hit anyone this week!"

"You know, Martha," I said, "they may find in the end that this kind of behavior is really chemically induced, a matter of the levels of neurotransmitters in these men's brains." The idea was shocking to her. She has spent years as a therapist working to help men control battering through insight and behavioral techniques.

41

The progress they make is slow and the setbacks many, but Martha's efforts were gratifying. Now I was coming along and suggesting that group therapy for people with poor impulse control may one day be obsolete. Is this what friends are for?

Yet suppose that, in fact, abusing others—verbally as well as physically—is symptomatic of chemical imbalance? Then the work these researchers are doing on mood-regulating brain hormones may lead to a chemical intervention that could save men like Martha's batterers—and their loved ones—years of suffering.

Anxiety: A Chemical Overload

Anxiety research took a big leap forward in the late seventies, when a receptor in the brain was discovered for tranquilizing drugs like Valium. Tranquilizers were found to relieve anxiety by boosting the action of the brain's own calming neurotransmitter, GABA.

In 1988, a press conference was held to hail the antidepressant clomipramine in the treatment of obsessive-compulsive disorder (OCD). A severely disabling anxiety disorder that had long resisted the efforts of psychotherapists, OCD responded dramatically to clomipramine. In many patients, symptoms ceased within weeks of starting the medication, as if a switch had been thrown.

Panic attacks have been found to respond to antidepressants. More generalized anxiety is often significantly reduced by the new serotonin drugs as well. As a result, attitudes toward what causes anxiety are changing. It isn't hard to imagine that some people's anxious personalities don't start in the psyche, says psychiatrist Arnold Cooper of Cornell Medical School, but are the result of "biologic dysregulation."

Speaking at a symposium in the mid-eighties, Cooper, past president of the American Psychoanalytic Association, was presenting his colleagues with a revolutionary idea: Many who are chronically anxious or phobic or have panic attacks may be suffering from "a hyperactive alerting system," the result of a small flaw in brain metabolism. GABA neurotransmitters—the body's calming agents—aren't firing properly.[38]

Ironically, Cooper's talk was given over two decades after

psychiatry had discovered that antidepressant medication stops panic. Today this treatment for panic is widely recognized.[39] Psychotherapy can be useful as well. It helps people "unlearn" the behaviors they developed to cope with the unpredictable switches into a panic state. But for the physically intense panic symptoms themselves—the "My God, I must be dying" sensation—nothing works as fast as medication. More and more therapists are recognizing this and suggesting that their panic-ridden patients seek help from a psychopharmacologist.

Analyzed but Still Panicky

Arnold Cooper tells the story of a woman who came to him complaining mostly of anxiety and whom he treated with analysis. Eventually, as he told his colleagues at the symposium, he came to have second thoughts about the treatment.[40]

The woman had had a history of depression. She was timid with men and terribly sensitive to rejection. Whenever she tried to have a relationship with a man, it was colored by her fear that the man would abandon her. This made her so anxious she behaved in ways that brought about the very outcome she feared.

Dr. Cooper thought his patient's anxiety was rooted in her childhood experiences. As a little girl she would become so anxious when her parents went out in the evening that it took hours for her to calm down. She also suffered from school phobia. Yet several genetic "red flags" in the woman's history would have put a psychobiologist on alert. Her mother had been chronically depressed. Her aunt had been hospitalized with an "uncertain" diagnosis of schizophrenia. (Mood disorders, especially bipolar depression, are often mistaken for schizophrenia.) Her father, when she was ten years old, went into a deep depression and became extremely withdrawn. Clearly, depression was the family illness. Such a strong genetic component points the finger at a biologically based mood disorder.

Dr. Cooper's analysis of the woman was directed at trying to get to the bottom of her anxieties. Gradually, the woman became more successful in her career and had somewhat better relationships with men. But the mood symptoms with which she entered the analysis—depression, anxiety, feelings of shame and worthlessness—came back repeatedly. Eventually, the end of her analysis was "successfully negotiated," says Cooper, even though the mood symptoms remained. Two years later, while she was on vacation, she found herself in a panic and called him. This time, he suggested an antidepressant. The woman responded dramatically, feeling relieved and reorganized, "as if some external intrusion in her life was now gone." Cooper told his colleagues that on medication his patient "had a feeling that she was in some way more in control of herself than she had ever been."

Arnold Cooper has been a spearhead in the movement to stop viewing drugs as mere symptom relievers. "There is a group of chronically depressed patients . . . whose mood regulation is vastly changed by antidepressant medication. The entry of these new molecules into their metabolism alters, tending to normalize, the way they see the world, the way they do battle with their superegos, the way they respond to object separation." He seemed to be implying that medication can actually exert changes in the personality. What would this do to psychoanalytic theory—and treatment?

It would have been fun to have been a fly on the wall at the Pittsburgh Psychoanalytic Institute when Cooper gave this talk in 1984. I suspect it caused quite a stir, so impassioned was his plea that analysts begin thinking differently about anxiety and mood disorders. He even suggested that had he offered his panicked patient antidepressant medication in the first place, things might have gone better, faster.[41]

Therapists often exhort people with mood swings to believe they have more control over the way they feel than they do. "It may be that we have been co-conspirators with these patients in their need to construct a rational-seeming world in which they hold themselves unconsciously responsible for events," Cooper admits.

The depressed look for reasons to explain their mood states. It is less scary to try to claim control "than to admit the utter helplessness of being at the mercy of moods that sweep over them without apparent rhyme or reason," Cooper explains. Therapists who use psychological interpretations to make their patients' mood swings comprehensible may be perpetuating "a cruel misunderstanding of the patient's effort to rationalize his life experience, and may result in strengthening masochistic defenses."

In other words, in encouraging people to construct a psychological house of cards for explaining their mood disorders, therapists may unwittingly extend their patients' suffering.

Bringing the Old and New Models Together

The schism between psychology and psychiatry is basically this: Therapists influenced by Freud's psychology see depression as a product of the *mind* and talk about it in terms of drives, defenses, regressions, and problems of identification and self-esteem. Those influenced by biological psychiatry see depression as a product of the *brain*, caused by shifts that take place among hormones and neurotransmitters. Shephard Kantor, a psychiatrist on the faculty of the Columbia University College of Physicians and Surgeons, looks for ways of bringing the two approaches together. The mental "productions" of depressed patients—negative thoughts and, with psychotics, hallucinations—come from chemical changes in the central nervous system and are *not* psychologically caused. Kantor no longer believes that the crazy thinking that accompanies depression is triggered by external events or is the residue— for example—of childhood interactions with parents. He believes the crazy thinking that accompanies depression is caused by the chemical state itself.

But what *is* the effect of childhood trauma? we may ask. Surely it can't be totally unrelated to depression. Kantor suggests that the mental changes of depression may be due to certain sensations and memory traces that go back to "the calamities of childhood." Such calamities produce changes in neurotransmitter levels or receptor sites, he theorizes. And it isn't just childhood trauma that does this. Emotional wounds at any point along the way might produce similar chemical alterations in the brain.

Studies with primates show that circuitry linking structures in the central nervous system is responsible for perception, memory, and emotion.[42] With this in mind, Kantor says, it isn't such a big jump to imagine how the tiniest of biochemical disturbances at any of these sites might evoke memories and moods whose origins lie in childhood.

Kantor has another idea. One of the breakthroughs of modern neurology was Wilder Penfield's discovery that stimulating certain areas of the brain with electrical impulses produces visual and auditory images and memories. Kantor asks this provocative question: Isn't it possible that the signals generated by neurotransmitters might function as "the internal equivalents" of Penfield's externally applied stimulating electrodes? If so, he says, it "would cause patients to report feelings, recollections and ideas generated not by conflict, fantasy, or drive derivatives, but by chemical stimuli."

Kantor's ideas have not yet been substantiated by research, but his thinking is far from wild, for much that has already been learned points in the same direction. In the meantime, Kantor stands firm in his conviction that psychiatrists should learn to understand—and accept—the chemical nature of mood disorders.[43]

Clearly, childhood events produce inner experience—feelings and attitudes that stay with us, affecting our lives immensely. The question psychiatry wrestles with now is how these powerfully resonant events interact with neurotransmitter deficits to produce shifts in mood state that are sometimes volatile, sometimes subtle. There are differences, after all, among all of us—differences in the amount of trauma or stress we experience and in the degree of chemical vulnerability we inherit. No one exists in a perfect state of chemical balance. Where, then, should the line be drawn with respect to neurotransmitter deficits? Do they exist in all who become mood disordered or only in those suffering from severe forms of these illnesses?

Shephard Kantor suggests a kind of equation between the severity of illness and the amount of chemical change. In people with mild depressions, the chemical alterations are minimal; thus, their effects remain mild and localized. With major depression, the chemical changes in the brain are greater, producing a ripple effect throughout the central nervous system. This is the point at which sleep, appetite, and libido become disturbed. Thought processes, including memory and the ability to make associations, are affected. Patients can, as my daughter did, develop psychomotor retardation, a slowdown of speech and thought that some have described as a feeling of being "weighted down" or "under water."

*   *   *

I haven't experienced Gabrielle's type of depression, although certainly I've been depressed. The difference, according to Dr. Kantor, is quantitative. The ebbing of serotonin is greater in more severe depressions. But it ebbs in milder depressions as well, producing changes that are discomfiting, although they may not be so drastically disruptive. We are all, when depressed, in need of serotonin or other brain chemicals that may be deficient. If the deficiency is mild enough, we may be able to boost it with sunshine, with exercise (endorphins, which are produced by exercise, bring about brain changes akin to those of serotonin), or by falling in love.

Yes, love, too, has been shown to produce boosting effects on mood-regulating chemicals. "When we fall in love," writes Maggie Scarf, "brain levels of norepinephrine and dopamine rise, flooding us with feelings of hopefulness and joy."

Relationships, romantic and otherwise, are affected by mood disorders. New research shows that chemical intervention actually changes the way people relate to others. "Antidepressant medication dramatically improves autonomous ego functioning," explains Eric Marcus of the Columbia University College of Physicians and Surgeons.[44] The ego, freed from storms of mood change, is better able to stand aside and observe itself and to test reality. Feelings flow more easily, and the person is able to regulate them rather than be overwhelmed by them. These capacities make interacting with others a joy rather than a burden.

Psychoanalysts aren't the only ones clinging to the old notion that mood disorders are rooted in the psyche. You and I are probably the ultimate resisters against the fundamental change being wrought by the new biopsychiatry. Devoted followers of Freud (whether we know it or not), we think about emotions and the psyche with an almost mystical fervor. We *believe* in the twists and turns the mind takes when childhood has left us insufficiently loved. We have spent our lives struggling to understand precisely what shade of our own arrogance is the result of father's narcissism and mother's submissive fusion with it. Where would *Death of a Salesman* be if Willie Loman had been diagnosed as having a mood disorder? Life is flattened, we feel, by a one-dimensional, chemical approach to the brain—flattened, trivialized, and made horrifyingly predictable.

There is also the fear that such an approach to mental disorders gives too much power to scientists and doctors. What will be the outcome if we start letting "them" manipulate the brain's chemicals to produce changes in mood and personality? And who knows what the long-term effect of all this may be. It might be better just to hunker down and continue eating our oat bran and B_6.

Ideas long held aren't easily given up. In reaction to political revolutions, people become frightened and dig in their heels, attempting to hold on to the old order. It is little different with scientific revolutions. We become cozy with our ways of thinking about things. What a great guy that Einstein was, we say. We are too young to remember how disturbed people were by $E = mc^2$. Probably we don't even understand $E = mc^2$, but someone does, we figure, and to the extent that it was around for a long time, it became a good and sturdy vehicle for glossing over the mysteries of the universe. When the new quantum physics came along, we resisted, inevitably. Even though something extremely exciting was in the offing, some new and far more sophisticated understanding of matter and energy and their fundamental sameness, a part of us didn't want to *hear* about it. Not the least of our distress came from the fact that the new physics is harder to understand, even, than the old. When will "they" stop changing the rules? we demand to know. And will the day ever arrive when the truth is finally fixed and knowable?

On the day after the dinner party at which I'd discussed what I'd been learning about mood disorders, I found myself thinking of the gut resistance many people have to the idea that depression is precipitated by metabolic malfunction of the brain. On some level we find it fascinating, but on a deeper level we are frightened. Depression an illness of the brain? That a predisposition toward this malfunctioning can be inherited seems to add to the overall sense of, well . . . futility. Forget that pharmacology has so improved things that mood disorders can now be successfully treated—and may one day be prevented. If four red pills on a counter are the answer to emotional well-being, can Orwell's vision for humanity be far behind?

CHAPTER THREE

What's Happening to Me?

Even with years of therapy, I'd never really identified a mood or anxiety disorder in myself or in any of my relatives. We were just your ordinary, neurotic family with good values and honorable intentions. And yet several times in my twenties, and once again, in my thirties, I'd had some very disturbing experiences. I never connected them with depression. I never associated them with anything. They were fluke experiences that seemed to have nothing to do with me. That continued to be the way I felt about it in spite of a long psychoanalysis.

The most upsetting symptoms had been anxiety and panic attacks that were accompanied by palpitations, vertigo, sweating, and tremendous fear. The attacks were always weirdly autonomous; they began with a bang and ended months later as abruptly as they had begun. Now it seems to me that beneath those unsettling symptoms there probably lurked a mood disorder. I can remember, at the time, feeling very odd, as if it were only I who had such symptoms—as if everyone else in my family were solid as oaks and I was in some way flawed, a fragile shrub that might not survive the winter.

My father used to say he had an addictive personality and would suggest that I must undoubtedly have the same, since I was his "genetic copy." He had worked hard to avoid falling into the trap of addiction, and I must do the same. He told me this when I was fifteen and he'd caught me in the local drugstore, smoking a Lucky Strike.

A scientist, my father was aware of the genetic connection

earlier than most. Still, I didn't want to believe him. I railed against his dire predictions, refusing a life as cautious as his, with his refusal to smoke, his rare travel or departures from routine, his strict regimen of two daily ounces of gin. So assiduously did he avoid situations that might have made him anxious that for years he didn't drive a car. Actually, he and I both had turned forty before taking up that perilous activity. And I didn't recognize my problem with driving until the man I was living with at the time protested against having to drive me everywhere. The argument lasted seven years. It took many analytic sessions to put a dent in what eventually I would classify as phobia, although I resisted the label for a long time. I had become adept at avoiding situations that made me anxious, including travel, certain kinds of social interactions (parties, especially, unnerved, me), and driving. Denying the degree to which I avoided things, I thought of myself as self-contained, self-motivated, well organized. For five years I lived in a rural village and either walked where I had to go or took a taxi. Visits to New York were brief and goal oriented: I went in to see my analyst and returned on the evening train. Often I would lie awake at night. Insomnia had become for me a way of life, cropping up whenever there was something new to do, some change in the routine, or extra demand, or new person to meet.

Searching further in my own past, I remembered that several years after college I had undergone a six-month siege of almost overwhelming anxiety. Its onset was dramatic—what psychiatrists refer to as "spontaneous," in that no specific event seemed to have brought it on. I had been at the Brooklyn Museum on a magazine assignment when a wave of vertigo hit me with such ferocity that I had to sit down and put my head between my legs to keep from fainting. An anxiety attack. The intense agitation that began at that moment rarely subsided for six months, almost to the day. I woke up one morning free, panic gone. I could read again, I could think again, I could relax and have fun again. But what had happened? At one point, a doctor had suggested that I see a psychiatrist. I had declined. I was twenty-three years old and wanted no further proof that I was (as I had often, during that episode, felt) a candidate for the psych ward.

Did I ever even describe the experiences to my parents? Probably not. I was a young woman trying to make it on her own in

New York. My attitude was "Get control of this thing. Try to rise above it." I didn't know at the time that one of my aunts was suffering from a mood disorder that would push her to attempt suicide. Nor did I find out until I was in my forties that my father's grandfather had killed himself in the attic one Thanksgiving day.

In 1972, a year after my marriage ended, the panic symptoms started up again, only beginning this time with an uncontrollable bout of tears. After my youngest child's sixth birthday party I started crying and couldn't stop for several hours. I felt unbearable hopelessness—over what, I had no idea. There was also a terrible sense of guilt.

This was the episode that finally sent me into analysis. We began our discussions with what had been happening on the night the most recent attack occurred. I was identifying with my young daughter, the analyst suggested; perhaps, on the night of her birthday, I had been struck by something that had happened to me when I was the same age.

For months we searched among the fragmentary memories of my sixth year but found nothing. The panic attacks had spread out into a generalized agoraphobia so severe that I had trouble staying in the supermarket long enough to shop. Movie theaters and restaurants became impossible. So did standing in line at the bank. The world in which I could operate freely became narrower and narrower. Fortunately, as a writer, I was able to do my work in the safety of my study. The palpitations and tremors and difficulty being with people remitted after about six months—the same timespan as the first siege. I thought my recovery was the result of my analysis.

Now I am far from sure of that.

Fear and Phobia: In the Brain or in the Mind?

Panic disorder affects 2 million Americans at any given time. It has recently been classfied as a separate form of anxiety. Today some scientists think panic disorder is partly medical and partly psychological. Others think it is entirely medical. Jeffrey Jonas, a research psychiatrist at Fair Oaks Hospital in Summit, New

Jersey, says the success of biopsychiatry in treating panic has resulted in psychodynamic theories of this type of anxiety being "quickly abandoned."[1]

They may have been abandoned by biopsychiatrists, but they certainly have not been abandoned by many therapists. And yet a great deal more is known about the illness these days. It has a specific course, and it responds to specific treatment. It is one of the easiest psychiatric disorders to dispense with, but most people struggle with it for months, even years.

"Unlike a person with generalized anxiety disorder, who is more or less always anxious, the patient with panic disorders becomes anxious in sudden and unpredictable bursts," explains Jack Gorman of the Columbia University College of Physicians and Surgeons. This was precisely the sort of panic I'd had in my twenties and thirties. Would that I had known then what it was that was happening to me. It would have been such a relief to know I wasn't going crazy.

Gorman describes a woman neurosurgeon who had her first panic attack driving to work one day over a bridge. "All of a sudden she feels her heart start to pound, she feels as if she can't catch her breath, and she shakes, trembles, and is sure she must be having a heart attack."[2] Finishing her trip to work in the slow lane, when she arrived at her hospital she convinced the emergency-room squad that she was having a heart attack. An electrocardiogram and several blood tests were normal. She was relieved, but that wasn't the end of it. She kept having the terrifying attacks, each lasting about twenty minutes. And they were occurring everywhere—at home, at work, in the car. Soon she was worrying about the next attack; "anticipatory anxiety," psychiatrists call it. She began avoiding the places where attacks had occurred in the past and found she couldn't go anywhere unless she had a friend with her. This is called *agoraphobia.* It is virtually always the end result of panic attacks that aren't psychiatrically treated.

It's been known since the late sixties that panic symptoms can be stopped in several weeks with medication. Most antipanic medications are antidepressants. They relieve symptoms so dramatically that biopsychiatrists wonder why psychotherapists are still trying to bombard patients with the old childhood theories of anxiety. Yet studies have shown that most people with panic still don't get offered medication.

Phobia is another type of anxiety. Phobias are based in irrational fears of specific events or situations that become so painful that people avoid whatever occasions they fear. To really classify as a phobia, a fear must seriously interfere with functioning. "A person who is afraid of skydiving does not have a phobia, because most of us live very nicely without jumping out of airplanes," Jack Gorman writes in *The Essential Guide to Psychiatric Drugs*, a book that's helpful to professional and lay readers alike.[3]

In recent years, phobia has been broken down into three types. *Agoraphobia,* as we have seen, is a complication of panic disorder. It is treated along with the panic attacks; once the panic goes, agoraphobia isn't far behind. Drug treatment is so effective, no one needs to suffer months and years with this illness.

Simple phobia is a fear of something very specific—heights, water, growling dogs. So many children have these fears that most clinicians consider them a normal part of development. There are no drug treatments for simple phobias, which usually respond to psychotherapy.

Social phobia is the fear of social situations—talking before a group, talking at parties, speaking up in class. Gorman says that some people with the illness can get uptight just having to sign a check in front of a bank teller. "Whenever they fear they are being watched," he writes, "people with social phobia become extremely anxious, have palpitations, shake, blush, and tremble. Then they think people can see them shaking and blushing and they get even more nervous."

Social phobia used to be called "performance anxiety," and people would spend years in therapy trying to get over it. I once knew the most marvelous violinist who had no trouble playing in a symphony orchestra but absolutely couldn't hack it in a chamber group. Suddenly, things got too small, too close, too visible, and she would suffer so from bow shake that she messed up everything. And yet she was able to make her living playing in the symphony because that situation didn't trigger her phobia. The last I knew, she had been working on the problem with a therapist for about five years. She loved chamber music and wanted desperately to be able to play in a group.

Recently, it has been found that social phobias respond well to medication, ideally in combination with therapy. Chapter 8 gives the details of medication for phobia and panic disorder.

Many people with panic disorders have relatives who have suffered from them or from mood disorders, or perhaps even both. Gabrielle said she never even knew she had anxiety problems—including social phobia—until she went on antidepressant treatment. Suddenly, the problems vanished. She was able to go to parties and mix and mingle easily. She was able to confront rude taxi drivers and get the bank to respond quickly when it messed up her account. Behaviors that I used to view as problems of dependency—the inability to stand up and take care of yourself—are, in those with social phobia, miraculously treatable. The shy, retiring person seems to stand straight up overnight, like a plant that gets a sudden shot of water.

Hudson and Pope think such problems are so interrelated and so intergenerational that people who are depressed can expect that their children may have panic problems or depression problems or will be vulnerable to addictions. The goal is to become familiar enough with the new, biological understanding of mood and anxiety disorders that we look for the signs—just as we would keep an eye out for measles or chicken pox in our children.

It was in the course of reading about Hudson and Pope's new spectrum hypothesis that I first began to think about how all of these illnesses—depression, panic, social phobia—have appeared in my own family. Obviously, my children had not just inherited their father's genes; they had inherited mine. Gabrielle's depression was not just a little island in our family, as her father's wasn't in *his* family and as my panic and periodic mood problems are not isolated examples in *my* family.

Is this depressing news, or is it hopeful? I think it's hopeful. The new treatments for these illnesses are so effective that people with extreme phobias and major mood disorders no longer need have ruined lives.

Nor need they spend months and years in therapy to gain relief.

Nor should they feel like pariahs—either in their families or in the world. These are genetic illnesses for which they bear—as Arnold Cooper tried to communicate to his colleagues—no responsibility. The question becomes one of trying to identify what's going wrong. People with panic shouldn't have to go running in fear to their cardiologists. People with depression should be able to say, "Oh, *I* know what's happening to me. I'm depressed!" And then get help.

Depression: The Experience

Joann was thirty-eight when she was freed of a depressive illness that had plagued her for her entire adult life. Before finally getting help, she felt lower than she'd ever felt before. "I was in agony, caught up in an excruciating, unrelenting mental anguish that worsened with each day. I could see no end to the blackness that engulfed me, and I knew I could not endure much longer."[4]

While a particularly stressful personal event might trigger such blackness, it can appear from nowhere. Or, as in Joann's case, it can creep up so insidiously that the illness is never fully acknowledged.

"Nothing had happened to make me feel so terrible," she writes. "Yet every drop of color had been slowly drained from my life—so gradually that I didn't notice it happening. Then, all of a sudden, there was no joy left in my day. There was no pleasure in getting up to a new morning, in being with friends, or in doing any of the million and one things I love to do. All that stretched in front of me was an aching loneliness and emptiness. Nothing had meaning. Nothing brought pleasure. I wanted desperately to laugh and have fun again, but the pain grew worse."

Remarkably, Joann kept working. At first, work was a distraction, a way of keeping her mind off her troubles. But eventually it became a trial in itself as she tried to keep up a pretense of normalcy. At the office, she avoided people. "It was terribly important to me to conceal my pain from everyone, especially since I couldn't explain it. I struggled to keep control of my emotions. I didn't understand what was happening to me, and I felt as though no one else would, either."

When a depressive episode goes untreated, it gets worse. After a while, Joann had to stop pretending that everything was okay. She was forgetting, avoiding phone calls, growing more and more irritable. "Mail, phone messages, and requests began piling up. I was so confused, I couldn't seem to clear anything away. I couldn't concentrate enough to read. Even minor chores began to seem very difficult."

Joann says that dealing with people used to be one of her strong points, but now she was misinterpreting others and blowing small incidents out of proportion. Things would make her cry, right out in the open.

Eventually, self-hatred set in. "I began thinking of myself as a terrible worker who had managed to fool people for a long time but who was about to be exposed as stupid and careless, someone who couldn't do her job." Life became "one long, confused haze." At this point, Joann was barely managing to get herself out of bed and to the office. At work, she spent her days choked with fear and anxiety, and when she got home, she felt exhausted. "I stopped cooking, cleaning, and even walking the dog. I lost weight. Sleep became my only escape, and I tried to sleep as much as I could. I never woke up really refreshed. At my worst, I would snap awake in the early hours of the morning with a terrible knot gripping my stomach."

That such total despair can be brought to a halt in three or four weeks is hard to grasp, but that's what happened. Joann eventually went to a psychopharmacologist for an evaluation. Her therapist had been recommending it for months, but Joann had been apprehensive. It was her last hope, after all. If the psychiatrist couldn't help her, *then* what would she do?

But the psychiatrist did help her. After taking a careful history, "he put the whole picture together," she says. He had found out about her childhood and adolescent mood symptoms and also about mood, anxiety, and addiction problems of her relatives. A thorough evaluation of this sort takes several hours. A great deal of data need to be elicited in order to ascertain what type of depression is operating. This, as well as the family history, will help determine the medication that's most likely to work.

Within a month of starting antidepressant treatment, Joann felt the leaden symptoms of her depression lift. What struck her, in retrospect, was how completely confusing everything had been before and how clear it was now. Neither she nor her friends nor even her therapist had understood what was happening to her, and it had gone on for months. "I'm an intelligent person," she says. "Why didn't I recognize my symptoms and know that I had

56

an illness called depression? Why didn't I see a connection between this episode and similar if not such serious ones in the past?"

A Confusing Experience

The term *depression*, used in so many ways, can be elusive. In common speech, it describes the "down" or blue state everyone experiences from time to time. But in psychiatry,[5] it refers to an inability to experience pleasure at all. The empty, hopeless feeling is known clinically as *anhedonia*. People who experience it tend to be able to describe it only in metaphors. "It is like a black cloud," they will say. "It cuts you off."

Anhedonia is a major symptom of depression. Another is trouble concentrating, which leads to loss of interest in things that were once stimulating. "The patient becomes bored very easily," Dr. Max Hamilton says.

Boredom may be how the patient describes it, but that sensation, or *lack* of sensation, is depression. "Objectively, it appears as a steadily increasing disinclination to take part in normal activities," explains Hamilton, in a psychiatry textbook.[6] Work becomes harder to accomplish. Concentration diminishes, decisions are put off, and the great pileup of untended tasks begins: laundry, bill paying, taxes. "The work eventually accumulates until the patient can't face it and finally gives up."

Interestingly, Hamilton says depressed women keep up with their tasks far longer than depressed men. "Even when they reach the stage at which men will have given up their work completely, [women] will often still be carrying on at a minimal, desultory level," he writes.

When Is Depression "Major"?

Psychotic depression and *neurotic* depression are terms that have largely fallen into disuse. A psychosis is a condition characterized by loss of contact with reality. While some depressions are severe enough to cause "psychotic" symptoms, such as hallucinations, most aren't.

The word *major* means that the depression is incapacitating

57

and vivid in its symptomatology. A person in the middle of a major episode can't escape. The mood change is unrelenting—and consistent. The little daily pleasures are gone. The big excitements, too, fall flat. No matter what happens, the person with major depression simply can't get very "up" about it.

Dr. Francis M. Mondimore says people can often date the onset of the change. One day they feel very differently, not their usual selves. Some will say they don't feel really depressed. "Usually, they seem to mean they are not sad and do not feel like crying, but they certainly are unhappy," Mondimore remarks. "They seem to be simply miserable, very irritable and short-tempered, impatient and restless, unable to relax, unable to say anything nice about anything or anybody."[7]

Major depression is present every day. It is pervasive and interferes with everything. "Many patients find that the mood change even intrudes on their sleep in the form of unpleasant dreams. Themes of death, loss, and pain are frequent," Mondimore reports in his book *Depression: The Mood Disease.* He reminds us that Abraham Lincoln, who undoubtedly suffered from mood disorder, had dreams of death and dying during the depressions that haunted him for years. "Shortly before his assassination, he told his wife he had dreamed of finding a corpse lying in state on a catafalque in the East Room of the White House. Whether this was some kind of mystical revelation of his own impending death I will leave to the parapsychologists, but it was certainly a typical symptom of the depression."[8]

People who are seriously depressed become preoccupied with thoughts and issues that didn't bother them before they became ill. Women with children become worried about their adequacy as mothers. When I had the crying spell the night of Rachel's sixth birthday, I was overcome with feelings of remorse. Suddenly—out of nowhere—came the feeling that I was a terrible mother. In general, I had always felt competent as a mother, so this experience represented a distinct and dramatic change. Suddenly, I was utterly, morbidly, guilt-ridden about my failure to take good care of my kids.

Those who have major depression find that their minds continually return to the same unpleasant things. "Even though they try to put such thoughts out of their minds, their mental activity is drawn to the same depressing theme as if by some force like magnetism or gravity," Mondimore says. In psychiatry, such ideas are called obsessional.

Some people never have symptoms severe enough to bring them to a doctor. "They simply go on in misery, perhaps thinking that everyone feels as bad as they do but that they can't cover it up as well as others," says Mondimore. "They become so accustomed to their chronic misery that they just learn to live with it."[9]

Dysthymia is the term for this type of depression: The prefix *dys-* denotes abnormal or impaired, and the root *thymia* refers to the mood. Dysthymic disorder is a new classification of depression. Dysthymia isn't as severe as major depression, but an episode lasts much longer. To meet the diagnostic criteria, a person must be depressed *most of the time for at least two years.* Though less severe, many of the symptoms of chronic depression are the same as those of major depression: appetite and sleep disturbance, low energy, low self-esteem.

Is it really so important what type of depression one has? Yes. Making a particular diagnosis helps determine which drug will likely be effective in getting the patient better. Not every type of antidepressant works on every form of depression. The doctor has to know what he's doing.[10]

Signs and Symptoms: "Phantom" Pains

Doctors know that many of the patients who come to them complaining of headaches and stomachaches are actually suffering from depression. Their fleeting and sometimes not so fleeting disturbances have been described as "phantom" because in the past they were not thought to be grounded in anything organic.

Today researchers have a different idea about the bodily aches and pains that so often are a fact of depression. They believe them to be a systemic reaction to falling neurotransmitter levels. A good physical workup will help to reveal whether aches and pains are caused by depression or some other disorder. The rest of the picture can be filled in with the results of one of the sophisticated new depression questionnaires now being used by psychopharmacologists.

Physically, depression may make salivation decrease; in fact, it may slow down *all* gastrointestinal activity.[11] It's no wonder dry mouth, stomachaches, abdominal pressure, and altered bowel function accompany the depressed state, Hamilton observes. In a sense, the gastrointestinal tract *itself* is depressed, as is the immune system. Simply, all systems are *not* GO.

The earliest gastrointestinal symptom of depression is a slight decrease in appetite that is sometimes accompanied by a bad taste in the mouth. Food becomes less and less interesting. The depressed person finds it necessary to remind herself to eat. As the illness worsens, she may have to be persuaded to eat at all.

Others who are depressed stop eating for a different reason: guilt. People sometimes feel that they don't deserve to eat because of their wickedness. Refusing to eat altogether is a sign of advanced depression and may be symptomatic of anorexia nervosa as well.

Disinterest in food results in weight loss, although weight loss is apparent even in those who haven't changed their eating habits. Friends notice the thin faces and loosely hanging clothes. Women, unfortunately, tend to value the weight-loss symptom. They may even get a transient mood lift from the fact that they've gotten thinner. A friend showed up at my house one day looking vastly thinner than she had only weeks earlier. She knew she was depressed but tossed off the weight loss, saying she had been wanting to lose some weight anyway. She was not a heavy woman to begin with. "How much have you lost?" I asked. "Ten pounds," she said. "Well, probably more like fifteen."

There is also the more rare, "atypical" form of depression in which people tend to both overeat and oversleep.

Loss of libido accompanies most depressions. Men may have difficulty with erections, and with the ability to ejaculate, and eventually can become completely impotent. Women may become anorgasmic. Loss of desire occurs in both men and women. According to Hamilton, lack of interest in sex is one of the earliest depressive symptoms to show up, and not uncommonly, it is one of the last to disappear as the patient improves.

Psychomotor retardation, a somewhat frightening clinical term, describes the slowing effect depression has in about half of those who suffer from it. (*Retardation* here has its literal meaning of "slowed" and has nothing to do with the term *mental retardation*, which refers to low IQ.) In the early stages, the signs of retardation can be subtle. There is a slight lessening of mobility in the face, a slight flattening of the voice, some rigidity of posture. During interviews with depressed patients, Hamilton tests for retardation by remaining silent for a while. In this situation, most people will become more and more disturbed, until they finally feel forced to break the silence. But not the retardedly depressed. These patients "sit silent and still, apparently immersed in their miserable preoccupations and entirely unresponsive to the breach of good manners."

Depressions accompanied by anxiety make people feel agitated. Three out of four depressed women are agitated rather than retarded. When anxiety is dramatic, it is frequently seen as the primary illness. An underlying depression—often the chief problem—may go undetected.

Among the less common symptoms of depression are vague and ill-defined paranoid ideas. They occur in about one out of ten patients, Hamilton says, and usually will only be elicited by careful inquiry.

Obsessive negative thoughts—"My life is a mess and everyone knows it"—will occur with the onset of depression and disappear with recovery. Compulsive rituals—hand washing, checking, counting—sometimes accompany depression and also disappear with treatment. Actually, full-fledged obsessive-compulsive disorders often respond dramatically to antidepressants, which leads scientists to think they may share with depression similar abnormalities in the brain.

Losing It

One of the most poignant symptoms of depression is the loss of one's cognitive powers. Says Hamilton, "There is a slowness or difficulty in thinking, often accompanied by a poverty of ideas, of which the patients are well aware." Some complain not so much of slowness or inability to think "as of thoughts that go round and round in the same circle." Many people who manage to get to the office don't really do much work once they're there because their thinking is slowed. A man I interviewed told me about a woman who functioned brilliantly when he first hired her but who seemed to get slower and slower. "I couldn't get her to do the work unless I literally stood over her, and even then she had trouble with it."

Did she have a drinking or drug problem? I asked. "None that I could detect," he said. "She never smelled of anything, she was never red-eyed, or pupil dilated, or jittery. It was just this slowing down, almost as if she were behind glass."

Once, the woman didn't show up for work for a week, and although she'd dutifully call in, it was never clear to her boss, or to those she worked with, *why*. "One of the secretaries needed to get something out of her desk, and she found all these pairs of shoes," her boss said. "A lot of people will do that, wear sneakers to work and keep shoes at the office, but this looked like Imelda Marcos run amok. Somehow Katy couldn't get organized, and yet in the beginning, she was fabulous. It just mystified me."

It's easy to imagine that many employers might be mystified by the fog that periodically descends on people who at other times are fine workers. It is equally mystifying for the people who are dragging themselves to the office and faking it for all they're worth, hoping "this thing" will go away.

Jim Dailey, a man with a long history of chronic depression, described vividly the effect of the illness on his ability to function as a lawyer. He had trouble "adapting" to his profession from the outset, he says, and he could never understand why. "People kept telling me I could do it. The standard test scores said I could do it. But over the years, the strain of trying and failing, and barely surviving, has been immense."

Jim's problem wasn't intelligence. "I have excellent writing skills—vocabulary, grammar, punctuation, a way with words, as people say—but I have an absurdly difficult time producing written work. It's as if I can't access my knowledge efficiently when trying to synthesize something coherent out of the information I've gathered."

Jim has suffered from this problem and been puzzled by it all his life. "I blast through standardized tests and consistently show up in the ninety-eight-plus percentiles, and yet I failed, outright, my history exam in college—all essay questions. I can't exaggerate the pain I've suffered around writing—the endless hours blocked, confused, unable to pull thoughts into consciousness, let alone get them on paper."

For Jim, the preparation of legal work is devastatingly difficult. "Sometimes the struggle to break through the writing block exhausts me. As time goes by, I have no product to show, and the stress is awful." And yet he has worked hard to break down the problem into specifics—to assess where his skills are intact and where the depression has interfered. "I can process concrete information very well in small chunks, and I can use language very well in the same way," he says. "I can answer a rapid-fire series of specific questions about a topic but have a lot of trouble responding when asked to tell all I know about the same topic."

Cloudy Thinking

Recently, neurologists have begun to pinpoint some of the ways in which depression impairs our ability to think and recall. When given a random list of words, people who are depressed have great difficulty remembering them, one study shows. When they come across new material, depressed patients are less likely to link it up to preexisting knowledge. They don't impose the organization that facilitates learning and memory, according to Harold Sackheim and Barbara L. Steif.[12]

The kind of neurological research that Sackheim and Steif are doing on depression is new and important. It will help people become more aware of the toll depression takes. Ultimately, what we know about such problems with thinking can be used to reassure those who are suffering them.

Sackheim and Steif say the kind of cognitive impairment depression produces will show up dramatically on tasks that require "complex processing, and/or independent structuring of information relative to preexisting knowledge." Creative work, in other words—essay questions on exams, law briefs, college papers, advertising copywriting, and heaven forbid, book writing.

During episodes of depression, Jim Dailey is puzzled by the fact that he can continue to do certain kinds of thinking but has such a tough time writing. Psychotherapists along the way have offered Jim various suggestions about what might be happening to him. "Fear of failure" and "fear of humiliation" topped the list. "Those may be factors, certainly," says Jim, "but to me they never seemed a satisfactory explanation for the amount of difficulty I was having."

After years of struggling at his job and just managing to keep his head above water, Jim finally went for neurological testing. He was vastly relieved to learn that his problems were not something he'd manufactured, but were in fact the result of his depression. "The cognitive impairment is subtle and has to do with paying attention to more than one thing at a time. It showed up in a test where I had to listen for three letters of the alphabet, then do some mental arithmetic, and then recall the letters. 'Letters? What letters?' In another test, a series of numbers were recited on an audiotape. I had to listen for the first two numbers, add them up and say the sum, listen for the third number and add it to the sum, and so on. I bombed these tests entirely."

Jim also had trouble making up a story about a drawing he was shown. "I could only describe very well what I saw on the paper. I couldn't create a story." This was not due to lack of language. Jim's verbal IQ score is above 150.

The type of depression Jim suffers from is chronic, with the greatest relief coming during less stressful periods of his life. Pushing to do his particular type of work is *adding* to his stress; not surprisingly, he doesn't like his job that much. Having discovered that his "cognitive deficits" (as neurologists call them) are real, Jim is now thinking about changing his profession.

One of the extraordinary findings of Sackheim and Steif is that the link between attention problems and mood disturbance may be so powerful it continues in those periods when mood state is normal. This certainly would be further reason to intervene early to treat mood disorder.

A Troubled Sleep

Four out of five people who become depressed approach bedtime with varying degrees of dread. They toss and turn, restlessly preoccupied with negative thoughts. They mentally obsess about something dumb they did, or think they did, at the party that night. They worry about money, taxes, and teeth falling out of their gums. When I became depressed after a long bout of anemia (chronic illnesses often produce depression), I found myself worrying about my studio tumbling into the stream that lies next to it. I knew it wasn't rational, but I felt helpless to control what my mind was doing.

The train of thought began with just the tiniest kernel of reality. The bank along my stream was etched away in places, damaged by heavy spring rains. As the level of my brain chemicals became altered, the erosion escalated in my mind—first to the loss of my studio; ultimately, to the loss of my home. Perhaps I should sell before my entire nest egg was swept away by the ravages of nature; on the other hand, the real estate market was so bad, maybe there would *be* no nest egg, and so on. After some rest, I would awaken, rationality restored. "My house has been sitting here since 1775. Surely it has a few years more." But in the middle of the night the same dire preoccupations would set in.

The biological underpinnings of these anxious thoughts became clear when, after taking iron for a month or so, my blood count returned to normal. Suddenly—really, from one week to the next—concerns about the imminent demise of my two-hundred-year-old farmhouse vanished. My daytime thoughts became bright and positive, and my nighttime thoughts returned to dreamland, where they belonged.

Waking early, anxious and disturbed, is considered a sign of depression rather than anxiety. Trouble falling asleep is usually anxiety related. In the case of milder depressions, only an hour or so of sleep may be lost. When depression is more serious, the loss can add up to several hours. Some people say they don't get any sleep at all, or they fall asleep shortly before the time they're supposed to get up. Those in their sixties, seventies, and eighties who have trouble sleeping should be evaluated for depression if no organic cause for the sleep loss can be found. Some physicians think poor sleep is inevitable in older patients. It isn't and should be treated.

Although disturbed sleep is considered one of the clear-cut symptoms of depression, it may not be the case with young people, who can be depressed without having a sleep disturbance. On the other hand, if Suzy is going to bed at midnight and getting up at one the next afternoon, it certainly isn't reason to think, Suzy has no problem sleeping. On the contrary, Suzy *has* a problem sleeping. Those who don't want to get out of bed are showing signs of pathology, which is as true of adolescents as anyone else.

Hypersomnia, it's called—the need for more than a normal amount of sleep. In depressions that are described as "atypical," hypersomnia often goes along with overeating. The brain chemicals are just having a different effect than in the typical depression, which is marked by difficulty in eating and sleeping.

No matter how the sleep disturbance begins, it will become more severe as the depressive episode gathers force, spreading to include other kinds of insomnia. There may be terrible, depressive dreams and abrupt waking in sobs.

Of course, lack of sleep produces daytime fatigue. People who are depressed are often tired. Fatigue can become so severe it dominates the clinical picture. Doctors and other health practitioners may come rushing in with any diagnosis *other* than a mood problem. Epstein-Barr virus and chronic fatigue syndrome (CFS) are often pronounced the culprits. These are particularly appealing diagnoses to practitioners devoted to holistic medicine. Anyone who remains fatigued for longer than several weeks should consider the possibility of depression before hooking up to an IV filled with vitamin formula in the hope of gaining relief.

Certain organic illnesses will produce symptoms of depression. These will usually disappear once the illness is treated. Low thyroid (hypothyroidism), which can produce severe depression, occurs more frequently than is generally recognized—especially among women. Thyroid levels should always be checked in anyone complaining of fatigue. Thyroid medication, in correcting the hormone levels, also corrects the depression—unless the person is also suffering from a mood disorder. Researchers have found that this is not infrequent. Actually, boosting the thyroid level is something psychopharmacologists try when depressed patients don't respond fully to antidepressants. Thyroid medication is known as a *potentiator* of certain types of antidepressants, improving their efficacy even when thyroid levels are in the normal range (see treatment, chapter 8).

Anemia is another illness that produces depression. Once the hemoglobin count is lifted into the normal range, energy level and mood are restored.

Certain hormones will make people depressed. Birth control pills are notorious for depression, although doctors often don't warn of this. Progestin, which is sometimes prescribed for heavy menstrual bleeding, can send women plummeting. Danocrine, a hormonal preparation used fairly infrequently to stop fibroid bleeding by putting women into artificial menopause, also produces depression. It is ironic that many of the drugs given women to treat problems having to do with their reproductive systems end up making them depressed (see chapter 4).

Chronic illnesses such as AIDS and multiple sclerosis will bring on depression. Chronic illness depletes the immune system, and there seems to be a connection between immunity and depression. Researchers are beginning to zero in on the depressive aspects of chronic fatigue syndrome. The overlap between CFS and major depression is so great that some scientists question whether it may, in fact, *be* a type of depression.

Because the elderly often suffer from chronic illnesses, they are often subject to depression and should be diagnosed and treated. For a long time, depression was associated with the mere fact of old age. "Well, of course she's depressed, she's seventy years old!" people would say. Today enlightened medicine recognizes that depression is as pathological in the elderly as it is in the young. Often mood disorders are mistaken for "senility," a concept that no longer has any clinical meaning. People are ill or depressed, or they are both, but they are not "senile."

Depression is an illness whose onset is subtle. It gathers force so gradually that those who suffer from it don't *see* that they're becoming ill. Something is wrong, but what?

At first, and for a long time, the illness manifests itself in symptoms that seem to represent some other problem. That is partly because we haven't been taught to recognize the characteristic symptoms, and so they remain, in a sense, secret.

Many who are depressed complain of feeling vaguely sick. They feel fatigued, sometimes profoundly so. Often there are elusive aches—the "phantom pains" discussed earlier. Gastrointestinal disorders, as has been noted, are common. So are headaches, muscular aches, and "heaviness" in the head or chest.

Once, our neighbor was rushed to the hospital in the middle of the night with chest pains. "Anxiety," said the emergency room physician, and sent him home with a muscle relaxant. It turned out the man was depressed as well as anxious, but like so many suffering from a mood disorder he went undiagnosed, his aches and fears continuing for many years. Whenever the heavy feelings in his chest came, he'd tell himself, "Anxiety," and stick it out. Meanwhile, he lived a narrow, controlled life as he attempted to keep his mood demons at bay.

Getting Better

For someone who is in the midst of an episode of major depression, the response to antidepressant medication is at first subtle. Friends and relatives are likely to notice the changes taking place before Mary actually feels her mood change. Dr. Mondimore writes, "A man notices that a week after she starts on antidepressants his depressed wife is taking more intense interest in her appearance, and he points out that her medication must be beginning to work. 'Are you kidding? This stuff isn't doing anything for me,' she says. 'I still feel terrible.' But a week later she has to admit her mood is better."[13]

Sleep improvement can be the first sign that the depression is remitting. Long before the mood lifts, the depressed person falls asleep more easily and sleeps through the night. Then appetite improves. Weight loss stops. It can be helpful to point the changes out. "Look, something's happening! You're sleeping again. Your food tastes better. Soon you'll be feeling *much* better."

Not everyone who's depressed will benefit from medical treatments, but experts agree that some—perhaps many—who are depressed suffer from an illness rooted in the biological or chemical functioning of the brain. For them, says Mondimore, medical intervention is necessary. Psychological treatment alone isn't enough.[14]

Relief from depression should be complete. That's the goal. Many people—and many therapists—accept incomplete recovery. "I feel better than I used to," the depressed person will say, and—still depressed—she thinks she shouldn't really expect more. Therapists, friends, and family should tell her to expect more. More is there; more is available. People who are not depressed feel tremendous pleasure in life.

"I spent this morning working in my garden," writes Joann, finally recovered from the illness that often caused her to become so withdrawn that she ended up losing friends and loved ones. In an account written for her psychiatrist, Joann describes the way she feels now.[15] "Although it is only mid-February, my daffodils are poking their heads up, and the roses are showing new bright-red shoots. I feel so much joy as I find each new wonder, and I marvel that my flowers are waking from another winter."

Everyone deserves to awake from winter.

CHAPTER FOUR

Biology and Women's Depression

It was not until after Ben was born that Hannah recognized for the first time that something was wrong. When she'd had Johnnie, it hadn't been like this. She was so exhausted she could barely stay awake. When the children napped, she fell asleep instantly and found it hard to drag herself out of bed when they awoke. Everyone had said raisng two children would be tough. Hannah felt as if she didn't have what it took to cope. She was tired and irritable from the moment she got up in the morning and worried about the effect her mood was having on the baby and on little Johnnie. She felt like a shrew. She felt as if she were becoming invisible, as if nothing she did or thought mattered in the least.

Hannah is recalling this scene from early motherhood as the two of us sit talking in my hotel room. What had been happening to her after her second child was born was an episode of mood disorder. There would be other such episodes. There would also be wild, inexplicable times—times of a high, charged, anxious energy—that she could never really make fit with the rest of her life. Once these weird periods, with their often strange behaviors, were over, Hannah would try to put them behind her. In between the ups and the downs, she was a good wife and mother. But when the huge shift in mood occurred (and in the early years, it happened frequently), she felt as if swept up in the eye of a storm. Talking about the experiences with me now, Hannah began to see that those mood storms had shaped the course of her life to a degree she'd never before recognized.

*   *   *

Hannah and I met for the first time after a lecture I'd given in Oklahoma. She'd come to see me because she knew I was working on a book about mood disorders and addictions, and she wanted to share her experiences. Today, Hannah lives alone and makes her living as a graphics artist. She has very fine, soft dark hair and large eyes. Her face looks so young that it's hard to think of her as a mother of grown children. She shows me pictures of her cottage and of the little studio set up in a corner of the living room. I note the extreme orderliness of everything, her brushes and paints, her kitchen equipment, the arrangement of cushions on the couch. She says it is the nicest house imaginable, much better than the tiny apartment she lived in for years before the cottage became available at a rent she could afford.

Several years earlier, Hannah had made some major changes in her life. She'd taken up meditation and quit marijuana, to which she'd been addicted for eighteen years. In recent years, she's lived a calm, mostly celibate life, but now she's started seeing someone several nights a week, and although she's up, she's also agitated. "This anxiousness always happens when I try to start up a relationship," Hannah says plaintively.

I ask her to begin at the beginning. Though she starts with the depression that came crashing down on her after Ben was born, she stops suddenly, recognizing that it had not been the first time, after all. "I got depressed in junior high, and I stayed that way throughout high school. I guess I've never before labeled what was going on in those horrible years as depression."

Depression, though, is what it appears to have been. When she was thirteen, fourteen, and fifteen, Hannah needed to nap every day after school. Mornings, she often couldn't get up in time to make the school bus and had to be driven to school by her mother, who reprimanded her for being lazy. In high school, Hannah always felt down on herself, had few friends, and thought herself a social failure. "I actually thought that everyone hated me."

In school, though, Hannah had always excelled. In college, she continued to do well, and suddenly—it must have been about her sophomore year—everything took on a rosier hue. To this day she thinks the sudden shift in mood was due to her booming social life. Boys liked her. She felt sexually attractive. Her spirits soared. "It's hard to imagine how I did well in school, because I was going out all the time. I was involved in a lot of stuff. I ran the school paper, acted in the plays, made dean's list, and was out all weekend long. I had this tremendous energy."

At this point, Hannah remembers that she had had tremendous energy as a little girl, too—*before* the time in junior high when everything folded in on her. "As a kid I was very creative, constantly doing projects. I kept a journal, I wrote plays, I was doing, doing, doing. Actually, when I think about it now, if I *wasn't* doing, I would just sort of go blank. I'd feel nothing, dead."

In her early twenties, Hannah fell in love and married a man she met on her first job, in San Francisco. "I got pregnant right away, and that first pregnancy was wonderful. Johnnie was born, and *he* was wonderful. But when I got pregnant with Ben, I felt low during the entire pregnancy."

The low dipped even lower after the baby was born, and Hannah was overcome with postpartum depression. As the months went by, her mood worsened. She was irritable, short-tempered, and tired from morning till night, but she never thought "depression." She thought, instead, of how annoying her husband was. The only way out of the dense fog that had encapsulated her was to leave. The marriage was suffocating her. She had married too soon, she hadn't really found herself, and now she had to get out and start her life over again.

But she was barely able to move! Still, she pushed herself to speak to her husband, Will, about splitting up. Hannah was convinced the freedom she'd gain by separating would pull her up.

Will was convinced she was in no shape to take her children with her. "I could hardly help but agree, since there was no such thing as day care. This was in the early sixties, remember. I thought that as soon as I got it together, my babies would come back with me again. It didn't work out that way."

Feeling suddenly energized—and, thus, sure that her decision was right—Hannah wanted to bring the marriage to a swift end. She was ready to *move*! She flew to Juarez to get a divorce, met a man there, and was divorced and remarried in less than a month. "Everyone begged me not to do it, but I felt great and thought I knew what I was doing."

This was the first quick marriage for Hannah, but it was not to be the last. She stayed married for only a few months ("Both of us looked at one another one morning and said, 'What are we *doing* here?' "), after which, depressed and insecure, Hannah remained alone for a year. She got by, waitressing. Then someone new came along, and she married again. By this time, she was twenty-five.

Earnest, intelligent, sober-sighted, Hannah today does not look like someone who'd careened through a volatile youth. There had been an abusive husband. There had been a suicide attempt. There had been a long, ferocious period of work in San Diego, where she'd hooked up with a repertory theater and worked night and day for six years. "It was one of those high-energy times. I didn't know what to *do* with all my energy. I practically ran the theater single-handedly. At night, I'd smoke marijuana in order to be able to sleep."

Through it all, Hannah missed her children enormously. They had never returned to her. It had been her main reason for marrying Number Three—he had agreed to help her get the boys back and rear them—but somehow the court had not seen things her way. The boys' father got custody. "Maybe it was for the best," she says, but she weeps saying it. Her sons' grandparents had sent them to fine schools. Today John is a lawyer, and Ben is studying to become a neurosurgeon. "We have pretty good relationships these days; I see them a couple of times a year. But of course it isn't the same."

Although Hannah had had a fair amount of psychotherapy over the years, now she was trying to manage with the help of meditation and a codependency group she'd joined. Her new boyfriend was a recovering cocaine addict, and though she herself hadn't had a toke in four years, he'd wanted her to join a twelve-step group. He thought she was too clingy. She wanted a future. He wasn't ready for that, he said. It made her feel bad.

Coming to the end of her story, Hannah said she'd always had trouble with relationships. Somehow the agitation she was feeling with this new man was so reminiscent of things that had happened to her in the past. She looked up at me and said tearfully, "I feel as if the only way I can stay on an even keel is by living this really narrow life—just work and meditation and exercise. I have to keep myself on a very tight path just to stay stable."

It turned out that Hannah had never before been asked to tell her story from beginning to end, so even *she* hadn't been aware of the roller-coaster nature of her experiences, their cyclicality. She had always attributed her troubles to her difficulties with relationships. It had never occurred to her that perhaps the volatility of her interactions with people might be due to a preexisting problem. Now, laying out the whole story, she saw for the first time that her entire life had been swept by mood storms. Not only had she had periodic depressions since childhood; she'd also had "highs," when she couldn't sleep and behaved in an impulsive way that had had tremendously negative effects on her life. She was not just a sixties child, a bright but misguided daughter who'd been ill prepared for life in the world. She'd been chemically unbalanced, and for that she had paid a terrible price. She had lost her children. She had never had a stable, mutually supportive relationship. She had never been able to do the creative work she was sure was in her. "I'm an intelligent person, and I feel I've never done the things in my life I ought to have been able to do."

Why Women?

Women are at much higher risk for depression than men. This is true for white, black, and Hispanic women—regardless of income level, education, or occupation. The ratio of depressed women to depressed men is about two to one. It's been established through careful epidemiological studies that the ratio is *not* the result of women's greater willingness to report their depressive symptoms. More women actually *are* depressed.

The question that everyone would like to see answered is, Why? If we could figure it out, we might be able to come up with ways of cutting down the numbers. Even up the score a little, as it were. God knows, women have *reason* to be depressed. All we have to do is look at the statistics on poverty, on wife beating, on sexual abuse of girls and women, and it becomes immediately apparent that women could hardly escape the psychological consequences. You could say it's a double whammy. Women suffer inequity, and they also suffer its emotional consequences.

The tricky part comes in suggesting that *some* of women's vulnerability to depression might be biological—a result of gender. Because we've suffered so long from Freud's "anatomy is destiny" ideas (he thought depression was rooted in little girls' grief over the absence of a penis), the mere mention of biology, when the subject is depression, becomes cause for alarm. We prefer to think that women's emotional problems are due to social causes, starting with our legacy of bias and mistreatment. We'd like to say, "Of course women are depressed!" and let it go at that.

And yet certain facts leap out at us, forcing a recognition that biology, while it may not be destiny, *is* involved in women's mood states. Look for a moment at a sprinkling of statistics.

One out of ten women, after a child is born, becomes seriously depressed.

Ninety percent of women report premenstrual mood symptoms. Not all of them are sufficiently mood disordered to qualify for PMS (premenstrual syndrome), but *something* disturbing is going on premenstrually with most women.

Women with PMS depression have lower levels of serotonin premenstrually than they do afterwards and lower levels of serotonin than women without PMS.

Postpartum depressive psychosis, though rare, is a striking illness. It hits without warning, and full force, within several days of the baby's birth, a phenomenon that obviously has no parallel in male experience. Who is susceptible? you may wonder. Mostly, it happens in women with no prior psychiatric history. Many researchers think postpartum psychosis deserves to be classified separately from other types of psychosis.[1] If this were to happen, it would become the first *distinctly female* form of psychiatric disorder. Actually, there is quite a protest taking place in the ranks of feminist psychologists to make sure this doesn't happen. They fear that any psychiatric disorder ascribed solely to women will be used to discriminate against them.

It could be that postpartum psychosis is a more severe form of the same sort of hormonal change that occurs at other times in a woman's life. What's needed is more research. Surely, in our defense of women, we wouldn't want to thwart scientific investigation that could end up liberating women.

The influence of feminism on the social sciences—psychology, in particular—has often had the effect of making it difficult for women to get their mood disorders treated. This is especially true of PMS mood states. Feminists do not want women's hormones impugned. And yet hormonal functioning cannot *but* be considered a factor in women's depression. Women have increased vulnerability to depression after birth, before the menses, and at puberty. Puberty, in fact, appears to be a kind of female Waterloo. In one study, thirteen and fourteen was found to be the age at which females were most likely to experience a major depressive episode. Patricia Cohen, a psychiatric epidemiologist at New York State Psychiatric Institute, surveyed 1,500 youngsters in the Albany area and was surprised to find that severe depression actually disables 7 percent of girls this age. "There's a tremendous risk for depression in girls in the years following puberty," Dr. Cohen says. Is it hormone-related?

Certainly this is an area that needs more and better research. It would be a great mistake to impose a quietus on biopsychiatry's efforts to understand the biological aspects of mood swings in women. That is what this chapter will focus on. First, however, let's look at some of the social conditions under which women live. Could these be the reasons more women are depressed?

Discrimination and Depression

In the sixties, Betty Friedan's ground-breaking book, *The Feminine Mystique,* found women to be depressed because they were undervalued by society and often found the job of full-time home-maker unsatisfying. Today, far fewer women stay home. Instead, they have full-time paid work, often in formerly male dominated professons, such as medicine and law. In the 1990s, most women feel they have choices. Many wait until their mid-thirties to marry or decide not to marry at all. The housewife "stuck in suburbia" idea seems as dated as Edith Bunker and *All in the Family.* And yet women are still twice as likely as men to become depressed. The question is, Why?

Certainly we can't ignore the fact that women continue to earn less than men and face blatant sex discrimination in hiring and promotion. Most women with both families and jobs still do the lioness's share of housework and child care—in essence, holding two full-time jobs while their husbands plunk down after work to watch *MacNeil-Lehrer.* As the saying goes, "Wouldn't *you* be depressed?"

Without even getting into the issue of whether or not vacuuming the blinds is boring, there remains the fact, teased out by epidemiologist Myrna Weissman, that anyone with a single role in life is at risk for depression. If that source of gratification dries up suddenly—as it does for full-time homemakers when their children leave home—mood can plummet. Work and social skills have gotten rusty, and mom feels tenuous about her ability to make it in the world. What is she going to do *now*, become a golden candy striper?

Having too few sources of gratification, Weissman's studies show, predispose women to depression.[2] On the other hand, women who work outside the home have problems, too. They are expected to be nurturing and passive in their relations with men but assertive to the point of selfishness at work. Janus-like, they have two faces—or "selves"—with which to operate: meek and seductive in the bedroom, outspoken and problem solving at the office. Some social scientists believe that the conflict between these two "selves" sets women up to become depressed.

Inferior-Feeling Girls, Depressed Women

There is also the inferiority issue. Studies show that because of their social conditioning females have a lower sense of their own competence. They interpret events more negatively, evaluate themselves more harshly, set lower goals for themselves, and rely more on external feedback in making judgments about themselves than do males. They're caught in a negative-thinking trap that leads to problems in motivation, achievement, self-esteem, and inevitably, or so this line of thinking goes, depression.

Before puberty, children either show no sex differences in rates of depression, or boys come out slightly higher. Then suddenly, as menstruation arrives, something dramatic occurs. Almost as if on cue, between the ages of thirteen and fourteen, females start becoming depressed in droves. Adolescent girls quickly outnumber boys two to one, and some studies have found the ratio to be much higher.

"Adolescence has traditionally been considered a period in

77

which most young people go through distressing self-analysis and experience frequent periods of anxiety and depression," says Susan Nolen-Hoeksema, a psychology professor at Stanford University.[3] The image of the teenage girl moping about, telling everyone how depressed she is, wolfing down huge quantities of junk food, and talking morbidly to her friends on the telephone has become a kind of cultural joke. Life for the adolescent girl is one big question mark. Does she look good enough, is she thin enough, smart enough, too smart, witty enough, popular enough, and so on. Parents wring their hands, hoping that by the time their daughters reach college, they will become distracted from all this self-involved worrying and—in part, by virtue of leaving home—get on a more realistic track.

In many, however, such adolescent preoccupations are not "age appropriate" but are symptomatic. The moods and behaviors of teenage girls require serious attention. Many are depressed, and this is a serious problem—both for the girls themselves and for society. After all, young women are the future workers and mothers of America. The child who is depressed (as we shall see in chapter 6) becomes the adult who is depressed—unless that child is treated and her depressive cycle is halted. In one study of thirteen-year-olds, *57 percent of the girls reported moderate to severe levels of depression!*[4] Only 23 percent of the boys rated themselves this way.

In another study of 150 fourteen- to sixteen-year-olds, 29 percent of girls reported at least moderate depression, as compared to 10 percent of the boys.[5]

Young people don't exaggerate when self-rating depression. Studies have shown that children's descriptions of their mood states correlate closely with psychiatrists' clinical evaluations of them and correlate poorly with evaluations made by parents and teachers![6] Often parents don't think their kids are depressed when the kids *know* they are.

Depression and the Abused Girl

There are certain stresses that females suffer far more frequently than men. Sexual abuse, for example. "Rates of sexual abuse of girls increase substantially in early adolescence, and many abuse victims continue to be abused throughout their adolescent years," writes Susan Nolen-Hoeksema.

In one recent random sample of 930 adult women, 12 percent had experienced some type of serious sexual abuse by a member of the family before age seventeen, and 26 percent had experienced serious abuse from someone outside the family by that time.[7] *The greatest increase in girls' experience of abuse occurred between ages ten and fourteen.*

Other studies have found that girls fourteen to fifteen have the highest risk of being raped of all age groups. Imagine what this must do to sexual and emotional development, as well as to intellectual development. Depression, as we have already seen, affects cognitive functioning. Many girls never talk about their rapes and thus have little chance to heal. They carry the wound within, and the depression gets worse.

As girls move through adolescence, things hardly get better. According to the American Psychological Association Special Task Force report on women and depression, *37 percent of women have a significant experience of physical or sexual abuse before the age of 21.*[8]

Twelve to 14 percent of all women have been raped either by spouses or acquaintances. Date rape and "party rape"—a kind of Ivy League version of the old gang bang—are widely known now to be prevalent on the finest campuses. In the fall of 1990, female students at Brown University were cheered by women all over the world when they protested their campus rapes by writing the names of perpetrators inside the bathroom stalls.

Battering is the chief cause of injury in women. According to FBI statistics, a woman in this country is battered every fifteen seconds by an intimate partner. The figure is currently 6 million women a year.

Investigation of the links between victimization and depression is just beginning, but the studies to date are revealing. Two found high rates of depression in both adolescent and adult women who'd been sexually abused as children. The type and severity of these women's psychiatric symptoms varied according to the age at which they were first molested and the length of time the molestation persisted.

Given the violent atmosphere in which we live, it is not surprising that girls and women feel that they have little control over the events in their lives. Violence produces the syndrome known as "learned helplessness," which some think leads to a vulnerability to depression.

Biopsychiatrists think *stress* can trigger depression, although only in those who are biologically vulnerable. Women, in any event, have particular stressors to contend with.

Women who've been abused often suffer from mood disorders that persist for a long time and may well require treatment with medication. Feminist therapists can be leery of this. The American Psychological Association Special Task Force suggested that "better therapy" might make it possible for abused women to "rely less on medication."[9] Such a warning implies that "relying" on medication is the result of a weakness, or character flaw, that antidepressants are to be avoided, and that psychotherapy is somehow "healthier" and better for you than medicine.

Of course, there are reasons for feminist concerns. Some years back, it was found that far more prescriptions for tranquilizers such as Miltown and Librium were being written for women than for men. Ads placed in medical journals by drug companies presented the anxious or depressed female patient as a complaining burden to her physician. "Here is a way to shut her up once and for all," the ad copy implied. Rightfully angered, feminist writers suggested that women were being overdrugged and not listened to. Once again, they were being placated and dismissed.

Pharmacotherapy has improved over the past thirty years, however. Antidepressants are not a "drug 'er and shut 'er up" type of medication. They don't dull feelings or in any way undermine a patient's ability to think for herself. On the contrary, they make it physically possible to *have* feelings and to express them. They make dulled and confused thinking disappear.

Depressed women aren't able to act on their own behalf because they can't feel much and they have no energy. They may be seeing unknowledgeable therapists who withhold medication, allowing them to remain in mood states that seriously disrupt their lives. While working on their "inner conflicts," depressed women drop out of school, refuse promotions, lead narrow social lives, and in all manner of ways remain cut off from growth and development. They become involved with abusive men, they abuse substances, they fail to mother their children adequately—in many cases, because they haven't been offered the medication that would correct their chemical imbalances and allow them, in surprisingly short order, to feel energetic and empowered.

This empowerment doesn't come "from the outside," as some therapists would have it, making women feel yet more victimized. It is precisely the same kind of empowerment any ill person feels when health is restored. There is relief, and there is joy. There *isn't* a feeling of "I haven't really done this myself" unless misguided friends or family bombard the depressed woman with that message. It is too bad when this happens, because she is down on herself to begin with and likely to take on any blame that others are willing to heap on her.

"Does She or Doesn't She?": The Great PMS Debate

Few subjects produce more ire among feminist scholars than premenstrual depression. Books are written in an attempt to document exactly how many studies have appeared in favor of its existence and how many against. Feminist writers question those who are pro-PMS, wondering what their (implicitly hidden) agenda might be. Some feminists seem to be more concerned with whether we say PMS exists than whether women are actually suffering from it and how they might be helped if they are.

The reason for the increasing attention PMS is receiving in the mental health field is the prominence of mood disturbance in most women who have menstrually related symptoms so severe they're driven to a doctor's office. "Large numbers of women throughout the country seek help from many clinics in departments of psychiatry that specialize in the study and treatment of this condition," write Sally Severino, M.D., and Margaret Moline, Ph.D. Severino is an associate professor of psychiatry at Cornell University Medical College, where Moline is an assistant professor of physiology in psychiatry. They are the authors of *Premenstrual Syndrome*, an evaluation of virtually all the research that's been done on PMS to date.

Mood disturbance seems to be a part of the PMS picture for so many women that the American Psychiatric Association decided to do the homework involved in deciding whether the disorder should be classified. Is PMS a psychiatric illness, that is, or isn't it? The very idea of clarifying this issue brought fear to the hearts of the feminist psychiatrists in the APA's Committee on Women.

In 1985, the physicians responsible for updating DSM-III, the American Psychiatric Association's *Diagnostic and Statistic Manual of Mental Disorders*, appointed a committee of experts to consider including PMS in the revised third edition. The first thing the Advisory Committee did was develop diagnostic criteria and consider names for the disorder. Because the symptoms associated with PMS can occur in women who don't menstruate (that is, women who have had hysterectomies in which ovaries are left intact*), the committee decided to drop "premenstrual" and finally chose the lugubrious "Late Luteal Phase Dysphoric Disorder" (LLPDD). Vigorous objection to this disorder being included in the DSM-III came from the APA's Committee on Women. Nevertheless, with the exception of two of its members, the Advisory Committee was strongly in favor of including LLPDD—thereby making it an officially recognized illness. A tremendous fight ensued, with feminist opponents mounting a letter-writing and media campaign against its inclusion. In the end, as a sop to the Committe on Women, the American Psychiatric Association included LLPDD (alias PMS) only in an appendix of DSM-III-R. "To date," write Severino and Moline, "opponents of the LLPDD category continue to campaign against the diagnosis based on their view that it is damaging to women. We do not believe that it is."

"PMS has been characterized as a double-edged sword," notes an article in *Women's Rights Law Reporter*. "If denied or treated lightly, researchers will ignore it and women whose symptoms could be treated will continue to suffer. On the other hand, since the menstrual cycle is one of the few real biological differences between women and men, when we do acknowledge menstrual problems, they are alleged to be evidence of our biological inferiority."

"It seems to us," Severino and Moline write, "that the issue of stigmatization really reflects the continuing stigmatization of mental illness, not the stigmatization of women." Moreover, that *some* women have a cyclic disorder associated with the men-

*Or even women whose ovaries have been removed, but incompletely—that is, some tissue remains.

strual cycle "certainly does not imply that *all* women who menstruate are ill."

In fact, it has been shown that most women don't have mood fluctuations with the menstrual cycle. But do women have a special vulnerability? "Yes," say Severino and Moline. "Just as men are vulnerable to developing certain disorders, so too are women. It is not 'anti-women' to recognize LLPDD any more than it is 'anti-men' to recognize the large number of illnesses that are more common in men."

It is probably true that an employer might be reluctant to hire a woman who acknowledges that she suffers from LLPDD. However, these scientists continue, with unassailable logic, "An employer might well be reluctant to hire a woman who acknowledges *any* mental or physical disorder that could impair her job functioning. If the woman truly is job-impaired, the employer's rejection is not unfair discrimination. If the woman is not impaired, then the solution to the problem of unfair discrimination in the workplace is certainly not to pretend that it does not exist."

Why Some Suffer and Some Don't

At one time or another, we've probably all wondered why menstrual cycles are so tough for some women and not for others. Researchers assume that the ovarian hormones estrogen and progesterone are involved. "Hormones are, by definition, substances that act as messengers at target organs," write Severino and Moline.

In PMS, the "target organs" are the brain, breasts, and uterus, with secondary effects occurring at the thyroid and the adrenal cortex. The brain is the focus of the new research. The regulation of the menstrual cycle involves complex interactions among brain neurotransmitters, pituitary hormones, and the female ovarian hormones. Thus, it is not simply the woman's ovaries that cause menstrual difficulties. Her serotonin, dopamine, and norepinephrine are part of the action as well. Somehow the ovarian hormones interact with the brain's neurotransmitters, and the end result is mood shift. How this happens—and why and when and in whom—is still the subject of rigorous study, if not debate.

Menstrual-cycle research is relatively new. Severino and Moline think we need to pay more attention to the *brain* "as an organ that responds to ovarian steroids, and that therefore has a role in producing premenstrual symptoms."

It is only recently that scientists have begun to focus on the contribution to menstrual mood change made by women's brain chemicals. They know, for example, that estrogen inhibits the production of the enzyme tyrosine, which in turn knocks down the amount of dopamine in the hypothalamus of the brain. Dopamine in the hypothalamus controls ovulation. What isn't known is *how* shifting ovarian hormones actually influence a woman's neurons to release neurotransmitters. When this is understood, we'll have a better idea of why Betty binges through her periods and Helen finds that her periods—especially the time beforehand—make her moody and irritated. Why is one woman beleaguered with PMS only a week out of every month and another three weeks? Why do some experience a mild feeling of being in the dumps and others severe, life-disrupting mood drops? And why do some swing through the whole cycle, as a minority do, as free and easy as a woman in a Maxithin commercial?

As we've seen in chapter 2, the brain's ability to regulate neurotransmitters is strongly influenced by genetics. Ovarian hormones are influenced by genetics as well. Thus, in addition to finding out how estrogen influences serotonin production in women in general, we need to understand how the individual woman's estrogen affects her particular ability to regulate serotonin. If she has inherited an abnormality in serotonin metabolism, it will certainly be a part of the equation that determines the symptoms and mood states her period brings on.

There is also the question of the female hormones themselves. Do they play a role in premenstrual mood swings? If so, what is the connection between female hormones and mood-regulating neurotransmitters in the brain?

"It is really only in the last twenty years," say Severino and Moline, "that we have come to realize that estrogen and progesterone directly affect nerve cell functions and, thus, have profound influences on behavior, mood, and the processing of sensory information—all of which are known to fluctuate during the normal menstrual cycle." One of the ways they do this is by modulating the action of the neurotransmitters.

The first research relating PMS symptoms to serotonin deficiencies appeared in the late eighties. Two studies found that in the week before menstruation women with PMS had lower levels of serotonin.[10] Another study found that women with PMS had lower serotonin *before* the period but not after, and that they were lower than the levels in women who are free of PMS.[11] Severino and Moline are struck by the implications. *It begins to seem as if women who suffer from premenstrual symptoms differ from women who don't in that they have less serotonin.*

The new research indicates that ovarian hormones are only a factor in female mood shifts—perhaps no more important than the fluctuating neurotransmitters at work in everyone's mood volatility—man, woman, and child. And yet every woman who suffers from menstrual mood shifts has at some point felt ashamed, helpless, and out of control. She may find the experience profoundly alienating. Who she *is* premenstrually is not the "real" her. She may fight with her husband. She may say terrible things to her children. She has no patience with the bank teller and chews out the school crossing guard. Moreover, she *knows* her behavior is irrational and hates herself for it. She probably feels guilty when her husband forms negative assessments of her, knowing that she *is* behaving irrationally. His reactions to her during such times cause her self-esteem to drop even lower. The whole thing becomes a miserable, self-perpetuating cycle.

Though physical in origin, the mood shifts and strange behaviors many women associate with PMS may benefit from a psychiatrist's help. Even getting the symptoms diagnosed can be a relief. This was true for Ellen, who suffered from a cluster of feelings, behaviors, and thought distortions that Severino and Moline say are typical of PMS—though to her they seemed strange and even, at times, horrible.

Thirty years old and divorced, with three small children, Ellen finally went to see a psychiatrist because she was angry much of the time and felt guilt about snapping at her children. She was prone to accidents. Sometimes she had fits of fury so irrational she could barely contain herself. Once, while preparing a meal for guests, she felt so angry over the fact that no one was helping her that she stopped cooking, went out to her car, and without knowing what she was doing, slammed the car straight through the garage door.[12]

What else was going on in Ellen's life at the time? Feeling bored at home and envying her husband's lack of domestic responsibilities, she had recently returned to work. Now she felt tired much of the time, and as her mother had before her, she got her oldest child, a daughter, to do much of the caretaking of the younger ones.

After a few months of therapy, something interesting turned up. Ellen's symptoms only occurred during the premenstruum. At that time of the month she developed what she called a "warp" in her thinking and felt she had no control over it. She told her therapist she felt "crazy," like "a witch riding a broom." As her history was unraveled in the psychiatrist's office, she began to see that her difficulties with her husband were not constant but happened only when she was premenstrual. She wondered how it could be that this had never before been noticed—by herself, her husband, her friends.

Before Ellen's mood changes were perceived as being monthly, she was diagnosed as having a neurotic problem— "unresolved oedipal conflicts." At that point, the psychiatrist had recommended insight-oriented therapy, but when it was clear that her behavior and mood changes occurred *only* premenstrually, her diagnosis was changed to PMS. Instead of focusing on Oedipus, the therapy turned to her damaged self-esteem.

Unfortunately, many women with symptoms like Ellen's harbor the fear that they might be going crazy and put off seeking help so as not to have the fear confirmed.

Depressed or Premenstrual—Is There a Difference?

One of the tricky aspects of PMS is its similarity to a major mood disorder. How can a woman know whether she's suffering from PMS, depression, or even, for that matter, hypothyroidism, whose symptoms closely parallel those of depression?

Diagnosis is an art. Those who are good at it know a great deal about a lot of different possibilities. When mood shifts are serious enough to interfere with a woman's life, they're serious enough for the diagnostic skills of a psychiatrist.

Marge was certain her problems were premenstrual ever since someone had told her that having at least "one good week a month" put you in the PMS category. Marge at least had this one good week. During her actual period, she had always been able to count on feeling okay. But now even that week was vanishing. Over the past six months, her cycle had shortened from twenty-eight days to twenty-three, so that now, any time at all of feeling good seemed to have disappeared.

Marge had long ago started seeing her pastor for counseling. Now she was so despondent that he suggested she see someone who could evaluate her mood. The psychiatrist she consulted found that after her mother had died a year earlier, Marge had suffered with a severe depression. Her sleep had been disturbed, she could barely eat, and even her speech had slowed down. Her depression had lifted a bit when she'd started talking to her pastor, but she'd lived with these mood swings for so long, she experienced them as *her*—a part of her "personality." It becomes hard to know as the years go by where our mood shifts end and we begin.

To begin teasing out the cyclicality of a mood disorder, it is helpful to go back over one's life looking for earlier episodes. Marge, for example, had had a moderately severe postpartum depression five years earlier, when her daughter was born. After that, she would become nauseated during her premenstrual week, and her mood swings started getting more severe. As time passed, *all* of the symptoms she'd always labeled "PMS" got worse—depressed mood, irritability, sleep difficulties. Fortunately, her pastoral counselor had recognized in Marge symptoms that required psychiatric expertise.

The psychiatrist found an important clue in Marge's family history. A maternal grandmother and an aunt had both had major depressive disorders. This information, along with Marge's postpartum depression, pointed to a major mood disorder. Since she would swing rapidly from euphoria to feeling that she was "at the end of the world," the psychiatrist decided she had a form of bipolar disorder and treated her with the appropriate medication.

Once mood disorders are treated, premenstrual mood changes disappear. Many women have low-grade depressions that go unnoticed except when they worsen premenstrually. Severino and Moline say that *any* type of psychiatric disorder tends to wax and wane, in tandem with the menstrual cycle. Women with panic disorders find their attacks coming nonstop in the week before their periods. Obsessive-compulsive women fret more than usual about the housekeeping. Bulimic women binge more. (One study found a higher rate of binging from days 15 to 30. Researchers think this may be because reproductive hormones produce in *all* women a biological drive to eat more during the premenstruum.)

Women like Marge who have a bipolar illness often find that their symptoms go haywire before their periods. Bipolar disorder requires medication and so must be distinguished from PMS. Severino and Moline think the treatment of choice for women whose moods swing up and down, and do so more volatilely before their period, is daily doses of lithium.[13] (See chapter 8.)

By now you may be thinking, But what can be done for plain old PMS?

A psychiatrist in Pittsburgh, Dr. Christiane Siewers, says that she gets good results treating women's PMS symptoms with diet, exercise, and vitamin supplements. But the program isn't easy. "They have to stay on a diet that's relatively low in salt and has no sugar, no caffeine, no alcohol," she says. And while they can eat plenty of complex carbohydrates, they must stay away from sugar. "People have a hard time doing that because with PMS you crave sweets, chocolate, baked goods, and so on." Most patients who stick to the program get their symptoms under control in three menstrual cycles, Siewers says, but a lot of people drop out. "What I'm asking them to do is hard, and I haven't found a way to make it easier."

The most common symptoms of PMS are irritability, depression, breast tenderness, and bloating. "Carbohydrate-craving and fatigue are in there somewhere, as well," says Sievers. The symptoms can be confusing. She asks anyone who suspects she has the illness to rate her symptoms from 0 to 5 on a daily basis. To qualify for PMS, a woman must have one week in the month that's symptom-free; otherwise, she's likely to be suffering from a mood disorder.

Those with mild-to-moderate PMS may respond to Dr. Sievers's basic nutritional plan, although it could require a major change in life-style. Patients are told to do vigorous aerobic exercise almost every day. "They have to do the equivalent of walking for one hour, five days a week. If they do more, fine, but less is not acceptable. It isn't going to produce enough endorphins to make a difference."

There is no doubt that endorphins reduce pain. Severino and Moline report that our bodies' natural endorphins are five to ten times as potent as morphine. The challenge is in doing enough exercise to keep that endorphin production pumping.

When PMS symptoms are severe—and in such cases, other psychiatric disorders are invariably present as well—medication is necessary.

It should be said that many psychiatrists and gynecologists eschew the vitamins-and-herbs approach to PMS, noting that there are few studies proving that it works. There is anecdotal evidence, however. And studies exist showing that vitamin B_6 helps the depressive symptoms of PMS. Higher concentrations of B_6 supposedly increase the brain's conversion of tryptophan to serotonin, which in turn alleviates depression. Very high doses of B_6, however, can produce toxicity.[14]

The Serotonin Connection: New Hope for PMS

At MIT, studies conducted by Dr. Richard J. Wurtman, a professor of neuroscience and specialist in brain chemistry, and his wife, Dr. Judith Wurtman, a cell biologist and nutritionist, have uncovered fascinating data on both the "why" of premenstrual carbohydrate craving and a new way of curing it. Their research indicates that depression, carbohydrate craving, and some other symptoms of PMS can be significantly reduced with a drug that affects—not surprisingly, by now—serotonin. D-fenfluramine is still in the trial stage in this country but has been used for carbohydrate craving in Europe for the past twenty years.*

Gabrielle and I interviewed Judith Wurtman in the office near her lab at MIT. She is a small, energetic woman, a scientist who may make a major contribution to relieving the menstrual suffering that afflicts so many women. Dr. Wurtman says she got the

*This drug is different from fenfluramine, which is on the market.

idea from the project because of women's stories about how they change their eating habits around the time of menstruation. "Right before they get their periods, many have an irresistible craving for sweet and starchy foods. You'll hear them say, 'I could *kill* for chocolate.' We wanted to know whether women actually do increase their food intake—in particular sweet and starchy food—or whether they simply *think* they do because their craving is so pronounced."

The Wurtmans' researchers tested a group of women who were experiencing PMS symptoms and another group who weren't. All were given a choice of a variety of foods—some high in carbohydrates (potatoes, rice, cookies, candy, pretzels) and others high in protein (chicken, cheese, tuna salad). "What we found," says Judith, "was that the women with PMS were eating large amounts of carbohydrate foods, but only for about three or four days before their periods. The control women—the women *without* PMS—didn't increase their food intake at all."

The PMS sufferers, who were all normal weight, increased their carbohydrates by about five hundred calories before their periods. The control group—those without PMS—didn't. The question the Wurtmans wanted to answer was, Why?

They had the same women consume a carbohydrate dinner at the beginning and at the end of their menstrual cycle. The meal consisted of a large bowl of corn flakes—"a neutral, high-carbohydrate food," says Wurtman. Before eating the dinner, the women's moods were tested—did they feel happy, sad, irritable?—and again, an hour afterward. Eating a large carbohydrate meal increases the level of serotonin in the brain. "And when brain serotonin is increased, there's an improvement in certain types of emotional states. People feel less depressed, more calm, less irritable, more focused, less confused, less distractable, more tranquil. We knew that if the carbohydrates—in this case, the corn flakes—were going to do anything, they would probably do it by increasing the serotonin."

After the meal, the women reported that they were indeed less depressed. "They were substantially calmer, substantially less tired and more alert," says Wurtman. "This was a wonderful finding, because it means that when women choose to eat carbohydrates at the end of their menstrual cycle, they're doing so in order to make themselves feel better. And it also confirmed for us that this brain chemical, serotonin, may be involved in some of the mood changes of premenstrual syndrome."

It's still not known what role serotonin actually plays or *how* its levels are altered by carbohydrate consumption. But for now, Wurtman thinks that before they get their periods, women should go into a "high-carbohydrate mode of eating." This will not go on forever, as it has its own natural beginning, middle, and end. And, of course, such a mode of eating doesn't involve fats. Wurtman suggests that premenstrual women eat complex carbohydrates like rice, potatoes, pasta, lentils, or beans, "along with, perhaps, some sweet carbohydrates if their craving is strong enough for those foods."

A new drug not yet on the market has been found to affect brain serotonin in a way that's similar to, but more potent than, carbohydrate consumption. D-fenfluramine, the Wurtmans have found in trial studies (see chapter 5), is successful in the treatment of carbohydrate-binging obesity. It, and drugs like it, may soon be marketed for the relief of premenstrual depression. The development of such medications will be the direction of future PMS research, Wurtman says. "Rather than manipulating hormones like estrogen and progesterone, which has been done for many years without having much success, the thing to investigate now is *what, in the brain, is causing these changes in emotional state*" (italics mine).

One antidepressant already on the market has been shown to relieve PMS depressions. The first study, reported in 1989, found that women rated themselves "much, or very much" improved on a tricyclic antidepressant, nortriptyline.[15] Although more research is needed, many psychiatrists already use antidepressants to treat moderate to severe PMS. Certainly any woman who suffers from mood swings and/or depression three weeks out of four might want to consider this type of treatment.

Lithium is also successful in treating certain types of PMS depression. In the early eighties, I met a businesswoman in Dallas who said she had been on lithium for PMS for a year and that it had changed her life. "Before then," she said, "I was a mess two weeks out of every four. I couldn't imagine what was wrong with me and neither could my family, but I was depressed and snappish those two weeks, then fine the other two. I can tell you, it was no way to live." Studies on the use of lithium to treat PMS were started in the mid-sixties, and successful reports of clinical treatment have been published more recently.[16]

A different research angle that heightens the connection between serotonin and premenstrual depression comes from the University of California at San Diego. Barbara L. Parry found that levels of melatonin, a hormone secreted at night by the pineal gland, are significantly reduced in women with premenstrual depression.[17] Melatonin is derived from serotonin, and its release varies rhythmically with the dark-light cycle. According to Dr. Parry, low melatonin in PMS women is evidence that disturbances in circadian rhythms, or imbalances in the body's biological clocks, may contribute to premenstrual depression.

In the future, light treatment may be used for treating PMS, just as, currently, it is used for people with seasonal affective disorder (SAD).

When Giving Birth Brings Depression

The birth of a child, usually regarded as a joyous event, paradoxically brings an increased risk of emotional illness to the mother. As mentioned earlier, one out of ten women has an episode of serious depression after childbirth. Experts in postpartum depression recognize three levels of the disorder. The mildest, "maternity blues," is a brief depression. It affects 50 to 70 percent of mothers. Mild postpartum depression includes crying spells, restlessness, feelings of unreality and confusion—and, less frequently, feelings of depersonalization, guilt, and negativity toward husband and baby. These symptoms may disappear within a week.[18]

It hasn't been determined whether "maternity blues" is caused by outside events in the woman's life or is due to endocrine or metabolic changes, or both. That hormones at least play a part, however, has become quite clear. Five days after delivery there's a dramatic drop in estrogen and progesterone and a large increase in prolactin. Studies correlating hormone levels with mood both before and after childbirth have found that the more the estrogen drops, the worse the new mother sleeps.[19] Plummeting progesterone also predicts problems. *The lower progesterone drops, the more likely it is the new mother will become depressed within the first ten days of giving birth.*[20] New questions arise as to whether these depressions can or should be treated preventively. Even brief depressions will have an effect on the infant-mother relationship.

Ten to 20 percent of postpartum women will experience a moderately severe depression that lasts six weeks to a year or longer. The specific content of postpartum worries seems to distinguish it from mood disorders at other times. Postpartum depressed mothers have extreme anxiety about their infants' well-being, and they doubt their ability to have normal maternal feelings toward the child.

A very small number of women—.01 to .02 percent—experience postpartum psychosis, a remarkable illness that hits between the third and fourteenth day after the baby has been born. (It has virtually *never* been known to occur in the first two days postpartum.) Although this dramatic and frightening mood disorder doesn't occur often, it is of great interest to scientists, many of whom now think of it as a unique psychiatric event.

When it happens, it happens fast. What at first looks like a mildly depressed mood can quickly intensify into an entirely different phenomenon. Obstetric nurses know to keep a sharp eye on any depressed new mother, for there is a chance that insomnia, exhaustion, agitation, and irritability could escalate to a full-scale psychosis, with alternating states of elation and depression, delusions, and hallucinations.

Not only does postpartum psychosis come on more rapidly, with symptoms turning severe in a matter of days, or even hours; in most cases there's no forewarning. Seventy percent of the time there is not even a prior psychiatric history.[21] Postpartum psychosis often bears no apparent relationship to events in a woman's life—other than the childbirth event. That this strange illness exists, even though rarely, adds weight to the biological view of mood disorders in general.

The Emotional State of the New Mother

A thirty-eight-year-old woman with her first baby described herself, within the first months following birth, as "losing it." She said, "I awake each day with dread. I can't face another day of feedings and diapers and small excursions to the neighborhood park.

The best I can look forward to is getting the baby dressed to go to the supermarket. I feel myself getting unhinged. Each day is endless and like the day before. I feel I made a terrible mistake."

In an effort to help new mothers like this one, Ruth Nemtzow, a social worker from the Jewish Community Services of Long Island, ran support groups that met weekly for twelve weeks. She says the women in her groups suffered from anxiety, role conflict, and "mild to moderate depressed mood, suggestive of postpartum depression." One of the women, for example, was concerned that she was going to end up "just like my mother. My mother worried about everything." Nothing about their family life was lighthearted. "Mother always imagined disasters. I couldn't go swimming, I couldn't roller skate, I couldn't even go on a class trip in a school bus. In all my memories of childhood, I feel my mother hovering. I promised myself I'd be different. Now I'm scared that I'm the same. I worry for an hour whether the baby needs a sweater. I don't want to be like this. All this worrying exhausts me."

The group, writes Nemtzow,[22] helped Linda "see herself as distinct from her mother" and supported her in the belief that she could set a different course for herself.

While few would contest that support is helpful to a new mother, leaping out from Linda's brief statement are signs of clinical depression, one that appears to be inherited and could easily affect her child. What a biologically oriented therapist would find noteworthy in Linda's report is that her mother was phobic ("I couldn't even go on a class trip in a school bus"), had negative thoughts about the future, worried obsessively, and was heavyhearted. It seems likely that her mother suffered from depression and may have had other psychiatric disorders as well. Linda sees herself going down the same path and wants to fight it. She reports that she is indecisive (it takes an hour to decide whether the baby needs a sweater), obsessional, frightened, and exhausted—all signs of moderate to severe depression. In light of her mother's symptoms, Linda's self-report takes on a distinctly biological cast. Although Nemtzow doesn't suggest it, her "Linda" has the sorts of symptoms that might well benefit from medical intervention.

Though therapists obviously need to be sensitive to events in women's lives, lending too much importance to social stresses can lead to ineffectual stabs at treatment. Therapists may over-emphasize marital discord, for example, as a cause of the new mothers' depression. Lord knows, detached husbands don't help, and statistics show that lack of support from a husband, or the feeling of being unloved by him, are major predictors of depression in women, *especially* following the birth of a child.[23] But therapists who minimize the biological aspects of depression overlook the fact that many women stay in marriages with unsupportive men *because* they're depressed.

In such a case, the solution is not shaping up the husband or finding a better one; it's treating the depression so that the woman has the energy and self-esteem to change her life in whatever ways she chooses. Biopsychiatrists are concerned about the problem of half treatment. It's possible for therapists to support women in a way that might ease their burdens temporarily, yet still leave them fundamentally depressed. If postpartum depression is as prevalent and as frequently serious as research shows, it may often require medical treatment in addition to short-term therapy.[24]

Mood Swings at Mid-Life

Whether or not menopause causes depression in women has for years been the subject of controversy. In the last decade or so, feminist scholars have searched to uncover a shred of evidence that would *prove* that women are at risk for depression when they stop ovulating. What they have come up with is precious little; some would say no evidence at all. "The link between menopause and depression was invented," says Dr. Ruth Formanek, chief psychologist of the Jewish Community Services of Long Island. This notion of menopausal depression as a made-up social construction has been around ever since feminists began their critique of gynecology some twenty-five years ago. However, this particular idea needs some revision.[25]

The controversy revolves around whether menopause *causes* depression, not whether women at mid-life become depressed; we all know that they do. The question is, Does their depression have to do with events in their lives or with the Sturm und Drang of hormonal shifts as the ovaries stop producing, or does it have to do with both?

First, the myths. Menopause was long considered an occurrence that signaled the end of a woman's worth. Passages from eighteenth- and nineteenth-century literature describe the sorry plight of women once they are no longer able to bear children. They are described as fat, frowzy, and listless and as losing whatever ability to think they might have been fortunate to possess in the first place. Mentally confused, apathetic, and without physical charm or energy, women were thought to have little choice but to wait out their remaining years in—it was to be hoped—silent endurance. This horror was all supposed to be due to the loss of estrogen that occurs when women's ovaries stop functioning—as well as to a woman's inevitable recognition that having lost her ability to conceive, she had no further function on earth. Men, of course, had no such diminution of powers at mid-life, but only grew richer, more powerful, and more "interesting" in appearance. Poor women! Doomed from the outset and doomed at the end. It is not surprising the feminist movement confronted this destructive stereotype and in so doing helped women reclaim the second half of their lives.

However, the question of what actually *happens* to women at mid-life remains complicated and requires a great deal of further research. Certainly women do undergo tremendous hormonal changes, and sometimes—as in, for example, the case of surgically induced menopause (the removal of ovaries)—it happens with shocking abruptness. Having hysterectomies is disturbing to many women, even when their ovaries are left intact. As we shall see, a new study from England shows that many women become hypothyroid at this time of life, a hormonal condition that invariably causes depression.

There's no question that any number of things can happen to a woman—physical events *directly connected to her menopause* that can cause subtle and not so subtle shifts in mood, energy, and even the ability to think straight.

The Subtler the Malaise, the Trickier the Diagnosis

"My eyes are crying, but I'm not," Ruth remembers telling her husband. In her case, tearing up without actually feeling sad was an indication that something was going on—a whole syndrome of symptoms that, after consulting her gynecologist, she decided were hormone related. Ruth, who was in her early fifties, opted for estrogen replacement therapy. "For me," she said, "the before and after is proof enough of the pudding. My estrogen levels were down, my follicle stimulating hormone was up, and I was in menopause, no question about it. I was also moody, edgy, and tired as hell. All of this changed once I began wearing an estrogen patch. Now I swim every day, I do aerobics, I'm writing two books, and I like sex again."

Because mood changes occur before, during, and after menopause, however, they can be interpreted as being *caused* by menopause. This may be the case, or it may not. Menopause is probably one of the big unresearched areas of women's health. The two-thousand-page *Comprehensive Textbook of Psychiatry* devotes a booming twenty-one lines to the subject!

Could there indeed be a mood change that occurs in some women once their estrogen levels drop? Many researchers think it likely, since similar types of hormonal change are known to occur at puberty, during menstruation, and after childbirth—other times when women seem subject to mood shifts. "Gonadal steroids have a profound effect on certain neurotransmitter-related enzymes and receptors in the brain, including receptors that are hypothesized to be the site of antidepressant drug action," write the noted researchers Myrna Weissman and Gerald Klerman.[26] Sex hormones, in their view, *do* have some kind of effect on mood, although the mechanism isn't understood yet. Weissman and Klerman think the relationship between endocrine physiology and mood is an important area for future research.

Some illnesses that are more likely to hit a woman at midlife may be bearers of depression. A recent study done in the U.K. indicates that low thyroid is the *likely* culprit when mood levels drop in perimenopausal women. Researchers did hormone profiles and standard psychiatric interviews with eighty-five women in the late premenopausal stage. Out of all the hormones checked—including sex hormones, follicle stimulating hormone, prolactin, and cortisol—the one that correlated best with high levels of depression was higher levels of thyroid stimulating hormone. (TSH). This hormone kicks in when the thyroid is underactive. The women in this group who were depressed *all* had underactive thyroids. The researchers were so struck by the finding that they suggested that low thyroid might have been the real cause of mood problems that showed up in other studies of premenopausal women whose thyroid levels had never been tested.[27]

Hypothyroidism is known to be the great "mimicker" of depression because so many of its symptoms are identical. It is possible to be symptomatic even when the thyroid hormone counts are low normal, which is called a "subclinical" state of the illness. Hypothyroidism is something women in particular should be on the lookout for, since 70 percent of those in whom this condition is found are women—and the problem is more widespread than is recognized. For many, the thyroid function may be all that needs correcting. Depressive symptoms will disappear within weeks of starting thyroid replacement therapy with synthetic thyroxine.

Certainly there are cultural stressors that could trigger depression in women at mid-life—poverty and the loss of friends, husbands, and children among them. The radical hormonal shift that occurs in mid-life women, *in combination with social stress*, could also push them into mood change. What is important is that women take their moods seriously enough to seek treatment. Having been told, perhaps incorrectly, that "menopause doesn't cause depression," women at mid-life may feel guilty about their mood changes and avoid seeking treatment.

Or they may feel loath to go to a psychiatrist and particularly nervous about taking medication. The safety record is clearer on antidepressants than on estrogen replacement. In the thirty years or more that they've been used in this country, antidepressants have never been connected with cancer. If women have mood problems at mid-life—and they can and do occur for many reasons other than menopause per se—they might consider trying an antidepressant for several months to see if it helps. Because antidepressants don't create dependence, they are easy to stop taking, although some require tapering (see chapter 8).

For women at mid-life trying to decide what to do about low mood, the situation is confusing at best. The good news is that scientists are at last researching the problems that are sometimes associated with women's reproductive system and are engaged in finding ways for women to feel better and function normally throughout the entire course of their lives. In the meantime, women should take any mood shifts they experience seriously, *whenever* they experience them, and seek treatment.

Getting Off the Mood Roller Coaster

Hannah called me four months after our talk to update me on what had been happening in her life. She had broken up with the man she'd been feeling so up—and so agitated—about. And she had decided, after beginning yet another intolerably volatile relationship, to consult a psychopharmacologist. She had been taking Parnate, an MAO inhibitor, for about a month when she had this conversation with me.

"When the doctor diagnosed me, he described the type of depression that I have as 'reactive.' Basically, I overreact to whatever is going on around me. If someone complements me or flatters me or gives me a present, I feel great, but I can just as easily plunge to the depths if I feel rejected or criticized."

Hannah recalled the irritability that had always made it hard for her to tolerate others. "If I'm standing on a long line in the bank or in the supermarket or someplace and there's someone who is doing something not quite right, according to my standard, it's not past me to make some kind of a comment. Or to my neighbor, or whatever, just to be a little bit of a bitch. That kind of thing never really sat very well with me. I always thought I should be able to tolerate some frustration some of the time without having to act out, but often I wasn't able to."

After eliciting Hannah's physical symptoms, her feelings, her ways of interacting with others, her doctor took a detailed history of her family. "He asked me if any of my blood relatives had any kind of mental illness or were suicidal, that kind of thing. Any kinds of addictions, any kinds of mood disorders. There were no addictions in my immediate family but there were definitely mood disorders. My father had no impulse control. He was very, very temperamental, very erratic. A lot of rage which he couldn't control. And my mother was very depressed and anxious, extremely so. And actually, I have certainly felt, particularly prior

99

to taking this medication, that I was becoming more and more like her."

The doctor concluded, before putting Hannah on Parnate, that she had a biochemical imbalance, the vulnerability toward which was genetic in her family. How had this news struck her, I wondered. "I was relieved," she said. "I have been trying so desperately to control myself for my whole life. For twenty-three years I've been really trying to achieve some kind of balance and fulfillment in my life, and although I think I've made some progress through a lot of stress-reduction techniques and controlling my diet and really getting my head straight about a lot of things, I've still felt basically out of control. And particularly when I'd get into an intimate relationship. I would just go bananas. And it didn't seem to matter how much therapy or how much . . ."

"Insight?"

"Right. Or how much I controlled my diet or how much I meditated or how much yoga I did. I still would be reacting in inappropriate ways, I felt. Overreacting. Like this last relationship. I really wonder whether I would have gotten involved in it in the first place if I had not been out of control emotionally."

"Can you be a little bit more specific about that?"

"There's a suggestibility. It's as if there are no boundaries. It's like an amoeba, and you hit it and— That's the way I sort of felt. Like one of these one-celled organisms. You do something and it immediately reacts, and then you do something else and it immediately reacts again. And there was no— I didn't have a sense of separation. . . ."

"How did that translate as far as living your life was concerned?"

Hannah said she had always felt unable to choose whether to react or not. "I'm now beginning to experience much more of a sense of choice over my responses."

I was interested in Hannah's experience with work and in her thinking—in particular, whether attitudes or feelings or work habits were changing since she went on the medication.

"I've always had tremendous difficulty concentrating on my work," she said. "I used to use grass a lot to help me paint. At least it would keep me sitting in one place."

"Was that because it relieved anxiety?"

"Yeah, I used it for painting. I used it for sex. After a while, for everything. But without grass, even with the grass, I used to fall asleep very often when I would try to paint. And it had nothing to do with how much sleep I had or how tired I was. I would just go unconscious. It's all about tolerating frustration, to me. Having control over my feelings, being able to stand on a line, all these things. So what I've noticed is, after about two and a half weeks of taking the Parnate, I began to experience much greater mental clarity and ability to focus. It showed up in different ways. I had an experience one morning where I decided to try my hand at something new, an approach to painting I'd never used before. And I sat down, and in an hour I did something I was actually excited about. Truthfully, the thought that this medication might actually facilitate my creative process might be even more exciting to me than the thought that it could make a relationship possible. I'm fifty-one years old, and I don't want to spend the rest of my years being an emotional infant, really, having to clean up the messes all the time and not being able to be as productive and mature a member of society as I'm capable of being."

I asked Hannah what she thought about the feminist concern with women taking medication to stabilize mood. "I don't see this as a feminist issue," she replied. "The issue is one of having a sense of control. I've been in therapy, all kinds of therapy, all kinds of human-potential-type groups. Codependency, in-depth, twelve-step programs. I mean I've explored every psychologically oriented or spiritually oriented type of therapy. I've looked at myself and my behavior intensively over the years. And I always thought of my emotions and my behavior in relationships with people as being something that I could fix. If I just cried enough or raged enough or prayed enough or learned the right concepts, or whatever, I could get this stuff under control. I mean, I really feel like I've been a *warrior* when it comes to this. Regular exercise. Walking almost every day. Doing yoga several times a week. I've eliminated drugs. I haven't had any drugs for six years. No alcohol, very little sugar. Minimal caffeine. And still the problem persists. Now I'm definitely seeing major improvements in terms of the stability of my moods. Although I would like to say, and I think it's important for people to know this, that this drug is not making me happy all the time. I feel sad, I feel angry. When I got my period I was irritable."

"Being on medication, then, doesn't make you feel stuck in one mood?"

"My mood fluctuates, but it's not— It's in a much narrower range. And it's tolerable. Even if I feel sad all day because I have good reasons to feel sad, I don't feel as though I can't tolerate it. I don't feel as though I have to do something, like I have to call my former lover or call all my friends to tell them how miserable and unhappy I am or think about suicide, or whatever. I can just feel sad.

"If I felt that this medication was hurting me, I wouldn't take it. And I've been very watchful and observant. I've taken notes every day on every reaction I've had. I've been in frequent communication with the doctor who prescribed it. And if I thought that this would turn me into any kind of a zombie or was somehow reducing my experience, my aliveness, I would not be taking it. For me, my life is about expanding my aliveness, expanding my creativity, expanding my ability to have intimate relationships."

Women and Medication: The Controversy

It isn't so surprising that women should vacillate about depression when our main mental health teachers—our therapists—will often push the idea that *conflict*, or the social system, is causing low mood and self-esteem, not the illness. Some will even say these medications are harmful, especially to women. Such ideas are outdated, and as long as they persist—for whatever reasons— women are being hindered rather than helped.

Women need to be aware that many therapists with no background in medicine misunderstand antidepressant medication. Some will tell you it helps only the symptoms, which is incorrect. Some will refer to medication as "chemical support," implying that medication is merely an adjunct to talk therapy. Some will make the unsupported statement that medication is dangerous for women. Psychologist Randy S. Milden admits that women with mood disorders—even milder ones—are often helped by medication, but she warns that women who take antidepressants "don't feel complete and in control of themselves. They have been told that they are ruled, during an episode, by their neurotransmitters, and that they are rescued by medication," she writes. "They understand that they are *neurobiologically incomplete*, and they need external materials to complement what they perceive as their *deficient selves*."[28]

Who tells them this? Obviously, doctors don't inform patients that they're "ruled" by neurotransmitters and "rescued" by medication. This is biased language.

Anyone who is ill has to rely on medication, as well as on the doctor who administers it. To benefit most from antidepressants, patients need therapists who will help disabuse them of any sense they may have of being "flawed." There is no perfect organism, and while one person may have knee problems and another poor vision, someone else may have faulty serotonin metabolism. Perhaps this is the point cautionary therapists like Dr. Milden are trying to make, but one gets the feeling from such writing that anyone who "has" to take antidepressants *ought* to feel deficient. Therapists risk conveying this when they warn patients against becoming "dependent" on drugs that stabilize mood, question whether a woman's mood is "bad enough" to warrant medication, or argue that those who are depressed can banish low mood if only they are willing to "confront" their fears and weaknesses. Depressed women—just like depressed men—have trouble confronting their problems *because* they are depressed, not vice versa.

Taking medicine can be difficult because it upsets our sense of immortality, our narcissistic belief that we are "above" becoming ill. We deny that we are feeling low, that our energy has been insufficient for some time, that we are having trouble concentrating on our work and feeling competent and relaxed with people. We dislike the idea of having to take medicine, yet when it's medicine for anything else, we tend to minimize our annoyance. Diagnosed with diabetes or chronic fatigue syndrome or flu, we are likely to be more sanguine about our frailty. "Everyone has *something* going on," we will tell ourselves. But why shouldn't we take this attitude toward mood disturbances?

We are confused about our moods and this may be heightened by confusion on the part of our therapists. *They* may see medication as something "external," something patients are "forced to rely on," or as something patients should hold off against for as long as possible. One woman we interviewed was told by her therapist that her depression wasn't serious enough to warrant medication. Then, one day, she told him she was afraid she was going to hit her child. This snapped him into action and he finally sent her to a psychopharmacologist. When her mood improved in three weeks, she began thinking she should have been offered antidepressant medication much earlier. She told her therapist she was angry that he had persuaded her to go without for so long. "He apologized, but said he didn't realize I was in such bad shape. He said, 'After all, Barbara, you weren't out of control.' I said, 'Were you waiting for me to be out of control before letting me have this medicine that has made me feel so much better?' "

Dr. Milden says some women may experience reliance on medication as "a prescription for regression." In their wish to have the problem resolved by something other than their own efforts, she says, they give up any sense of autonomy they've gained.

In 1990, in its report, *Women and Depression: Risk Factors and Treatment Issues*, an American Psychological Association Special Task Force sounded warnings similar to Dr. Milden's. "We need to know if there is a danger that antidepressants may encourage dependency, passivity, and a victim psychology in women, which could reinforce depression over time," it stated.[29]

Concerns such as this seem to be based on a fundamental misunderstanding. There's no reason why a woman who's worked hard to resolve her conflicts and improve her sense of independence would relinquish it by deciding to take medicine that will help treat her illness and make her feel better. If women have dependency problems, and I'm certain they do, they need help in solving them. Women with mood disorders may find that this help comes in part from a nonaddictive medication that restores both energy and a feeling of power. The women Gabrielle and I interviewed who'd been prescribed medication for depression had a sense of control over their lives that they hadn't felt in a long time. They went back to school. They progressed in their professions. They found themselves gaining new friends and improving their relationships with old ones. Depression debilitates. Halting it makes people feel whole again.

What happens to a lot of women when they *aren't* prescribed mood-restoring medication is this: They stay months and years in therapies that may help them to function but do not touch their low mood and irritability. They learn to assert themselves, to analyze their feelings about their therapists, to keep dream journals, to set priorities, to be nice to themselves, and they still don't feel well. Such women may end up feeling deficient and passive not because of some internalized sense of inferiority but because—once again—they have not been properly treated.

CHAPTER FIVE

Compulsive Eating: A Disturbance in the Brain

"When I was in high school no one really knew about bulimia," writes Gabrielle, recalling the social atmosphere in which she began her innocent dalliance with some eating behaviors that would lead her, eventually, into a full-blown disorder. "But everyone was talking about anorexia. Most of the anorectic girls were unmistakable, as they became unbelievably skinny and their hair began to thin. Their 'mental illness' was fodder for the gossip mill, and anyone who lost a lot of weight became suspect. 'Do you think Lisa (or Karen, or Gina) has . . .' we would whisper to each other in the hallways. Secretly, though, many of us were envious of their slimness. As we struggled with our own weight, devising a crazy new diet for each one that failed, the anorectic girls seemed to lose weight effortlessly. Not that we wanted to look like Auschwitz victims. If only you could have 'a little' anorexia, we silently wished.

"When Mary Jamison announced in the girl's locker room that she'd tried to make herself throw up so she wouldn't gain weight from all the junk food she'd eaten the night before, some of us were very interested. *I* was interested. My first, and only, thought was, What a great idea! If I could make myself throw up, I could eat anything I wanted without worrying about it. No more dieting! A couple of days later, I gave it a try and found that it wasn't too difficult. And the more I did it, the easier it became. It felt liberating to be able to eat as much as I wanted without worrying about gaining weight. I had no idea I'd stepped onto the path of a disease that would end up dominating my life for the next six years."

Bulimia, doctors now know, is closely associated with depression. Its roots, like depression's, are in the metabolic functioning of the brain. When Gabrielle was suffering from the illness, that discovery was just being made, and news of it had not yet trickled out of the psychiatric research laboratories. In the early eighties, women with eating disorders were thought to be seriously psychologically disturbed, to have severe conflicts about sexuality, independence, their relationships with their mothers. The idea that the illness might in fact be physical in origin was inconceivable. Later, when data supporting this notion emerged from the laboratory, many psychotherapists found it dubious. Hudson and Pope's book *New Hope for Binge Eaters*, published in 1984, was received eagerly by bulimic women themselves but with skepticism, to put it mildly, by their therapists.[1]

At my urging, Gaby saw a therapist, though briefly. She had the distinct feeling that the talking wasn't getting her anywhere. I took her lack of interest in psychotherapy to mean she was afraid to face her problem. Everyone I'd met who claimed to know anything at all about eating disorders said one couldn't get well without therapy, *years* of it. "In some women these things never go away," two psychiatric nurses who'd founded an eating disorders clinic in Toronto told me in 1981. "They can be forty, fifty, and still bulimic." A therapist in Macon, Georgia, who talked with me after a lecture I gave there, said, "I've got women patients in their seventies who are still vomiting."

Still, and miraculously, Gabrielle's binging and purging ended the year she turned twenty-one. Eventually, we would learn why. "I always thought it stopped because I'd struggled so hard," Gabrielle says, "but after reading the research, I can see I didn't struggle any harder with my bulimia at the end than I did in the beginning. The binging and purging stopped when the bulimia went into remission. It really had nothing to do with me."

As scientists began uncovering the roots of this strange and debilitating illness, we eventually found that Gabrielle's helpless binging and purging had *not* resulted from her personality, her psychosocial background, or the strength or weakness of her will.

The binge-purge syndrome is the disturbing result of a condition that's *physical*. Changes in certain neurotransmitters, such as serotonin, in Gabrielle's brain had caused her draining and obsessive involvement with binge eating and vomiting.

Biopsychiatrists don't yet understand the association between brain chemistry and bulimia, but they do know that correcting that chemistry stops the binging and purging in the great majority of cases. They also know that when the illness isn't treated, it will eventually remit by itself, just as depression will, and, untreated, may well return. *Or* it may be replaced by other addictive or mood-related problems.

Gabrielle's bulimia stopped without treatment. For six long years the illness held her in its grip like a whirlpool. Then, one day, as abruptly as it had swept her up, it dropped her on another shore. Suddenly, the urge to binge and purge just wasn't there anymore. But her depressive episodes became worse.

Women and Food

Studies show that frighteningly large numbers of young women today are obsessively involved with food and dieting. Many go on to become adult women who are preoccupied with dieting—or eating. Some become hooked on diet pills. Others, locked in cycles of losing and gaining and losing, never seem to be able to get off the dieting pendulum. The struggle with weight becomes a constant in their lives. For many if not most women, eating is not a natural and pleasurable experience. It is fraught with anxiety and a kind of drivenness.

Social pressures to be thin and beautiful have long been thought to be the cause of women's problems with food, but in the last decade, biology has added a new view. Eating affects—and is affected by—the same chemicals in the brain that regulate mood. The new information that science has uncovered about the relationship between this illness and mood disorders is important for *anyone* who feels "out of control" about eating, not just those with full-fledged eating disorders. Disturbed eating behaviors are symptomatic of a biological condition—and, happily, they are treatable.

Eating disorders afflict millions of women and a small percentage of men. Although the numbers vary somewhat from study to study, they are consistently disturbing. One survey of female graduate students found that 12 percent were bulimic.[2] In a study of high school students, 20 percent claimed to be binging, and another 27 percent said their eating was "out of control."[3]

Bulimia usually hits women in their early twenties, although it's been known to appear as early as age twelve. In the extreme, the illness can persist for years and is devastating both psychologically and physically. Some women end up with severe erosion of tooth enamel, or disturbances of electrolyte balance and, rarely, perforations of the esophagus.

The mental effects of bulimia—the obsessional thoughts about food and eating, the guilt and self-disparagement—are no less brutal. Bulimia is usually associated with depression and with abuse of drugs or alcohol as well. Clearly, these women are having a rough time of it. *At some point during their lives, 20 percent of those who are bulimic attempt suicide.*

When Gabrielle came down with this illness in the late seventies, few knew how widespread it was. Bulimia is easy to hide, since the binging is done in secret and weight can be kept more or less normal. The deep guilt and shame women felt about what they were doing was heightened by the belief that they were the only ones doing it. Eventually, they discovered that they were *not* the only ones. A new illness had entered the annals of medical literature: bulimia nervosa. Recognized as separate from anorexia, bulimia was found to be far more prevalent. Soon the media were promoting it as the bizarre, new illness of the eighties.

Compelled to Binge

In the early 1980s, Dr. Katherine Halmi of Cornell University Medical College reported the startling findings of a study she'd conducted at the State University of New York. Of 355 students surveyed, 13 percent met the official DSM-III criteria for bulimia.[4] Hers was one of the first studies to show how widespread eating disorders had become. Fascinated, James Hudson and Harrison Pope, who were doing research on bulimia at McLean Hospital outside of Boston, applied Halmi's figures to the general population and estimated that 5 million people in the United States have had bulimia at some time in their lives.[5]

Hudson and Pope decided to sample seniors from two schools in the Boston area. At College A, "a prestigious rural college for women," 14.7 percent turned out to have full-fledged eating disorders, and another 10 percent binged at least once a week. "Even more striking findings emerged from College B, an urban coeducational university," they wrote. "Of 102 women respondents, bulimia, anorexia, and once-a-week binging brought the grand total of eating compulsions to an alarming 32.5 percent.[6]

Although their findings correlated with those of other researchers, Hudson and Pope remained skeptical. The figures seemed so high that the psychiatrists thought they must not be correct. Another study was clearly needed. After working up a new questionnaire and testing its validity, Hudson and Pope went off to suburbia. "We stood in the middle of a mall and offered every woman shopper a dollar to fill out the same confidential questionnaire and deposit it in a sealed box." This was research grass-roots style. In all, 300 women participated. "When we opened the box and scored the results, we were stunned."

Over 10 percent of Hudson and Pope's shoppers met the DSM-III criteria for bulimia. But in the younger women, the illness apparently was rampant. In the thirteen-to-twenty age group. 17.7 percent were, or had been, bulimic. After adjusting the prevalence rates to reflect the difference between the age distribution of the shoppers and that of the American female population, Hudson and Pope came to the conclusion that *some 10 million American women have a history of bulimia.*

As high as these figures are, they still don't represent the full gamut of people who have serious problems with eating. They do not, for example, include those who binge but don't purge. Over a third of college students reported eating binges, according to Hudson and Pope's studies. Obese people, too, are often bingers, although those who don't purge don't meet the criteria for bulimia.[7] Scientists have recently determined that binge eating, too, is an eating disorder and that it's caused by the same chemical deficits in the brain that cause bulimia. As we shall see later in the chapter, studies of new medical treatments for this disorder are very hopeful. Many who binge-eat—with or without purging—

find they are able to stop with a pill that corrects brain metabolism.

Obsessed Females

Other forms of abnormal eating behavior are constant dieting and the use (and abuse) of diet pills. The large majority of dieters and pill abusers are female, and often they are very young. In a study of 500 girls conducted by the University of San Francisco, almost half of the nine-year-olds and 80 percent of those aged ten and eleven were dieting. Few of the girls were overweight!

In the fall of 1990, experts testifying before a House subcommittee investigating the weight-loss industry expressed concern about the numbers of girls who diet excessively and abuse over-the-counter weight-loss products. "Our investigation found that juveniles are dieting more obsessively than ever, and that many are suffering adverse health effects and even death."[8]

"Diet pills containing the drug phenylpropanolamine, or PPA, pose a very serious health risk to adolescents," Vivian Hanson Meehan, president of the National Association of Anorexia Nervosa and Associated Disorders, testified. The subcommittee reported, according to Meehan, that at least one out of ten teenagers engages in dangerous eating practices—starvation diets, binging, the abuse of laxatives and diet pills. While such practices don't always lead to full-fledged eating disorders, it can be said that with rare exceptions *no one becomes eating disordered who doesn't start out with some extreme method of dieting.*

Eating compulsions lie on a spectrum, and many people are caught up in unhealthy eating rituals that may be less severe than anorexia and bulimia but which still are wreaking havoc on them physically and emotionally. By studying the more extreme forms of eating disorder, scientists have gained insight into how *all* eating compulsions work.

Bulimia is related to a category of behaviors that are called "obsessive compulsive." People with full-blown obsessive-compulsive disorder (OCD) may wash their hands dozens of times a day or count obsessively. In all obsessive illnesses the behaviors and thought patterns seem to have a life of their own. In bulimia, the compulsive component is uncontrollable binge eating. The binges are followed by purges accomplished by self-induced vomiting, the consumption of large quantities of laxatives, or fasting, intense exercise, or a combination of these. The binge itself has a strikingly compulsive, automatic quality. It's as if "the normal shutoff mechanisms fail, almost as if some piece of circuitry had been miswired in the brain," say Hudson and Pope.

As distinct from a bout of overeating, a true bulimic binge continues unchecked until something external ends it: abdominal pain, falling into a stuporous sleep, some unexpected social interruption, or self-induced vomiting. The total amount of food consumed can be staggering. Psychiatrists at the University of Minnesota have calculated that between three and four thousand calories are consumed during an "average binge," which lasts slightly over an hour. But binges can be worse. Some patients report eating for as long as eight hours and consuming eleven or twelve thousand calories in a sitting. A few have even described eating up to 50,000 calories a day, in roughly ten 5,000 calorie binges—the equivalent of what some people eat in a month![9] Rapidly consumed, the food is barely tasted. Patients have described grabbing frozen pastry dough from the freezer, running it under hot water to thaw it, and then gobbling it down half-thawed. This is not unlike the alcoholic slugging booze straight from the bottle. Something frantic is going on, something entirely unmediated by reason. Biopsychiatrists think that what's going on is primarily *physical*.

In their book *New Hope for Binge Eaters*, Hudson and Pope describe the development of bulimia in a woman they call Sally, who was attending a women's college in Massachusetts. Sally's preoccupation with food began in her sophomore year, when she became depressed. Little by little, her thoughts turned to food, and her concerns about losing weight increased. A strict diet seemed in order, but though at first she felt pleased when she began losing weight, the crash was soon to come. One night, she found herself devouring a package of chocolate cookies. Craving more food, she went out for a gallon of ice cream. Back in her room, she began eating it straight from the carton. Soon the entire gallon was finished. Feeling sick, sedated, and filled with self-disgust, Sally collapsed onto her bed and slept for twelve hours. The next morning, she saw that she'd gained seven pounds.[10]

Over the next week, Sally lost the weight she'd gained, but then a strange, uneasy feeling began to build inside her. On the eighth night, she did it again. Her binges soon settled into a regular pattern, occurring every fourth or fifth night, with rigorous dieting in between. Sally began to recognize the building tension that heralded the approach of another episode. She would make elaborate plans for it, stocking food in advance and arranging her affairs so that she wouldn't be interrupted. As the cycle developed its own momentum, Sally tried to break free, but no matter what schemes she devised, the compulsion continued.

For those who've never suffered from bulimia, the illness can be difficult to understand. Friends and relatives, even therapists, frequently urge women like Sally to "just stop," unaware that bulimics can no more will themselves free than can those with leukemia. "Not to mention the fact," says Gabrielle, "that if women could simply *choose* to stop, they certainly wouldn't need others telling them to do it."

The obsessional nature of an eating disorder is hard to recognize at first, partly because the female preoccupation with size and weight is so prevalent that it's considered normal. But such thoughts can become so all-consuming that they interfere with functioning. "We have seen patients who weigh themselves forty times a day," report Hudson and Pope. "Between weighings, they obsess about whether there might be some slight error in the scale, or perhaps some anomaly of the humidity, which might cause it to register a shade lower than the true weight, or some angle of the light that causes them to slightly misread the dial."[11]

For the woman with an eating disorder, almost no aspect of life goes untouched. She feels that she is in the grip of a frightening addiction. Friends and lovers go by the wayside as her involvement with food and dieting increases. Once-pleasurable activities are forgotten as her waking hours become dominated by binging, the preparation for binging, and its aftermath.

Gail, a woman who'd been bulimic for twelve years, told Gabrielle about a journal she'd kept during her illness. It detailed plans for her binges—the restaurants she would go to, the food she would order. Gail said she would binge far from home because of her fear that people she knew might find out. What could be going on here, we wonder, as we observe this terrifying cycle of behavior in people we know—or in ourselves. Surely something so powerful, so overwhelming, could not simply be a matter of behavioral dysfunction. The question is, How does the ordinary, if neurotic, preoccupation with one's figure turn into an uncontrollable illness that can continue for years?

The Depression Link

Scientists have found that women with bulimia are also likely to suffer from other psychiatric disorders. Major depression is most common. It occurs far more frequently in bulimics than in the general population, and it also shares certain features with the eating disorder—notably, the characteristic disturbances in sleep, energy, and mood. And in both there is often a drastic decrease in sexual desire.

Although some researchers view depression as a reaction to the eating binges, many studies suggest that the depression comes first. Half of all bulimic women have had a depressive episode a year or more before the onset of bulimia. Eighty percent will experience such an episode at least once in their lives.[12]

The most intriguing link between the two illnesses is that bulimia responds to antidepressants. When bulimic women are treated with antidepressants, any depression they have is relieved as well. But fascinatingly, *bulimic women who aren't depressed also respond to antidepressants*. In other words, it isn't the depressive symptoms of bulimia that are being treated with the medication. The bulimia, *in toto*, is—the binging and purging, the obsessive thoughts about weight, food, and size, and any mood disturbances that may accompany these symptoms.

Biopsychiatrists are struck by the cyclical nature of the binge-purge illness, the almost automatic predictability of the behavior. After a binge, women go into the starvation phase of the cycle, dieting to the extreme to make the dreaded pounds disappear. As they approach their base-line weight level, a mounting uneasiness and craving for food again become intolerable. At that point, another binge is triggered, and the cycle starts again. Hudson and

Pope have noted that a depressive cycle often accompanies the binges, as if the two illnesses were riding in tandem.

Bulimia and major depression both seem to arrive and depart spontaneously. In depression, the dark mood and thought distortions can appear without provocation, like a virus that's flown in through the window. In bulimia, the binging and/or vomiting just seem to start one day and very soon are out of control. Bulimia also appears to end spontaneously. Many recovered bulimics believe that they were able to conquer their illness through willpower, but scientists question whether a condition that has been so utterly uncontrollable as bulimia would suddenly become manageable simply through an exercise of will.

It's always tempting to think that an illness has improved as a result of our efforts. We *want* to believe that. It gives us solace to think that we can control anything bad that has happened to us. But what patients actually experience when their binging comes to an end, Hudson and Pope believe, is spontaneous remission.[13] The illness stops, that is, because it stops. So far, no one knows why it chooses a certain biological moment in time to stop any more than why it chooses a certain biological moment in time to begin.

Binging, Boozing, Stealing: A Syndrome of Compulsive Behaviors

Therapists have found that bulimic women often abuse drugs and alcohol. Hudson and Pope say that as many as 25 percent of the women they've treated have been alcoholic. Some actually began as alcoholics and then developed bulimia shortly after they became sober. "They broke the addiction through Alcoholics Anonymous, professional counseling, or sheer self discipline; and almost immediately found themselves victims of a new affliction: compulsive binge eating," the scientists report.[14]

Both alcohol and cocaine raise neurotransmitter levels in the brain. Hudson and Pope think that bulimics, like people who are depressed, may be using drugs and alcohol to "self-medicate"— that is, to compensate for low neurotransmitter levels. Unfortunately, the mood boost brought about by alcohol is short-lived, and, as is explained at length in chapter 7, chronic abuse ends up depleting the body's supply of natural opioids—morphinelike chemicals that have been discovered in the human brain. As they are reduced in number, the urge to consume artificial opioids is renewed, and a vicious cycle sets in. Dr. Jeffrey Jonas has put forth the idea that opioids "may be globally involved in most addictive or compulsive behaviors."[15] At a 1988 meeting of the Society for Neuroscience, held at the Addictions Research Foundation in Toronto, a number of papers, including Jonas's, suggested that bulimia and alcoholism are neurobiologically related.[16]

Besides depression and alcoholism, at least six other psychiatric disorders occur more frequently among bulimics than in the general population: anorexia nervosa, bipolar disorder, obsessive-compulsive disorder, panic disorder, agoraphobia, and kleptomania. "People are invariably shocked when we report that about one-third of our bulimic patients—many of them affluent, law-abiding people with sterling reputations in their communities—regularly engage in thousands of dollars' worth of compulsive shoplifting," write Hudson and Pope.

In the study mentioned earlier of bulimic students at the University of Minnesota, two-thirds reported stealing behavior. Most of what they stole was stuff they didn't want or need, and yet they felt compelled by an irresistible urge. Hudson and Pope describe such behavior as a "breakdown in the voluntary control mechanism." Most of us turn off urges to do things that are inappropriate or harmful dozens of times a day. "The process is so rapid and automatic that we are hardly aware of it—we take our voluntary impulse control for granted."

Voluntary impulse control, Hudson and Pope explain, "has its seat in a network of ordinary nerve cells somewhere in the brain, and these are as vulnerable to illness as any other organ of the body." Just as the person with epilepsy can't control seizures, people with bulimia and kleptomania may be incapable of turning off the urge to binge or steal.

Hudson and Pope are currently conducting trials on the use of antidepressants to treat kleptomania. They were struck by the discovery that shoplifting bulimics who were treated with antidepressants stopped their stealing as well as their binging. They also located ten large studies of shoplifters and found that in eight of them subjects had shown elevated levels of depression. They've had initial success treating kleptomania with antidepressants. It is notable, they wrote in the *Journal of Clinical Psychopharmacology*, that these women "responded to drugs that affect serotonin neutrotransmission, and serotonin has been associated with effects on mood, appetite, and impulsivity."[17]

The Old Theories

An important theory about eating disorders evolved in late 1970s, when Dr. Hilde Bruch wrote that they afflicted young women who'd grown up in overcontrolling families.[18] Parents in such families prevent children from becoming attuned to their bodily needs, she said. Feeding routines become organized around the mother's needs, not the child's. Mother's tendency to become overinvolved with her female child made things worse. Bruch saw anorexia and bulimia as part of the adolescent's struggle to gain control over herself and her environment. But since her death in the late seventies, studies of the parents of eating-disordered people have failed to bear out the theory that these illnesses are caused by controlling mothers.[19]

Society's Child

Ideas about families causing eating disorders soon were attacked by feminist psychologists, who hoped to get the focus off mother and onto society. Papers began being published claiming that the value our culture places on slimness heightens some women's problems with self-esteem and creates havoc with their eating behaviors. This approach to bulimia and anorexia was in part a product of the political climate at that time. In a campus atmosphere that was fiercely feminist, contempt arose toward psychological ideas that were considered male-constructed and antiwoman.

In the late seventies, Marlene Boskind-White and her husband, William White (she is a therapist, and he a clinical psychologist), learned that a surprising number of women at Cornell were suffering from eating problems, including full-blown bulimia. White and Boskind-White interpreted the students' disordered eating patterns as "cover-ups" for deeper feelings of inadequacy.

"Because of their low self-esteem, these women feel unworthy of being loved and can attribute this feeling to their temporary self-disgust about binging or being slightly overweight," they wrote in *Bulimarexia* in 1978. Conditioned to devalue themselves, the women were "ripe" for disorders like bulimia, the authors said.

Bulimarexia was welcomed by therapists and counselors who found themselves facing a baffling new syndrome and wanted guidance in treating it. Binging was a way of "filling up without needing others," the authors stated. It was a way of "warding off people with a wall of (perceived) fat." A bulimic woman was presumably "locked into a struggle between two parts of herself"—the wish for total control versus the wish to be out of control. Believing herself to be unlovable, she became supersensitive to the reactions of others. Eventually, "the most minor or insignificant slight is exaggerated and distorted, creating massive self-loathing that propels the woman to further binging." The solution, according to the Whites, is for women to gather insight about their negative social conditioning. "Once women come to realize that they have embraced the same legacy of helplessness and hopelessness that their mothers have lived out, they can free themselves to choose a different way of living."

The Whites write, "We are convinced the women we work with are not 'sick,' or 'mentally ill,' as many clinicians suggest." But what, possibly, could bulimic women be if not ill?

These therapists have decided that bulimia is "learned behavior," and that, as such, "it can be unlearned." This unlearning is the focus of the Whites' model of treatment. They try to zero in on "maladaptive patterns" their patients have come to rely on presumably because of "the way they've been socialized, as women."[21]

The "psychosocial" approach to bulimia continues to influence many therapists today. Disturbingly, it fails to incorporate new and important information on the biological component in eating disorders. Treatment plans that address only the psychodynamic aspects of bulimia can keep women in therapy a long time without relieving their urge to consume huge quantities of carbohydrates. There is, as we shall see, a better way. But many therapists in this country remain strangely blindered to it. In the spring of 1991, Gabrielle and I attended a day-long conference held by the American Association of Anorexia and Bulimia in New York. We were especially interested in seeing how the 123 therapists who attended would respond to the two talks scheduled on biopsychiatry's contribution to the understanding and treatment of bulimia. On the day of the meeting, we arrived to find that the two lectures had been canceled. Only two people had signed up for the talks. Apparently the therapists weren't interested in finding out what science had learned about eating disorders!

Most therapists today still try to treat their bulimic patients by the slow uncovering of "inner conflicts." Often such therapy doesn't help the binging and purging. "I've had years of group therapy and one-to-one, and while both have given me a lot of insight into interpersonal problems, they haven't touched the binging," a woman from Los Angeles told me. She was thirty-eight, with a highly successful business escorting out-of-town celebrities to press interviews and media shows. But while she was able to organize and run the business and also take care of a family, she was *not* able to control the binges that seemed to make a mockery of her success. She told me sadly, "I've been binging and vomiting since I was a teenager. Nothing I've done has ever really put a dent in it!"

Hudson and Pope, who have treated patients with many psychiatric disorders at McLean Hospital in Belmont, Massachusetts, have been struck by the particular pain inflicted by eating disorders. "We have seen few other patients with such manifest suffering and with such a desperate desire to be freed from their illness."[22]

Medical Help for Bulimia

The history of treatment for eating disorders had not shown much promise when Hudson and Pope first experimented with medication to stop the binge-purge syndrome. "Clearly, a rapid, dependable, and inexpensive treatment, effective for both bulimia and its associated symptoms—especially depression—would be welcome," they wrote in *New Hope for Binge Eaters*. "Now we may have one: antidepressant medications."

The use of antidepressants in treating bulimia had begun in the late 1970s. The first success was reported by Dr. Daniel Moore of Yale in 1977. Moore used amitriptyline to treat a woman with both anorexia and bulimia. For four months she had no further binging. The medication was stopped, and within two weeks, as Moore described in the *American Journal of Psychiatry*, the woman "became preoccupied with food, calories, eating, and vomiting, to the exclusion of the other therapeutic issues on which she had worked so well for the past four months. The next week, she called in tears to say that she had been eating and vomiting continuously and would like to resume the amitriptyline." The bulimia stopped within two days, and her preoccupation with weight faded into the background.

In 1982, Hudson and Pope published the first study of a group of bulimic patients. Although the study was small and used no control group, it was distinctly encouraging. Six out of eight patients improved within weeks of starting on antidepressants "despite having binged continuously for as long as four years prior to treatment."[23]

A twenty-one-year-old woman with a history of severe binging had an especially poignant story. Before being treated with imipramine, the woman used to binge twice a day. Both times, she'd consume a gallon of ice cream drenched in maple syrup, along with assorted candies, doughnuts, and other sweets. To purge, she took as many as twenty diuretic pills and 500 ml of milk of magnesia a day. She also vomited. Emotionally, as you might imagine, she was in bad shape—depressed, insomniac, and with intense suicidal ideation, especially after her binges. Hudson and Pope treated her with imipramine, checking her blood serum level to see how she was metabolizing the drug, and increased her dosage several times. Once her dosage was raised to 300 mg a day, her binges dropped to one a week, and she reported improved mood and a complete disappearance of her thoughts of suicide.

Dr. Timothy Walsh of Columbia University reported the case of a thirty-seven-year-old nurse who'd been bulimic for ten years, with episodes of binging and vomiting three and four times a day. Food was costing her hundreds of dollars a week. She'd had six years of psychotherapy, as well as some behavior therapy, and small doses of tranquilizers and tricyclic antidepressants—all without effect. Three weeks after beginning treatment with phenelzine (Nardil), an MAO inhibitor, the woman reported she no longer felt depressed and had lost the urge to binge and vomit.

In the next ten months of treatment, she binged only three times, all during periods of high stress.[24]

Studies done in the early 1980s were larger and added substantially to the credibility of antidepressant treatment. At the Mayo Clinic, Dr. Patrick Hughes established complete remission of bulimia within ten weeks of treatment in fifteen of twenty-two subjects.[25] The depression and other associated symptoms showed striking improvement. Dr. Hughes had tested blood levels to be sure the dose he was prescribing was adequate. In some cases it wasn't, and when he increased the dosage, the symptoms remitted. *This was the first study to show the importance of blood-level testing and adequate dosage.*

Therapy Versus Antidepressants

Most studies that appear to raise doubt about using antidepressants to treat bulimia have serious flaws, say Hudson and Pope. Either the dosage used was too low, the studies were conducted over too short a period of time to measure fully the medication's effect, or (unlike what happens in clinical practice) patients were not offered another type of antidepressant when the first one didn't work. Unfortunately, these flawed studies are often mentioned by therapists as a reason *not* to steer their bulimic patients to a psychopharmacologist.

A widely cited study by Dr. James Mitchell, published in February 1990,[26] concluded that treatment combining antidepressants and psychotherapy was only negligibly more effective than psychotherapy alone and that treatment with antidepressants alone was significantly less effective than psychotherapy alone. The study, however, was seriously misleading. In those cases in which the medication didn't work, a new medication wasn't offered. *This is key.* Many studies have now shown that it can take two or three tries to get good results. "Any study comparing antidepressant treatment to psychotherapy which doesn't allow additional antidepressant trials is effectively no comparison at all," Harrison Pope told us. Indeed, Dr. Mitchell's own group found that many of their patients who had failed in an initial trial of imipramine "responded quite nicely to a subsequent trial of an alternative drug"—often an MAOI, fluoxetine, or desipramine. However, by a fluke of academic publishing, the results of the second trial were published in 1989, *before* the results of the first. But this was not acknowledged when the original study was finally reported, in 1990.[28]

As of 1989, there has been only one study—Hudson and Pope's—in which patients who didn't respond to the first antidepressant were offered one or more additional trials with drugs from other families.[29] *In it, 73 percent of sixty-five patients achieved either a marked reduction (greater that 75 percent) or a total remission of their bulimic symptoms.*[30]

By 1991, at least fourteen blind and well-controlled studies had shown that antidepressants are effective, and that evidence is mounting that their benefit is maintained, or even improved, over the long run. "Antidepressants have documented efficacy in decreasing the binge-purge cycle," wrote Michael Gitlin, M.D., in *The Psychotherapist's Guide to Psychopharmacology*. The decrease in binging—*across studies*—averaged 75 percent.[31] "A variety of antidepressants have been used, with the majority showing positive results," Gitlin reports. He emphasizes that "when one antidepressant is ineffective, a different one will work, so that several trials are warranted in the patient who fails to respond."

Hudson and Pope's method of treating bulimia with antidepressants is detailed in appendix B. Women with this illness can compare it with the treatment they receive currently.

Eating Disorders and Neurotransmitters

In the late eighties information began to emerge from the field of neurophysiology on *why* antidepressants work with bulimia. Changes in brain chemistry seem to produce the symptoms of binging and purging as well as the obsessional ideas about food, weight, and eating. An article in the *American Journal of Psychiatry* described how the starvation anorectics inflict on themselves *lowers* their supply of norephinephrine. "Anorexics may be lessening their own anxiety by lowering their levels of norepinephrine," observes Dr. Maurizio Fava, a psychiatrist in the Clinical Pharmacology Unit at Massachusetts General Hospital in Boston.

"Lessening their anxiety by starving themselves may reinforce the severe diets that anorexics adopt and may encourage them to repeat the process whenever they begin to feel anxious."[32]

Helping to perpetuate the starvation diets may be the euphoria that results when the brain opioids, or endorphins, are increased. Extreme dieting "elevates levels of opioids, producing a sort of high that may also reinforce the behavior," Dr. Fava said.

Serotonin, too, as mentioned earlier, is altered in people with eating disorders. Bulimic patients have lower than normal levels of it. As we've seen, serotonin deficiencies are associated with depression and anxiety. They also reduce the sensation of having eaten enough—which may in part explain why bulimics feel compelled to binge.

Relief for Carbohydrate Cravers

Judith Wurtman uncovered an important reason why diets so often fail. The way she explained it to us, in her office at MIT, was as follows: Many people get on a destructive pendulum, swinging between overeating and fasting. Initially, afraid they won't be able to control the carbohydrates they crave, they cut them out entirely. Soon their brains go into "serotonin deficit." At this point, "they can't stand the diet anymore," says Wurtman, "and they go back to binging again." Such dieters inevitably gain weight. Emotionally, they become trapped in a negative cycle, feeling deprived without carbohydrates and guilty when they gorge on them.

The solution, Wurtman has found, lies in understanding—and, to a certain extent, managing—one's serotonin supply. This means *managing*, not avoiding, carbohydrates. Cutting them out entirely is the worst thing to do because it drives down the serotonin level, pushing the dieter into a carbohydrate feeding frenzy. Part of the trick is in the timing. To illustrate. Dr. Wurtman tells of a college professor who sought her guidance because she felt stressed and would overeat during the school year. "She came to see me one summer, hoping to avoid her usual pattern in the upcoming semester. She said doctors had always told her she shouldn't eat carbohydrates, although that's what she *wanted* to eat. Being told it was bad for her made her feel out of control. Yet when she allowed herself to eat carbohydrates—'self-indulge' was how she put it—she always felt calmer."

The woman had her worst urges between midafternoon and bedtime, which is typical. Wurtman has found that accommodating rather than denying such urges is what works. "I put her on a carbohydrate diet from four o'clock in the afternoon until bedtime. She was to eat vegetables, fruits, and some dairy products, but mostly complex carbohydrates like cereals, bread, and pasta." The new eating plan turned the teacher's mood around. "Her stress went, and she maintained her weight. She couldn't believe it was so easy."

Because stress depletes serotonin, the teacher felt a greater desire to eat carbohydrates during the hectic school year than she did in the summer, when she was more relaxed. Struggling with her craving, she would try to cut out carbohydrates completely. This would deplete her serotonin even more. At this point, Wurtman says, her patient's carbohydrate binging became virtually inevitable. It was as if she *had* to have them. Her brain *demanded* them. Not understanding the purely physiological basis of her need for carbohydrates, she felt guilty. She was "out of control." A vicious cycle ensued.

Wurtman got her client out of the cycle by teaching her how to eat to alter her brain chemicals. "Giving her the carbohydrates that she clearly wanted satisfied her brain's need to make more serotonin," Wurtman explains. "This is what made her feel good and put her eating back into control."

These studies by Judith Wurtman and her husband Richard Wurtman lead to the conclusion that diets low in carbohydrate are bound to fail. "People need the opportunity to eat carbohydrates unaccompanied by protein. That's why liquid protein diets will provide such dramatic shifts," says Wurtman. First, the big weight loss, then the crash, then the weight gain. "Drinking two shakes every day and having a dinner of protein, you can lose a great deal of weight, but as we've actually shown with animals, you also produce a detriment of serotonin levels in the brain. As a consequence—and we saw this with the animals—you have a period of carbohydrate binging to restore the serotonin levels. The animal does this for maybe a day or two, and then its serotonin levels go to normal. The animal, of course, has no residual emotional overlay, no 'I feel so guilty because I ate so much lab chow.' " So the animal is likely to rebalance itself. In humans, however, the guilt may trigger a new bout of carbohydrate deprivation. Then up and down and up again it goes. When Oprah Winfrey lost sixty pounds on a liquid diet, she was exhilarated by the results, which she presented to an admiring audience pound by pound. The end point—it took only several months to accomplish—was a size-ten pair of jeans. Then came the crash. The mashed potatoes, which Oprah says she craves daily, were back in the picture again, and Oprah's weight began to rise as dramatically as it had lowered.

On the Drawing Board: A Drug That Prevents Weight Gain

Looking for a more direct method of relieving carbohydrate craving, the Wurtmans have been conducting trials of the drug D-fenfluramine. They first tried the drug with women who were overeating premenstrually (as was seen in the previous chapter). "We found that D-fenfluramine relieved the mood symptoms in most women suffering from PMS and showed 100 percent efficacy in normalizing food intake."

D-fenfluramine enhances the release of serotonin in the brain cells as well as delaying its degradation. Interestingly, the drug didn't lower carbohydrate intake when the women were consuming normally, at the beginning of the menstrual cycle. Premenstrually, it only brought their food intake back to what it was at the beginning. Thus, the Wurtmans believe, D-fenfluramine won't be abusable. It won't be able to be used by normal-weight women to become unhealthily thin.

Like depression and panic, and even some addictions, carbohydrate binging is episodic. Wurtman says clinicians need to learn that in any given patient obesity will return and that when it does, it should be treated. "You don't wait until a person is suicidal before putting him or her onto an antidepressant," she notes. Once drugs are available, "doctors won't have to wait until someone's gained seventy-five pounds before using them."

Because episodes of overeating are often predictable, efforts at weight control have been cast in a new light. "Let's say a woman is sliding into menopause and the luteal phase of her menstrual cycle is twenty-one days every month. That's an aw-fully long time to overeat. You can imagine that considerable weight could be gained in that situation. You can *predict* that. You can also predict that if someone is under prolonged stress, that person is likely to gain weight, since eating carbohydrates relieves the serotonin depletion produced by the stress. If there's a significant change in exercise level, *that* predicts weight gain. Quitting smoking predicts weight gain."

The way the drug trials are going, the Wurtmans think D-fenfluramine may be able to be used episodically for weight control. It will be similar to the way antidepressants are used. "You treat a person for depression, and after a while you with-draw the antidepressant. It may be years before the person be-comes depressed again, or it may be six months. But no psychiatrist would ever say, 'I treated you in 1987 for depression. You have no right getting depressed again.' "

Carbohydrate binging, then, is rooted in the physiology of the brain. The Wurtmans' work breaks new ground in placing epi-sodic binging squarely within the realm of medicine. Carbohy-drate craving is real—a physical need that results from inadequate mood chemicals in the brain. I asked Judith Wurtman if she would hazard a guess as to the number of obese people who suffer from chemically induced carbohydrate craving. "With women, it's probably as much as 80 percent," she said. "Many females have this carbohydrate craving—if not chronically, then certainly when they're premenstrual."

Carbohydrate craving is less prevalent in men. Wurtman sus-pects obesity in men is often related to alcohol intake. "And alcohol certainly has an effect on serotonin. You could say that in men that's the substance that's consumed rather than carbohy-drates."

It made me think of how often men eating out will order liquor after dinner. Their wives will order dessert.

Children in Pain

....

Once . . . he wrote a poem.
And he called it "Chops,"
Because that was the name of his dog, and
that's what it was all about.
And the teacher gave him an "A"
And a gold star
And his mother hung it on the kitchen door,
and read it to all his aunts. . . .

Once . . . he wrote another poem.
And he called it "Question Marked Innocence,"
Because that was the name of his grief, and
that's what it was all about.
And the professor gave him an "A"
And a strange and steady look.
And his mother never hung it on the kitchen door
because he never let her see it. . . .

Once, at 3 a.m. . . . he tried another poem . . .
And he called it absolutely nothing, because
that's what it was all about.
And he gave himself an "A"
And a slash on each damp wrist,
And hung it on the bathroom door
because he couldn't reach the kitchen.

Written by a 15-year-old boy two years before he committed suicide.[1]

Can a child actually suffer from depression? Until ten years ago, it was thought not. Traditional psychiatrists believed prepubertal children lacked the emotional and cognitive "depth" to suffer from true depression. "You can't mourn a loss if you don't know you've lost something" was the idea. To put it crudely, it was as if children didn't know enough to become depressed.

As the new, biochemical information on depression began to change psychiatry's understanding of mood disorders, researchers started wondering if children as well as adults might have such illnesses. In the last decade, studies have shown that young children and adolescents not only get depressed; they suffer from all the forms of mood disorders. Depression actually is disturbingly prevalent among children, and it goes largely unrecognized.

Some researchers today think we may be seeing in kids the end result of generations of untreated mood disorders and substance-abuse problems. Unfortunately, very few clinicians have the information to make a thorough assessment of children. "It has gotten complicated," says Virginia Hamilton, an addiction counselor connected with New York Hospital who, on an outpatient basis, treats primarily middle-class abusers, many of them children. "These kids come in here on all kinds of street drugs. They have underlying psychiatric disorders that are very sophisticated—atypical depressions, bipolar disorders, atypical bipolar disorders."

It used to be thought that kids were bored, immature, and street drugs were available, so they got addicted; *then* they went crazy. New studies show that the opposite is closer to the truth. As we shall see in this chapter, research from Yale and New York Hospital and information from hands-on clinicians like Virginia Hamilton make clear that in most cases—Virginia says 70 to 80 percent of the time—the kids are sick first. They get into booze and drugs at nine, ten, and eleven *because* they are ill. "They self-medicate," says Hamilton.

And then they become addicted. Once addicted, they are treated as addicts. Their illnesses are almost always overlooked.

Because of the unwitting psychiatric bias against children—the idea that they're too immature to become depressed—many if not most children with major mood disorders have been diagnosed as schizophrenic. Doctors still tend to lump all bizarre delusions, grandiosity, and flights of ideas into the "schizophrenia" bag. Parents, terrified by what is happening to their child, usually feel they have no recourse but to accept the diagnosis. This is tragic, since a mood-disordered child cannot get well on the type of medication used to treat schizophrenia. Also, mood disorders are far more responsive to treatment than schizophrenia; the children, then, are being shunted into hospitals and programs that are bound to keep them sick because their illness hasn't been correctly diagnosed.

Steven, whose mother sent him to a New York City psychiatrist, was at least recognized as depressed. But his story, told by both the boy and his mother in separate interviews, illustrates the many problems a child faces in a society that isn't prepared to diagnose and offer good therapy to children with psychiatric disorders.

Steven's Story

Steven had begun to become depressed in the fall of his senior year in high school. He had been, compared to his brother, the good kid, the one who'd always done wonderfully in school, the one about whom there were never any worrisome reports. But now he couldn't concentrate and had stopped doing his schoolwork. One night, he called his mother, Esther, on the telephone— she and his father had been separated for several years, and he had chosen to live in the city with his dad—and said, "Mom, I want you to call someone and find out why it is I keep having these thoughts about death. I feel like I can't get my mind off it. I'm too young to be having thoughts like these."

Esther was a school psychologist. She was taken aback, for Steven's announcement had come out of the blue. He'd always been happy and well adjusted. But she knew that thoughts of death and dying were serious—something that she, as a mother, was not equipped to deal with. "Steve, I think you should talk to someone directly to find out why you're having these thoughts," she said. "I'll find a therapist for you."

Steven agreed and was sent to a psychiatrist, the friend of a friend of someone in the family. The psychiatrist said Steven was definitely depressed. His thoughts of death and dying had suicidal implications. The doctor felt the boy should go on antidepressant medication immediately but warned that tricyclic antidepressants will sometimes trigger a manic episode. When assessing a young person, it can be hard to tell whether the depression is unipolar or bipolar, and in the case of bipolar, tricyclics can trigger mania. Other substances can trigger manic episodes as well—cocaine, amphetamines, and hallucinogens, among them. When street drugs produce this effect, it is usually because an underlying bipolar disorder has been triggered by the biochemical stimulus.

Steven had never heard of mania before his psychiatric consultation, but he was a serious young man, and he paid attention. The doctor had told him to call immediately if he began to feel himself going "up." This isn't just a matter of feeling good, the doctor had said. "You'll notice nervous energy, increasingly rapid thinking, the feeling of being out of control. Mania may feel okay at first, but it soon becomes very uncomfortable."

The antidepressant didn't seem to help much, but Steven stuck with it for a couple of months. And then, one night, Esther got another phone call. Steven's father was out of town on business, and Steven was feeling very anxious. "I think I might be getting manic, Ma," he said. "I'm pacing back and forth, and I can't sit still."

Esther told him to go across town to her mother's apartment and to stay put until she got there. Then she drove the two hours to the city. Steven was asleep by the time she arrived, but the next morning, a saga would begin that included a power struggle between the divorced parents, what may well have been medical negligence, although no lawsuit was initiated, and mood storms of terrifying proportions. Steven, the good son, the good student, bright, inquisitive, thoughtful, and caring, would soon—in a matter of days—find his world turned upside down.

Steven's intuition about what was happening to him had been right. He *was* becoming manic. He was quickly put on lithium to prevent the mania from escalating. The medication worked, and within a week Steven was feeling more himself. He was advised, however, to continue the medication.

Steven never felt very comfortable about taking the drug. He didn't like the idea that he needed to take medication in order to feel well, and he wasn't convinced he really needed to, anyway.

After all, he'd only experienced a little sleeplessness, a few racing thoughts. He had never really become fully manic.

Still, his mood *had* evened out on the lithium. He was no longer racked by depression, and he wasn't swinging up and down and feeling out of control. Under his psychiatrist's guidance and with urging from his parents, Steven agreed to continue taking the drug. He was more or less stable during the summer, although the mood swings of winter and spring had taken their toll.

The stigma of any medical problem, but in particular a psychiatric disorder, is especially difficult for adolescents to contend with. Steven had had no psychotherapy to help him come to terms with his illness, and he felt afflicted by it. That fall, however, he went off to college, hoping for the best. He fell in with the guys and began to enjoy his first time away from home. His weekly meetings with the psychiatrist assigned him by the school health service struck him as odd, however. He didn't relate to the psychiatrist and didn't know what to talk about. Soon his weekly sessions had been reduced to a ten-minute check-in and occasional blood-level tests.

As for having to take those pills before meals and at bedtime, the whole thing made him feel weird, as though he were different. He'd mentioned his experience to a couple of his friends, and while they weren't particularly uptight about it, nobody seemed to *get* it, either. How could he expect them to? *He* didn't get it. Steven also found it hard to go out drinking on a Friday night, because after having a couple of beers he slurred his words and acted as if he were out of control. Steven had begun to think that his main problem in life was lithium. In November, he went to the health service and told the doctor he wanted to go off it.

The psychiatrist, who'd never really liked the lithium idea to begin with—this kid had never had a full manic episode, so why had he been put on this medication in the first place?—said okay. Steven could go off the lithium as long as he checked in every few weeks so that the psychiatrist could see how he was doing.

Steven didn't check in. He plunged into life as a college student, hoping the whole depression thing was behind him. Which it seemed to be. One day in March, he began feeling hyper. The agitation increased until he wasn't sleeping very well. At this point, Steven went back to the psychiatrist and said, "I'm feeling really weird. I think I should go back on the lithium."

The psychiatrist said, "Why don't we give it a few days? Come back on Monday and let me check you out again."

Steven was attending school in Canada, where psychiatrists are more leery of psychotropic medications than they are in the United States. When Steven returned a few days later, he was feeling quite pleased with himself. "Everything's changed," he said. "I don't need the lithium now. I'm feeling great, just great."

"Great," said the psychiatrist. And Steven was off—and flying. Within days, he would be completely out of control, running around barefoot, taking beer in to his exams, singing as he strutted down the streets of Montreal. "I felt great," he said, recalling the early days of the high. "I felt like a god." A god who was barely eighteen years old, and who was at the mercy of a psychiatrist who didn't know how to treat bipolar depression.

Finally, one of the resident adults in Steven's dorm took things in hand and got him to a hospital. By the time Esther arrived the following day, she said, "I could barely recognize him. This was not my son. Steven was screaming and hostile and utterly abusive. They had to put him in restraints. It was terrible. What had happened to him? To this day, when I think of it . . ."

Steven, the hospital psychiatrist explained, was in the midst of a full-blown manic episode—a psychosis. "The nurses said, 'Don't worry,' " Esther recalled. " 'We've seen this before. Your son will be himself again in a few weeks.' I don't know what I would have done if they hadn't told me that."

The chief resident put Steven on Tegretol, an anticonvulsant medication frequently used to treat rapid-cycling bipolar disorder as an aid to the lithium. Within a week, Steven's symptoms had begun to subside, but the ordeal had taken a terrible toll. "I don't feel that I've fully recovered," he told us six months after the episode. "I feel like I'm still getting over it."

How Many Suffer?

Since 1980, childhood depression has become an accepted clinical entity, although there are still professionals who will argue that it isn't possible for children to become depressed. A preponderance of evidence disputes this. One recent study shows that as many as

8 percent of preschool-aged children show signs of clinically significant depression.

As children get older, their chances of becoming depressed increase. A 1982 study of almost three thousand children in grades three through nine found a whopping 15 percent with symptoms of depression. The same study found that by the time they reach fifteen, one out of five is depressed.

Depression in children isn't just a passing phase. The average episode of major depression lasts seven months—and in some children, much longer. The younger the child, the longer the episode, according to Maria Kovacs, one of the country's chief researchers in childhood depression. Early onset, she says, also has a less favorable prognosis, especially when the depression isn't recognized and treated.[2]

Once a child has had an episode of major depression, the chances are high that he or she will have another. Seventy-two percent of the children Dr. Kovacs studied had a recurrence of major depression within five years.

While acute major depression is a terrible thing to see in a child, it is actually easier to treat than milder dysthymic depression. Dysthymia, in children, says Dr. Kovacs, is "the most chronic and the most complicated" of depressions. The illness lasts much longer—an average of *three years*. For some reason, dysthymic depressions are almost always accompanied by other psychiatric conditions.

Children and adolescents suffer from all sorts of mood disorders and can become just as ill as adults. When their mood disorders go untreated, they get worse. The clinical use of antidepressants and lithium in children and adolescents has become much more prevalent in the last decade as the serious effects of mood disorder on childhood development have become better understood.

Diagnosis of depression in adolescents isn't always easy. As Fred Goodwin and Kay Jamison, authors of a textbook on manic depression, point out, depression is often mistaken for something else. Decreased energy levels and lethargy, particularly in an ordinarily active adolescent, can easily be mistaken for some other illness. "In addition, mood is not always affected, the child may have age-specific problems in communicating moods and other subjective states, and physicians tend to think of depression and manic depression as illnesses of adulthood," the scientists write.[3]

Hypomania is a form of depression that in children can easily be confused with hyperactivity. Several features distinguish it. It is characterized by mood swings, mood disorders in the family history, and hyperactivity that is episodic rather than day-to-day. When children with bipolar disorder have been compared with those with attention-deficit disorder, the manic children showed greater overall behavior pathology and maladjustment. Bipolar illness in adolescents can become confused with antisocial personality disorder, since the two are marked by impulsive behaviors such as shoplifting, substance abuse, aggressiveness, and getting in trouble with the law. Factors that are useful in identifying bipolar children are the association of antisocial behavior with elevated or irritable mood, the absence of a conduct disorder, and a relative lack of peer-influenced behavior.

Goodwin and Jamison say that among preadolescent children, alcohol abuse is very closely associated with mood disorders. In one study, seven out of ten cases of adolescent alcohol abuse or dependence were bipolar or cyclothymic, and the remaining three had closely related depressive disorders.

That manic episodes are painfully disruptive to anyone who suffers them is particularly true of a young person who hasn't fully developed his identity. "Mercifully," one psychiatrist wrote in a medical journal, "much of what happens during a manic episode isn't recalled by the patient."

But that very lack of recall, in combination with being treated strangely by doctors and nurses and family, can be utterly unnerving.

Medication Is Not Enough

Steven spent a week in the hospital in Montreal lying in restraint. "I've never been able to figure out why they had to keep me in a straitjacket," he says. "It was horrible. My body got so stiff from it. I was having these religious experiences the nurses made light of. I felt they weren't taking me seriously."

Esther wanted Steven to stay in the hospital until he had recovered completely, but Edgar, Steven's father, a successful New York restaurateur, flew to Montreal and insisted the boy come home as soon as possible. "I'll take care of this," he said. He didn't like what was happening. Things were out of control, had been ever since the boy had gone to that first psychiatrist in New York and started on all this medication business. "But obviously he's sick," said Esther.

"He's sick now," said Edgar. "Who knows how sick he'd be if he'd never started on this stuff."

Edgar flew Steven to New York with him, and Esther drove to her home in upstate New York. It wasn't long, though, before Steven was back in the hospital. The stress of trying to deal with it all—with his father, who didn't fully acknowledge his illness, and with his mother, who was arguing daily on the phone with his father—was too much. He tilted into mania again. Although it was brought under control in a couple of weeks, this time he stayed in the hospital a month and a half.

Shaken by what had happened to him, Steven nevertheless returned to college in the fall. His mother had vacillated, trying to decide whether to let him stay home a semester to recuperate or whether to get him back on the main track as quickly as possible. Steven is glad now that he returned, but at the time he wasn't at all sure he could make it. He had been through something huge and frightening and wasn't even sure what it was.

Steven, unfortunately had been offered no therapy. A psychopharmacologist in New York had given him instructions on how to take his medication and had said that he would, if necessary, consult with the Canadian psychiatrist on the telephone. Esther had set that up. She was painfully aware that the health-care system had failed her son—in particular, the college psychiatrist. If it hadn't been for this doctor's casual attitude toward medication, Steven might very well never have had a full-blown manic episode. And yet Esther knew she had to work within the system. What else could she do?

Before Steven took the trip back to Montreal, Esther telephoned the school psychiatrist in the hope of prodding him to assume more responsibility. "Steven *must* stay on this medication," she said. "He can't be allowed to go off, as he was last year." She told the doctor what had happened to Steven, and the doctor actually apologized. He swore that this time he'd "stay on top of it." Esther felt somewhat reassured.

A month later, worried because Steven was sounding low on the telephone, she called the psychiatrist. Should his dosage be increased? she wondered. The doctor said, "I'm in charge here."

In another few weeks, Esther called to tell the psychiatrist that now she was really worried. Steven had said he was still feeling low and complained that he didn't have many friends. Returning to his sophomore year after the experience of the summer was obviously very trying for him. Esther asked the psychiatrist, "Isn't there some group he can go to where there'd be others who've had experiences like his?" The psychiatrist replied, "When he forms an attachment to me, he won't need any group."

Esther didn't know what to do. It had been her first experience with a mood-disordered child. Shouldn't the psychiatrist know best?

This one apparently didn't. Steven got through another year of college and, taking his lithium, was able to avoid another manic episode. His sense of identity, however, was severely shaken by what had happened to him. He needed therapy, but what he was getting from the school psychiatrist was little more than monitoring—is he too high, is he too low, is he more or less stable? "Can't you send him to another psychiatrist?" I asked Esther when she told me about this. "This one's covered by the school's insurance," she said. "I doubt that his father would pay for an outside psychiatrist. He still hasn't accepted the fact that Steven is sick."

Esther didn't have any money, and Edgar used his to try to control a situation that deeply disturbed him. He had had his own bouts of depression, and although he'd never been hospitalized, he'd had experiences that his son suspected were manic. "I've seen him shouting and waving his arms around," Steven told us. "He's very irritable and fast-paced, and he loses it. So *my* being sick really gets to him."

Steven felt he had to cope as best he could on his own. There were a number of problems he had to contend with, many of which involved his feelings of being "different." For example, he didn't like the idea of taking his pills in front of his friends and would try to remember to do so before mealtime, in the secrecy of his room. In short, he felt ashamed.

In adolescents, the sense of stigma associated with a psychiatric disorder is especially strong. Said Steven, "It's hard to talk about it with friends, and I don't like when my mother mentions it around me. I feel as if my interactions with people are a little off. I guess I have in the back of my mind that the experience I went through sets me apart."

There is much in the day-to-day life of this nineteen-year-old to remind him that he *is* apart. "There are things I can't do when I'm on lithium. I can't drink alcohol, can't miss sleep. If you miss out on a night's sleep, it can exacerbate your manicness. The whole thing is limiting my experience. Actually, I'm trying to figure out ways around it. For example, drinking. That's what we do every weekend, almost. It's hard, because if I have too much, it has some kind of synergistic reaction where I just become very confused and I start not making any sense, jumbling up words and stuff. On New Year's Eve, I went to this party in New York, and it happened. I got confused, I just didn't know what was going on, so I got in a cab and went home."

Steven has a little program he's worked out to try to get around this problem. "Let's say a big night is coming up where I'll be finished with exams or something and we're going to go out and we all want to have a good time. I find that if I miss two days of my medication, I can maintain my level within like a tenth or two, and it kind of lessens the effect of the alcohol. Which I'm not supposed to do, but . . ."

Steven is playing with fire, and on some level he knows it, but he desperately wants to be able to fit in with his friends. Also, it's possible that he isn't getting sufficient relief from depression and that he is drinking to self-medicate. In any case, Steven should be getting help from a therapist and not trying to second-guess the situation on his own. Actually, he's quite aware that he's got more on his plate than he can handle, but he can't ask for help. "I don't feel comfortable telling my parents that I need to talk some things out with a doctor," he says. "My father would take that to mean that there's something wrong with me, that maybe if I'm seeing a psychiatrist then things aren't okay. Somehow he takes it as an offense to him."

I suggested that perhaps that was his father's problem. "Sure it's his problem," said Steven, "but it doesn't make me feel comfortable. And my mother would have to pay for it, and I know she can't afford it."

Less obvious to Steven is that if he were to see a therapist, it would make his illness more real to him, something he had to contend with in a more conscious way and come to accept. As it is, he denies much of the impact that his illness is having on him, trying to put it in the past. "I like to feel like I'm independent and that I'm not sick, that I'm mentally independent," he says.

Someone should be helping him with that fragile sense of independence. While young people with mood disorders can be successfully treated with psychotropic medications, they are in even greater need of adjunctive psychotherapy than adults. Almost inevitably, a young person's experience of a psychiatric disorder is damaging to his self-esteem. In addition, his relationships with family members—the very persons on whom he must rely for support—can become disrupted. As happened in Steven's case, parents can find psychiatric illness in their children threatening. Often the parents of a mood-disordered child haven't come to terms with their own mood disorders, and so things are covered up.

Catching It Early

Depression has serious and far-reaching effects on a child's life. Joaquim Puig-Antich, the first psychiatrist to devote his career to the study of depression in children, reported in 1985 that while *all* psychiatric disorders will affect children's social relationships, depression is by far the most impairing.[4] It's damaging to school performance and interactions with friends and family. The relationship with the mother in particular is likely to become distant. According to Puig-Antich, even after children have been treated medically for depression, their relationships are likely to continue to be impaired. With mother, things may improve moderately, but the relationship will lack "depth," he says. School performance seems to improve faster than the depressed child's social relationships.

The situation with peers is often not great. Depressed children tend to have fewer close friends, and their friendships don't last as long as those of nondepressed kids. Puig-Antich says that depressed children are not only shier than other children, they are more likely to be teased. This, of course, affects self-esteem, and the depression becomes reinforced.

As with adults, mood disorder affects a child's cognitive abilities. In school, depressed kids can end up being placed at levels below their intellectual capabilities. Often they find it difficult to concentrate, which leads to lack of interest and motivation. They are easily distracted and fatigued, all of which affects their ability to do schoolwork. Depressed children score significantly lower than nondepressed children in reading, writing, and arithmetic. Poor scholastic performance makes them feel even worse about themselves. If the underlying mood disorder isn't treated, academic problems and their effects on self-esteem can continue into adulthood.

Childhood depression shares many of the features of adult depression, but some symptoms that are notable in adults, such as guilt and hopelessness, may not be apparent in children. Important in evaluating depression in children is understanding that symptoms change with a child's level of development.

In children, symptoms of depression can be thought of—and often are—as more or less "normal" behavior. Refusal to attend school, for example, can be a sign of depression in children, and parents and teachers often don't recognize it. Poor academic performance is also key, although a child can do wonderfully in school and still be clinically depressed.

Parents usually aren't able to identify mood disorders in their children. Most of the kids who get into treatment do so because their troubles are noticed at school. One woman we interviewed said that as a child she was so "hostile" in nursery school that the private kindergarten she was slated for wouldn't take her.

What tends to get picked up in mood-disordered kids, explained family therapist Karen Gainer, in an interview, "is attentional difficulties, poor academic performance, or an attention-deficit disorder, which teachers think of as 'hyperactivity.' Or the kids have some kind of conduct disorder or behavior problem. Or they may be accident-prone." Thus, when the child who is depressed is taken for evaluation, it is usually because he or she is "acting up." The behavior is annoying to someone.

Children whose behavior is *not* annoying are often left untreated—until they are in serious trouble. Yet when a developmental history is taken, says Gainer, "you'll begin to hear from parents, 'Oh, my goodness, yes. He or she was always like that. He *always* was very temperamental, he *always* would fuss over very small events and have trouble with calming and self-soothing.' Or, you hear, 'She *always* had these periods of being very giddy and silly and laughing for no particular reason. One minute she'd be like that, and the next minute there'd be temper tantrums and irritability.' When clinicians hear this we think, 'agitated depression.' It actually shows up more clearly in kids than it might in adults."

When parents see temper tantrums and irritability, they rarely think, Agitated depression. They think, What can I do to get away from this kid?

Signs and Symptoms

The quiet, "good" child may be suffering within. Girls especially seem to be silent sufferers. Psychologist Anita Gurian points out that "parents and teachers view the docile or withdrawn girl as socially more appropriate than the docile or withdrawn boy."[5] For this reason, parents tend to seek help sooner for a withdrawn son than they do for a quiet, submissive daughter.

Age plays an important role in *how* a child reveals that he or she is depressed. Dr. Gurian, a senior psychologist and specialist in child development at Long Island Jewish Medical Center, says, "The infant may fail to grow physically, the toddler may have prolonged tantrums, the nursery school child may be overly aggressive or withdrawn, the elementary school child may avoid school, the adolescent may refuse to hear."[6] Unfortunately, the trend in diagnosing children is to focus on the symptoms that characterize *adult* depression—namely, fatigue, suicidal ideation, low self-esteem, and social withdrawal. This is a mistake, says Dr. Gurian, since depressed kids may not have such symptoms or may have others that present more vividly.

A baby of nine months, for example, may show failure to thrive. Perhaps its very young mother has frequent crying spells and suicidal ideas. The baby is unresponsive, seems to sleep more than most, "looks withdrawn and distant," notes Gurian, and is growing too slowly. A pediatrician, looking at this syndrome, should think "depression."

Seven-year-old "Celia" can't get herself to go to school in the morning. She's afraid of being teased and of not being able to do her schoolwork. (When Celia was two, her mother became depressed and had to be hospitalized.)

A ten-year-old daydreams in school, never gets her homework done, and zones out on TV and as many cookies as she can get her hands on. She's often in bed by late afternoon, comes down for dinner, and goes back to bed afterward.

An eleven-year-old does very well in school but constantly chastises herself for the way she does things. She frets over her homework every night and before a test will lie awake half the night worrying.

In general, says Dr. Gurian, the symptoms of depression are more diffuse in very young children. Feelings of guilt do not seem to set in until later in adolescence. Some therapists believe that hopelessness doesn't present until adolescence, although this seems at odds with the fact that children commit suicide.

It is true that younger children often don't express feelings of sadness openly, but they will appear sad and bored, will lose interest in activities they once liked, and may increase attention-getting behavior as a way of communicating their distress and/or getting relief from low mood. If you see a small boy or girl acting up around the house, unable to sit still, interrupting adult conversations, pulling the dog's tail, and generally behaving like Dennis the Menace, you may find, in the same house, a mood-disordered mother or father—or both.

If asked directly, Dr. Gurian says, children may use words such as "rotten," "bad," or "gross," to describe their feelings. While many depressed children won't use "sad" to describe their feelings, a boy named Peter is able to do so quite clearly. "This is a child who says, 'Yes, I feel sad. I feel sad almost all the time,'" says Karen Gainer. "The only thing that he was able to identify that made him feel better was riding his bicycle."

At age four, Peter witnessed his mother murdering his father.

Today, two years after the initial trauma, he is still depressed. If you were to meet him, however, the last thing you might think is "This child is depressed." In fact, Peter looks *anything but* depressed, says Gainer. "This is a boy who, when you sit with him in a room, is all over the place. He seems very hyperactive. But if you look at the broader picture, you can see that what he has is really an agitated depression."

The Bipolar Child

It isn't yet clear why, but bipolar disorder is on the rise in children and adolescents. Doctors aren't picking this up. A 1985 study found that of forty-four children who had bipolar parents and who also had clear symptoms of depression, *none had been diagnosed with affective disorders, even though all had been seen previously by a variety of mental health professionals.* The study, conducted by Hagop Akiskal, a world-renowned authority on mood disorders,[7] found that, instead, the children had been diagnosed as having schizophrenia, adjustment reaction, or conduct disorder. The major reasons for their having been referred to Akiskal in the first place was bizarre behavior, drug-related problems, suicidal ideation or attempt, and failing in school—all characteristic of mood disorders. When Akiskal studied the children, he found a high incidence of acute depressive episodes, dysthymia, and cyclothymia (a milder version of bipolar disorder). The children were followed for three years. *None of them had, or ever developed, schizophrenia.* Thirty-nine percent, who'd earlier had minor mood swings and polydrug abuse went on to develop full-fledged bipolar disorder.

What does bipolar disorder look like in children? Younger children generally show intense, cyclic symptoms. As Dr. Robert DeLong describes it, "The touchstones of the clinical picture of juvenile bipolar illness are the *intensity* and *cyclicality* of the symptoms." All emotions are abnormally intense, but "irritability, anger and rage are particularly salient in these children. The more intense, hateful, venomous and protracted the symptoms, the more likely the child is to be lithium-responsive."[8] This means, of course, that the bipolar child can be treated.

Silly, giddy, overexcited, overtalkative behavior with expansive and grandiose ideas are also characteristic of bipolar kids. These children may manifest the type of depression that's expressed by withdrawal and inhibited behavior, or they may show it by extreme agitation, which sometimes merges with rage.

In 1990, at the annual meeting of the American Psychiatric Association, De Long suggested that many behaviors previously considered "oppositional" may in fact be forms of bipolar disorder. The first clue he looks for in children is a family history of manic depression in relatives (especially if these relatives are known to be lithium-responsive). He is especially watchful for any undiagnosed conditions in relatives that might represent manic depression—certain types of sociopathy, for example: substance abuse, suicide, marked cyclic depressions, and postpartum depressions.

De Long and his research team at the University of North Carolina have found that fecal soiling is strongly associated with bipolar disorder in children. When fecal soiling coexists with some behavioral problem, such as unusual obstinacy, or with obviously cyclic moods, a diagnosis of juvenile bipolar disorder and lithium therapy should definitely be considered, says De Long. Fifty percent of the children he has seen with intractable fecal soiling have responded to lithium treatment.

Also important in diagnosing bipolar disorder is the child's *cognitive profile*. It, too, is characterized by intensity. Bipolar kids have intense interests and may concentrate on something that they like for hours on end. Bipolar kids are willful and self-directed. "They may be quite distractible, even rejecting, when faced with something that doesn't interest them," DeLong says. These children are attracted to visual-motor tasks and love to draw, which they do "assiduously and well, with great attention to detail, imagination, and complete absorption."

Other pursuits, often intellectual, may be equally absorbing. It is quite characteristic of bipolar children that they have great mental energy, are imaginative and vivid in thought, and, as younger children, have active and rich fantasy lives. Computer games may absorb them for hours. Also, intellectual "fantasy" games like *Dungeon and Dragons*.

In young adolescents, bipolar disorder is often of the rapid-cycling kind, and it can be mixed with irritability and anger. These "mixed states" can appear spontaneously, or they may be precipitated by drugs or alcohol. Among preadolescent children, alcohol abuse is very closely associated with mood disorders, according to Frederick K. Goodwin, M.D., and Kay Redfield Jamison, Ph.D., who have written a definitive textbook on bipolar illness.[9] In one study, seven out of ten cases of preadolescent alcohol abuse were bipolar or cyclothymic in nature; the remaining three individuals had other depressive disorders.

Bipolar illness in adolescents is often confused with antisocial personality disorders. "The two disorders are marked by overlapping behaviors, such as impulsivity, shoplifting, substance abuse, difficulties with the law, and aggressiveness." When these kinds of behavior occur during periods of irritable or elated mood *and* there is a family history of affective illness, bipolar disorder is the likely cause.

The biggest error in diagnosing manic depression in adolescents is clinicians' tendency to mislabel the disorder as schizophrenia. In a recent study of severely disturbed children, almost half of those who were bipolar had earlier been misdiagnosed schizophrenic.

Even psychiatrists can be thrown off when they see grandiosity, thought disorder, and bizarre delusions in children. However, parents should be aware that solid, standardized criteria exist for making the distinction between schizophrenia and bipolar illness in children.[10] The tendency among clinicians to misdiagnose is so widespread that if I were told my child was schizophrenic, I would seek a second and possibly even a third opinion immediately—from the most experienced and sophisticated psychiatrist I could afford. A consultation, after all, is a one-time fee—and it could change the course of everything.

If I have learned anything in the course of working on this book, it is that widespread ignorance of mood disorders exists among clinicians in this country—and the ignorance is especially pronounced in the case of children. The study of mood disorders in children is so new that much of what's been learned hasn't trickled out to the medical profession as a whole.

Psychiatric diagnosis should never be considered a one-time-only thing. If a child is not getting better after a few months, a second consultation should be sought—and the possibility of new diagnosis considered.

The Silent Sufferer

Studies have shown that even when a child's symptoms are severe, parents often don't recognize them. A child may be contemplating suicide without his parents having the least idea that something is wrong. In fact, it is more than likely to be the case. In a 1989 study of fourteen suicidal children, Dr. Javad H. Kashani found extremely disconcerting the fact that only two parents had been aware of their children's suicidal tendencies.[11]

Robert, age twelve, was diagnosed with major depression after he tried to commit suicide by swallowing the contents of a bottle of aspirin. A quiet, well-behaved kid, Robert had entered high school a year earlier. He spent several hours a night studying. Though he earned excellent marks, he was always afraid of failing. The night before an exam, Robert would be unable to sleep. He'd lie awake worrying about how he was going to do on the test. As the hours passed, he'd become increasingly convinced that the test would have a question he couldn't answer.

But Robert kept his worries to himself, and the difficulties he was having weren't apparent to others. His teachers viewed him as something of an overachiever. That he was on the quiet side and didn't participate in school activities didn't seem so unusual for a serious kid.

Robert's parents weren't really aware of his school anxiety, either. When Robert was quite young, his father began telling him how important it was to do well in school and to get into a good college. It was an opportunity *he* hadn't had. Although he was quite intelligent, Robert's father had never managed to "pull it together" in high school, and his grades were mediocre. He'd gone to a local junior college, found himself bored, dropped out after the first year, and gotten a job in a supermarket.

Although he'd moved up over the years and was currently a senior manager, Robert's father felt he'd missed a lot in life because of his early failure. He was relieved his son wasn't following the same path. "Sure, I sometimes thought Robert studied a little too hard," he told us. "But that seemed better than not applying himself enough."

Robert preferred spending his free time alone and had few friends, which his mother chalked up to his "seriousness." "Robert's very bright," she said. "I thought the other kids just didn't

145

interest him, that they weren't at his level. And Robert's always been on the quiet side. Even when he was six or seven, it was difficult to get him engaged in a real conversation. Unless he was asked a direct question, he didn't speak up. Sometimes you'd get the impression he was more interested in his own mind than he was in other people's."

Taken one by one, Robert's symptoms—low self-esteem, anxiety, and social withdrawal—could be regarded as more or less normal. However, when these symptoms are looked upon as a piece, the picture becomes clearer. Robert's mother, worried about her son's behavior, was rationalizing when she thought of him as "too smart to be interested" in other kids. All children are interested in other children unless there's a problem. It isn't normal for a child to be anxious about his schoolwork, isolated, and untalkative, no matter how bright he may be. And children ought to be able to do schoolwork without worrying.

Unfortunately, as often happens with children who are depressed, no one suspected Robert's illness and stepped in to help. Robert's depressed mood wasn't recognized until he took a desperate step and swallowed the aspirin.

Clinicians used to rely primarily on parents' reports to diagnose depression in children and adolescents. It was assumed that parents knew everything about their children and that children themselves were not reliable historians because they couldn't articulate their feelings as well as adults. It is now recognized that children can be very reliable informants of their own symptomatology as long as appropriate interview techniques are used. Developmental stages must be kept in mind as well. Age-stage-relevant questions should be used when probing for mood disorders. Also, the clinician evaluating very young children should rely on nonverbal communications, such as sad or apathetic expression and stooped posture as well as tempo of speech, if he is going to tease out the underlying condition.

It can be difficult for a depressed child to express how he or she is feeling. Often a child will not say, "I feel sad," but as Puig-Antich points out, it doesn't necessarily mean he or she is not depressed.[12] Rather, a child may identify with feeling "blue, down, low, very unhappy, empty, feel like crying, or having a bad feeling inside that is with you most of the time."

Karen Gainer says that if you ask kids directly how they feel

inside—Do you have a sad feeling? Or do you have a bad feeling?—
"they will tell you, 'Yes.' They will be able to say that. And you
ask them, 'Does it ever go away?' They can tell you, 'No, that
feeling never goes away. It stays there all the time. I feel sad, I feel
bad all the time.' Or they'll be able to tell you, 'Well, it's there all
the time, except when I ride my bicycle,' or 'I feel better when I
ride my bicycle.' Or, for young ones, you just draw a picture of a
happy face and a sad face and say, 'Which of these is the way that
you feel? And they'll point, and they'll show you.' "

While adolescents can express themselves better, they, too,
should be offered alternative labels to describe how they feel.

In addition to depressed mood, at least four of the following
eight symptoms are necessary for a diagnosis of major depression:

1. appetite disturbance
2. sleep disturbance
3. loss of energy, fatigability, or tiredness
4. psychomotor agitation or retardation (Pacing is an example of agitation; slow speech, an example of retardation.)
5. feelings of excessive or inappropriate guilt
6. loss of interest or pleasure in usual activities
7. difficulty concentrating or thinking
8. thoughts of death or suicide

After the age of six, clinicians can use structured and semistruc-
tured interviews to assess depression. A number of good ones
have been developed.[13]

Talking Suicide

"The whole process of listening to kids is letting them know that
you take what they're saying very, very seriously," says Karen
Gainer, "that if they talk suicide, you're going to take it seriously."

Sometimes parents are in denial and rationalize that their
children are healthier and safer than they are. When this is the
case, Karen will say to them, " 'I'm quite concerned about this.
Your child is expressing this, and I'm feeling right now that we
need to do some intervention.' And if I have any doubt that the

child is not going to be safe and if the parent is unable to come up with a suitably protective plan, I take the position that I'm not comfortable letting anybody leave the office. The parent has to be *getting* it. He or she has to be saying, 'Okay, I'm hiding the knives.' I mean, a girl who sat in the office and said, 'I think about stabbing myself, and I've gone to the kitchen drawer and I've taken out knives' and actually found herself standing in the kitchen with a knife in her hand, a knife poised at her stomach, and not remembering how she got there—*that's* out of control. . . . Well, I would want to know what the mother was going to do, even over the next twenty-four hours, until we got a second opinion. And if the mother had any doubts, if there were any doubt in *my* mind that that mother wasn't going to remove the knives and wasn't going to supervise the kid appropriately, then I would take the kid to an emergency room right then and there for an evaluation. Sometimes I've had to really debate about releasing a child into the parents' custody because of the parents' denial."

Depressed Parent, Depressed Child

Depression runs in families, handed down from generation to generation. "It's in your genes," says Dr. Mark S. Gold, former head of depression research at Fair Oaks Hospital in New Jersey. Although the proof of a genetic predisposition to mood disorders has not yet been finally established, the evidence is extremely strong and is mounting. In the meantime, the family picture that's been drawn by epidemiologists is so persuasive that "few doubt there is a strong genetic component to affective illness," says Dr. Gold. Children who receive the affected gene or genes are vulnerable, predisposed to mood swings when under stress— the very same stress that *doesn't* produce mood swinging in people who *aren't* predisposed.

Identical-twin studies have produced some of the most convincing evidence. If one identical twin has a mood disorder, the other, because he or she would have precisely the same genetic structure, should also develop one. This happens 40 to 70 percent of the time, depending on the criteria used to define depression. Just as happened when schizophrenia was studied, some have raised the question of whether one twin becomes depressed merely by "copying" the other, but further studies indicate that twins raised apart show the same degree of "concordance" as those raised together.

The work of this kind of science progresses on two fronts: *molecular genetics,* which searches for a specific gene that might be the cause, and *population distribution genetics,* which studies first- and second-degree relatives to see whether specific illnesses cluster in families. While molecular genetics has not yet uncovered a gene for depression, twin and adoption studies have established clear evidence of genetic vulnerability to all forms of depression. The Epidemiological Catchment Area Study found that a child of a parent with major depression stands a 30 percent chance of developing some form of depression during his or her lifetime. When *two* parents are depressed, the child's likelihood jumps to 70 percent.[14]

A joint NIMH-Yale Family Study shows that children between the ages of six to seventeen with depressed parents are two to three times as likely to develop major depression as children of normal controls. The children also showed a threefold risk for *any* psychiatric diagnosis. If the parents not only were depressed but had panic disorder or agoraphobia as well, the risk of major depression and anxiety disorders in the children increased.[15]

As these facts have emerged in the last decade, the interest in further study has increased, fired by the knowledge that where predictability exists, the possibility of prevention lies. Perhaps the black bird of depression is not so arbitrary a creature, after all. The questions lying before scientists now are, Can its landing be forestalled, its stay shortened, its arrival even prevented?

Kerim Munir, director of Pediatric Psychopharmacology at Cambridge Hospital, in Cambridge, Massachusetts, says that in the past ten years, the use of drugs in treating the psychiatric disorders of children and adolescents has come of age. The disorders and behaviors considered most likely to respond to medication include attention deficit–hyperactivity disorder, separation anxiety disorder, major depression, obsessive compulsive disorder and certain agitated/aggressive disorders, including bipolar depression. However, he warns that drugs alone are never enough in the treatment of children. When administered rationally, Munir says, "medications can help alleviate suffering, but their use needs always to be part of a comprehensive treatment addressing complex psychological, educational and social issues."[16]

Because the child is young, and in the process of both emotional and intellectual development, much ground can be lost to a psychiatric disorder. The suffering child needs a full phalanx of support. Neither therapy nor the possibility of medication should be overlooked.

When Sobriety Is Not Enough

In June of 1990 Daniel Goleman, a science writer at *The New York Times*, told the story of a woman who had been depressed and overweight as a teenager, until a friend turned her on to amphetamines for lowering weight. By the time she was seventeen, she was taking them regularly, having experienced, besides the weight loss, an unexpected dividend. "They also made her feel confident, even buoyant," Goleman reports.[1]

That was the beginning. At nineteen, a boyfriend offered her cocaine. Within a week, she was addicted. "By 24, she had an out-of-wedlock child, a chaotic life and a $5,000 a week cocaine habit that she supported by helping to distribute the drug. She was hospitalized twice for the deep depression that would come whenever she tried to stop taking cocaine."

At Harvard Medical School, research was being done on the use of various kinds of medications to help people get away from the substances they were abusing—and stay away. This woman was treated by Dr. Edward J. Khantzian, a psychiatrist at Harvard, in a startling and controversial way. She was given small daily doses of the stimulant Ritalin, whereupon she recovered dramatically. Khantzian reports that she has not had cocaine in eight years. Why did the Ritalin work? Khantzian theorizes that it is effective in weaning patients from cocaine because it acts on the dopamine receptors in the brain.

"For several years, scientists have suspected that at least some drug addicts suffer imbalances in brain chemistry that make them vulnerable to depression, anxiety or intense restlessness," reports Daniel Goleman. "For such people, addiction becomes a kind of self-medication in which drugs correct the chemical imbalance and bring a sort of relief."[2]

"Self-medication" is one of the more important ideas about addiction to emerge in the last decade. Proposed originally by Dr. Khantzian, it suggests that people use drugs, however inadvertently, to relieve painful mood states. Moreover, *what* they end up abusing is to some extent determined by the drug's ability to relieve the particular psychiatric disorder from which they suffer. "Clinical work with narcotic and cocaine addicts has provided us with compelling evidence that the drug an individual comes to rely on is not a random choice," writes Khantzian in the *American Journal of Psychiatry*.[3] Opiate abusers, he says, are trying to calm intense, violent, aggressive feelings. Cocaine abusers are trying to treat depression.

At least half of the almost 2 million American people with chronic mental illness abuse drugs.[4] If the self-medication hypothesis is correct, it would mean that many drug abusers are driven by an underlying and often treatable psychiatric disorder. There have been a number of studies that support the hypothesis. Some have found underlying mood disorders to be common in cocaine abusers. Others have shown that when treated with antidepressants, depressed people who abuse cocaine experience not only relief from the depression but decreased craving.[5] "Subtle neurochemical differences" among individuals may predispose to drug or alcohol abuse, explains Harvard psychiatrist James Ellison. Whether hereditary or acquired, these neurotransmitter differences may account for the often subtle psychopathology that can turn people into drug abusers.

Scientists have come to believe that spotting an underlying psychiatric disorder and intervening medically will help treat the drug abuse as well as the disorder. (Therapy, of course, is also necessary. Ellison warns that medication alone is *never* adequate treatment for drug abuse, although once medication has made the drug abuser feel better, he or she will be more receptive to therapy.)

A revolution in the treatment of drug dependency and addiction seems to be under way. Many psychopharmacologists consider medication an essential part of addiction treatment for those who suffer from mood and other psychiatric disorders. Ellison says, "Recognition and treatment of these disorders may allow many individuals to be spared the ravaging effects of long-term drug abuse."[6]

Alcohol, tobacco, and caffeine have been the "recreational" drugs of choice in America since colonial times. In the last few decades, other drugs have been catching up. After alcohol, marijuana abuse is the most commonly diagnosed drug disorder in the United States, affecting an estimated 4.4 percent of the adult population. Abuse of opiates, hallucinogens, and cocaine are each under 1 percent. Taken together, 6.2 percent of the population have a history of dependence on or abuse of controlled drugs, but statistics jump rapidly in the younger age groups. In those under thirty, 22 percent abuse drugs.[7]

Alcohol is the substance most commonly abused by far. Thirteen percent of the American population over a lifetime suffer from alcohol abuse, with even higher rates among those who have other types of psychopathology. "In my opinion," says Michael Gitlin, M.D., in the *Psychiatrist's Guide to Psychopharmacology*, "alcoholism is the most commonly missed diagnosis by mental health professionals, including myself."[8]

According to the Alcohol, Drug Abuse, and Mental Health Administration, about 18 million Americans have problems stemming from alcohol abuse. Only half a million are in treatment. The mortality rate for alcohol abusers is horrifying. Half of all accidental deaths, suicides, and homicides in the United States stem from alcohol consumption. Among young people, it is clearly a problem that has gotten out of hand. More than one out of three high school seniors reports drinking five or more drinks in a row in any given two-week period. Nearly 5 percent of high school seniors drink every day.

It isn't just kids. Recent studies show that alcoholism is disturbingly prevalent among middle-class professionals. White-collar workers are at far greater risk for both alcohol abuse and depression than previously was thought. When two thousand managers and professionals at Westinghouse Electric Corporation were evaluated, 23 percent of men and 36 percent of women reported experiencing major depression in their lifetimes. Sixteen percent of the men and 9 percent of the women abused alcohol.[9]

* * *

Why some people and not others fall prey to drugs has always seemed mystifying. "Even if we agree that individuals who develop one compulsion or addiction are likely to develop another, we are still forced to ask why do only some individuals develop addictive behaviors. This inevitably leads to an exploration of a neurobiological basis for the behavior," says Jeffrey Jonas, who has studied addictions and eating disorders intensively.[10]

Researchers like Jonas have come to think that *who* is likely to succumb to addiction may have a degree of predictability. Some of us are marked—by genes, by environment, by the amount of stress we face. Together, these factors produce an imbalance of brain chemicals that can lead to addiction. When the imbalance is corrected, the newest research shows, addiction may be prevented—and those who are already addicted but have managed to achieve abstinence have a better shot at avoiding relapse.

Today there exists a clearer understanding of how the brain turns a user into an abuser. Theories have developed about the biology of craving. One emerging theory of alcoholism considers that "opioid processes" involving natural, morphinelike substances in the brain may be critical, and drugs can be developed, as effective adjuncts to treatment.[11] The idea of using drugs to treat a drug addiction has always been abhorred by people who promote traditional methods of rehabilitation. It takes some understanding of the relationship between neurotransmitter metabolism and addiction before one can glimpse that using a drug to treat an addiction may not be so contradictory.

In the past five or ten years, medical researchers have found that medications can be used to diminish craving and help people remain abstinent. This chapter will explore some of the theories that have led to medicine's new methods of substance-abuse intervention and describe some programs that are offering this help. The use of medication in the treatment of addiction is very new and very controversial. I've come to the conclusion that neither traditional rehab programs *nor* psychiatric approaches stand alone as solutions to addiction. Both camps have help to offer, and each needs to integrate what's valuable in the other.

Both, however, can take better advantage of what science has learned about the biology of addiction.

It's in the Family

Some of us are more vulnerable to addiction *from birth*. With alcoholism, for example, evidence of a genetic factor has been mounting. According to the National Institute on Alcohol Abuse and Alcoholism, at least 50 percent, and perhaps "nearly all," of those treated for alcoholism come from families with histories of the illness. Scientists think children of alcoholics inherit differences in their brain's ability to metabolize alcohol. They face a high risk not only for alcoholism but for mood illnesses. Children of alcoholics show high levels of anxiety, depression, and compulsivity. This syndrome is not simply produced by the trauma of growing up with a short-fused, unpredictable alcoholic parent. It is, to some degree, genetic.

In the early seventies, scientists at Washington University School of Medicine studied individuals reared apart from their biological parents who had either a biological parent or a surrogate parent with a drinking problem. They found that children were significantly more likely to have a drinking problem if their biological parent was alcoholic, regardless of whether the surrogate parent was alcoholic.

In a study of 5,483 Danish men who were adopted in early childhood, the same researchers found further support of the genetic theory of addiction. Sons of alcoholics were more than three times as likely to develop drinking problems as were adopted sons of nonalcoholics—and at an earlier age.

Investigations carried out at Washington University involved daughters as well as sons.[12] One study included 862 men and 913 women who'd been adopted by nonrelatives before the age of three. Thirty-five percent had at least one biological parent who abused alcohol. Of the sons of alcoholic biological fathers, 22 percent were alcoholics, compared to 14 percent of the sons who did not have an alcoholic biological parent. Ten percent of the daughters of alcoholic biological mothers were alcohol abusers, compared to 2 percent of daughters who did not have an alcoholic biological parent.

Interestingly, alcoholism in the adoptive parents was *not* a factor in predicting whether adoptees would become alcoholic. The studies show that the main determinant in predicting alcoholism is genetic. Home environment—even when adoptive parents are alcoholic—is virtually irrelevant. "For people who are biologically predisposed, the first drink or dose of the drug is immensely reinforcing, in a way others just don't experience it," said Ralph Tarter, a psychologist at the Western Psychiatric Institute and Clinic in Pittsburgh. "Many recovering drug abusers tell me, 'The moment I took my first drug, I felt normal for the first time.' It stabilizes them physiologically, at least in the short term."[13]

Some people drink to ease anxiety. Underlying the behavior is an imbalance in the brain's receptors for GABA, a neurotransmitter that regulates anxiety, among other things, according to Dr. Howard Moss, a psychiatrist at the University of Pittsburgh. In a 1990 study published in the *Journal of Biological Psychiatry*, Dr. Moss showed that sons of alcoholic fathers had lower levels of GABA and higher tension levels than men whose fathers were not alcoholic. But when they drank a glass of vodka, the GABA levels of the first group rose to levels equivalent to those of the other men, and their tension declined.

"Those sons of alcoholics who are unusually anxious drink to ease their tension, which is due to a perturbation of GABA," said Dr. Moss. "Our hypothesis is that this GABA irregularity is a trait marker linked to a genetic vulnerability to alcoholism."[14]

Other alcoholics, whose behavior is impulsive and aggressive, "seem to have low levels of serotonin," says Dr. Moss. "We're not sure just where the deficit is. It might be that their neurons release too little serotonin or their receptors do not respond well to the serotonin they're sent." But whatever its exact cause, deficiency in serotonin is related to the inability to rein in impulsivity, scientists are finding.

Daniel Goleman reports the case of a man with a heroin addiction who, since childhood, had always been quick to become enraged. By the time he was in his early thirties he felt deeply embittered because so many of his relationships had ended, due to his quick temper. A pharmacist, he had easy access to morphine, which he said calmed his bitter resentments and his feelings of mounting rage.

The angry pharmacist is typical of more than four hundred patients that Dr. Khantzian has treated for narcotics addiction. "Their histories reveal life-long difficulty handling rage; opiates like heroin and morphine, they say, help them feel normal and relaxed," Goleman writes.

A Shift Occurs

Early alcoholism research focused on alcohol's effects on the brain and the central nervous system. In the early 1970s, the emphasis began to shift to the mechanisms underlying "craving behavior." Today, out of an enormous accumulation of data, there has emerged a new understanding of the role neurotransmitters and receptors play in addiction. "We began to see that their availability and balance, and the action at receptors, are keys to reward: pleasure, feelings of well-being, and euphoria," writes Kenneth Blum in *Alcohol and the Addictive Brain*.[15]

Over the past two decades, genetic research on addiction has pointed to malfunction that begins in the gene. Environment can trigger, worsen, or to some degree lessen the genetic predisposition, "but the determining factors," Blum says, "are biogenetic and biochemical."

Addiction, he and others believe, progresses by degrees and slowly produces chemical changes in the brain. Once the illness reaches a certain stage, willpower alone cannot bring it to a halt. The addicted brain needs chemical rebalancing if it's going to heal. Abstinence permits the brain to rebalance its own chemicals over time, but for many who become addicted, abstinence is hard to achieve. And it alone *won't* do the job for those who, in addition to addictions, are suffering from mood disorders.

Occasional drug users are more likely to slip over into addiction—and faster—when they have mood disorders. "These patients may have a more rapid transition from initial use to dependence," according to Roger Weiss, who heads the Alcohol and Drug Abuse Treatment Center at McLean Hospital.[16]

Serotonin and Craving

In the late eighties, eye-opening data on the biology of alcoholism came from studies using rats. Researchers headed by Ting-Kai Li found ways to breed strains of heavy-drinking rats and light-drinking rats who were then taught to self-administer alcohol and other mood-altering drugs by hitting a lever. The idea was to try to duplicate in rats normal drinking and the compulsive drinking of alcoholics.

Li compared neurotransmitter levels in the brains of both types of drinkers. The rats that hit hardest on the booze lever had consistently lower serotonin levels. Li speculated, "There must be an inverse relationship between the amount of serotonin in the hypothalamus and alcohol craving behavior." The lower the level of serotonin, that is, the greater the rats' inclination to drink.[17]

Would it be possible to increase serotonin in the brains of the alcoholic rats and cause them to abstain or at least cut down? Because fluoxetine (Prozac) makes more serotonin available in the brain, Li's group tried injecting it into the heavy-drinking rats. Eureka! The rats cut back significantly.[18]

The next question was obvious. What would happen if humans who abused alcohol were given Prozac? At UCLA, scientists studied two groups of patients, one receiving fluoxetine and the other a placebo. Both groups had free access to alcohol, hourly, for twelve hours each day. The group taking Prozac drank significantly less than the control group. "These results are consistent with Li's finding in rats, and suggest that serotonin is a possible controlling factor in human alcoholism," wrote D. A. Gorelick, who headed the research team.[19]

Early trials of antidepressants in the treatment of alcoholism were disappointing. Roger Weiss says this may be because the doses given in these studies were too low. Newer studies are more promising. Antidepressants acting directly on the serotonin system have been shown to reduce drinking even in alcoholics who aren't depressed.[20]

Craving has historically been seen as a primitive urge to surfeit oneself with heady euphoria, to escape moral responsibility and normal human pain. The biology of craving is changing this view. First of all, those who crave compensatory chemicals aren't simply suffering the normal discomforts of life. Craving, like hunger, is the painful state that ensues when the organism isn't getting what it needs. Instead of looking upon craving as depravity, scientists are now recognizing it as a medical alert—the brain's signal that something is missing and replenishment is required.

Endorphins Also Help

While some scientists are hot on the trail of serotonin's relationship to alcohol craving, others are pursuing the role of endorphins. In 1987, Christina Gianoulakis and Alca Gupta at McGill University shed light on how endorphins and enkephalins affect alcohol-craving behavior. The scientists came up with some intriguing information. First, they'd found that alcohol-preferring mice have fewer endorphins. In both high-drinking and low-drinking mice, ingesting alcohol prompted the release of more endorphins in the brain.[21]

Recently, these researchers extended their work to include high-risk humans with a family history of alcoholism and low-risk humans without such a history. They found that drinking releases substantially more endorphins in the high-risk humans. After drinking, the low-risk group showed a slight decrease in the body opiates, while the high-risk group showed a 170 percent increase. "We believe that endorphin release in these subjects is responsible for the reinforcing properties of alcohol," says Gianoulakis.[22] In other words, since alcohol doesn't increase endorphins in low-risk people, it doesn't dramatically alter their mood state, so there is little reinforcement for drinking.

Such studies have helped create a clearer idea of what happens to the brain during a developing addiction. Genetic vulnerability, stress, and the chronic abuse of the substance itself are all factors that contribute to neurotransmitter deficiency. Thus, the high-risk person has a genetic vulnerability to begin with. The biological changes produced by stress heighten that vulnerability, as do the biological changes produced by the drug itself. Ultimately, the brain's metabolism changes and the "craving" becomes a constant. At this point, the person is hooked.

The Opiate Theory

Opiates have been used for medicinal and recreational purposes for centuries but the mechanism through which they produce their effects in the brain has only recently become clear.

"It is now well-established that opiates produce their pharmacological actions by interacting with specific receptor molecules," says Ellen Unterwald of Rockefeller University. These receptors were first discovered in 1973, at several different laboratories.[23] The questions their discovery left unanswered were, Why did the receptors exist? What natural substances were meant to fill them? Scientists didn't know, but soon were hot on the trail of finding out. They achieved their goal rather quickly.

Evidence for the existence of endorphins and enkephalins, natural opiatelike materials in the brain, was first presented at an international conference of narcotic researchers at Arlie House, Virginia, in 1975.[24] Several different scientists reported discovering a mysterious peptide, or compound of amino acids, which seemed to interact with the opiate receptors and had morphinelike effects. One called the mystery compound "X." Another called it "MLS," for morphinelike substance.

A decade later, Sidney Spector, at the Roche Institute of Molecular Biology, announced that his research group had discovered morphine in both toad skin and rat brain.[25] This led to an intriguing question: Was there also morphine in the human brain?

Because they needed people they could be sure hadn't used any morphine, Spector's group decided on nonaddicted hospital patients who hadn't been exposed to any drugs at all for several months. Tapping the patients' cerebral spinal fluid, they found significant quantities of both codeine and morphine.[26] The discovery suggested an inevitable hypothesis: *In the normal person, the brain produces enough natural morphine to provide a feeling of well-being. The person whose brain doesn't produce enough of this morphinelike substance feels a need, or craving, and may try to satisfy it with such substances as morphine, heroin, or alcohol.*

At the same international conference, the narcotics researchers finally settled on a name for the mystery substance whose presence apparently makes people feel good and whose absence can make them miserable. "Endorphin," a contraction of *endogenous*, which means "within," and *morphine*, was the term they decided on. Some scientists use the term "opioid" or "natural opioid" or will say, "The brain's own opioids." Since this substance had been found in pigs, rats, and camels, and, finally, in the human brain itself, many researchers in this field think they have a tiger by the tail. Still, as Ellen Unterwald noted at the 1988 meeting of the Society for Neuroscience, "The complete biosynthetic pathway for morphine in mammals has yet to be demonstrated," and the role of such compounds in the brain is also not entirely clear.[27]

Still, it is easy to see why narcotics researchers have gotten excited. The existence of a natural, morphinelike substance in the human brain would explain why alcohol, morphine, and heroin initially seem to have salutary effects. In the short term they ease stress and provide a sense of well-being. But very quickly "the craving becomes uncontrollable and more and more of the drug must be taken to achieve less and less relief," as Kenneth Blum sees it. Blum, who conducts his addiction research at the University of Texas Health Center in San Antonio, proposes that when enough receptors fill with endorphins and enkephalins, well-being results. When these opioids drop off and too few receptors fill up, the brain creates an urgent sense of agitation.[28]

Too Few Endorphins to Feel Good

When the brain is so low in natural opioids that a painful psychic state results, the organism may be pressed to seek relief. Scientists from the "opioid deficiency" school think people turn to drugs like alcohol, heroin, and cocaine because they substitute for the missing opioids. Boosting depleted brain chemicals may allow the drug taker to feel great for a while, but the situation changes the more the drug is consumed. Thus, too many artificial opioids will cause a boomerang effect, lowering the body's already diminished supply of endorphins. As the drug wears off, "the feeling of need becomes greater than ever," Blum explains. "Craving gradually overcomes willpower and becomes the dominant force in the person's life."[29]

Scientists think that in predisposed humans *the production of endorphins and enkephalins in the brain is abnormally low from birth*. Low levels of these mood-regulating chemicals result in anxiety and a feeling of need that is extremely uncomfortable. It is this bad feeling that makes people susceptible to the brief mood-lifts provided by drinking and drug taking. They are not really looking for euphoria. What they long for, what their bodies are trying to achieve, is the state of chemical balance that those of us enjoy who are fortunate to have enough neurotransmitters in the first place. But in trying to make up for what they don't have, they get caught. Habitual drinking or drug taking generates a physical need, which strengthens the habit, which worsens the need, until the undertow of addiction has sucked those who are vulnerable into its grip.

Stress, too, affects the body's opioid levels, researchers have found. People with a lot of stress are at special risk for being swept into an addictive cycle. Studies of Korean and Vietnam war veterans have produced dramatic proof that the worse the stress, the greater propensity for addiction. Nearly two-thirds of those who had not seen combat never developed an alcohol problem, while two-thirds of those who did see combat were either alcohol abusers, active alcoholics, or alcoholics in remission. The *severity* of their alcoholism, moreover, correlated with the amount of time spent in combat. One study found that the relationship between combat stress and excessive alcohol consumption persisted for more than a decade after the stressful events took place.

The Cocaine Connection

In the late eighties, Roger Weiss conducted studies of cocaine addicts. Since McLean is a private psychiatric hospital, many of his patients were executives. Over half were suffering from mood disorders as well as addiction. Thirty percent suffered from unipolar depression, and another 23 percent had either bipolar or cyclothymic depression. (Interestingly, those addicts who suffered from bipolar mood swings didn't perceive themselves as self-medicating for depression. They said, rather, that they used cocaine when they were already feeling "up" because they wanted to stay "up.")

In some people—those with attention-deficit disorder, for example—cocaine has the effect of "helping to focus undifferentiated, often uncontrolled energy," says Harvard psychiatrist James Ellison. This may be due to the paradoxical calming that drugs with a stimulant effect have on people with certain psychiatric disorders. For example, children with attention-deficit hyperactive disorder (ADHD) are calmed by psychostimulants. Most adults with ADHD go undiagnosed, yet follow-up studies of children with attention deficit have revealed that a significant proportion continue, *as adults*, to be overactive, impulsive, and unable to concentrate. Unwittingly, these people may turn to cocaine to calm the chaos. Weiss's cocaine abusers report having gotten temporary relief from their inattentiveness and impulsiveness when they first started using cocaine.[30] Thus, he believes chemically treating attention deficit may improve the chances for recovery in substance abusers who suffer from it.

In most people, cocaine causes stimulation and euphoria, in part by partially increasing dopamine activity in the brain. But chronic use causes a boomerang effect. It depletes the brain's supply of dopamine, which produces both withdrawal and craving.

During the first few hours of the withdrawal "crash," people look as if they're in the middle of a major depression. They oversleep and they want food. When, over a period of days, their energy returns, their mood remains flat and depleted. Then the craving begins to increase markedly, often leading to relapse. "Strategies for treating cocaine users have focused on increasing brain dopamine in this post-withdrawal period," Gitlin writes. The idea is to reduce craving. Of the various medications that have been tested so far, evidence is strongest for the antidepressant desipramine. Effects are seen within one or two weeks.

As an example of someone whose recovery from cocaine addiction was aided by treatment with an antidepressant, Gitlin cites the case of a patient he calls Barry. For a while after a big binge, Barry would go to his CA (Cocaine Anonymous) meetings, but he always ended up using again. When things got so bad that his girlfriend was threatening to leave him and he was afraid of being fired, Barry consulted a psychiatrist who specialized in cocaine addiction. Desipramine was suggested as something that could help him stay off cocaine, but *only* if he attended twelve-step meetings regularly. When Barry agreed, he was prescribed 175 mg daily of the antidepressant. He had one relapse soon after beginning treatment, but over the following three months his cocaine craving diminished. At that point, the medication was tapered off and stopped. "Barry continued to work in the CA program and has now been clean for seven months." Gitlin reports.[31]

People who suffer from mood disorders are at increased risk for cocaine dependence. Roger Weiss says evaluation is important

163

for cocaine abusers because so many have prior mood disorders. Clinicians need to look carefully for these mood disorders—especially cyclothymia (the milder version of manic-depressive illness) and attention-deficit disorder. When they are treated, says Weiss, the cocaine addict has a far better chance of getting well.[32]

Roger Weiss and Jack Mendelson, psychiatrists who are well known in the field of addiction research, recently conducted an overview of the studies done to date on the use of antidepressants in treating cocaine dependence. Of eleven studies, nine showed that tricyclic antidepressants may help people get off the drug. (Of the two negative studies, one used dosages too low to be effective.) The psychiatrists point out, interestingly, that the anticraving and mood-elevating effects of antidepressants were observed *even in cocaine abusers without a major mood disorder.*[33] Further research is needed, but the medical approach to addiction treatment looks very hopeful.

For those interested in such treatment, it should be noted that giving a trial to any old antidepressant would be unwise. A cocaine abuser should not hit up his or her GP for Prozac, say. Antidepressants with stimulating effects have been known to give cocaine abusers a jittery, anxious feeling—even a high, or a rush—and in such cases may increase cocaine craving. The medication chosen for trial use with an abuser of *any* sort of drug must be carefully matched with the particular patient's history of drug use, psychiatric history, and family psychiatric and drug history. What this boils down to is the need for a specialist—ideally, a psychopharmacologist experienced in eliciting such histories from drug abusers and devising an appropriate treatment plan.

Until very recently, AA (Alcoholics Anonymous), CA, and NA have shown little interest in the genetic factor in addiction or the effect of mood disorders on people's attempts to get straight. As we shall see, this has been a tragic oversight. "Many traditional treatments for alcoholism may be unsuccessful because they do not address the disturbances that predisposed the person to alcoholism in the first place," said Dr. Tarter.[34]

"A combination of early detection and pharmaceutical intervention is the most sensible way to proceed," Dr. Fred Goodwin, of the Alcohol, Drug Abuse, and Mental Health Administration, told the *New York Times*. Moreover, he thinks that in the near future, medication will begin being used for prevention. Researchers are beginning to think that for some addictions there may be a critical time, such as late adolescence and early adulthood, when the risk of addiction is highest. "Offering a medication that corrects the vulnerability during those years is one potential treatment strategy," Goleman reports. In the case of those with a susceptibility to alcoholism due to low serotonin, Dr. Goodwin said, "if they are protected by a drug that enhances and stabilizes serotonin during those years when they are most vulnerable to alcoholism, then later in life they may be able to drink socially with low risk."[35]

Addiction researchers see the need for new medications designed to correct the precise brain chemical abnormalities being identified with each addiction. Dr. Goodwin says the Alcohol, Drug Abuse, and Mental Health Administration is launching "a major medication development program to find drugs that react with the specific receptors to reduce craving."

How many might benefit from such medication? Goodwin says that 80 percent of those in therapy programs who leave too early do so because of craving.

Family Addictions, Family Moods

Psychotherapist Eileen Fitzpatrick had spent years in therapy and in Alcoholics Anonymous before she decided to try antidepressant medication. "Everyone said the depression would go away after I'd been abstinent for a while. The depression didn't go away."

What convinced Eileen to seek medical help was her discovery in her late thirties that both alcoholism *and* depression had run in her family for generations. Why had she never known about her family illness before?

Once she'd achieved sobriety, Eileen decided to stay away from others in her family to protect herself. "So many of them drank, I avoided them," she says. But after she had been sober seven years, she felt strong enough to reconnect again and mailed out Christmas cards. "Several months later I heard from my cousin's daughter. One night we got together for dinner and started talking about the family." Her cousin, she found, was in recovery from alcoholism, as were several of her sisters. Their father had almost died from alcoholism.

Eileen's cousin became severely ill before anyone recognized that she needed treatment. She told Eileen, the night they had dinner together, of several suicide attempts she'd made. "The last time was serious," Eileen said. "She almost died."

It was striking to Eileen that her cousin had been in recovery almost five years when she made the last suicide attempt. "It was only because she ended up in a psychiatric facility that she finally got antidepressant treatment. She told me it worked wonders."

The conversation Eileen had with her cousin suddenly put things into perspective. "She reported so much depression in the family, I had one of those 'Aha!' experiences. I thought, So *that's* what's going on with me!"

The drinking problems in her family were more pervasive than Eileen had ever guessed, but "the part that really surprised me was the depression." Her father had always been an anxious man, yet his anxiety had not been associated with depression. Now Eileen believes his depression had been masked by anxiety, just as hers was.

It took persistence on Eileen's part to get from her first "Aha" to an appropriate treatment plan. First, she brought it up with her therapist, who claimed not to have been aware that she was depressed. "Maybe I was hiding it," she says, minimizing the fact that her therapist had never properly diagnosed her in the first place. The same had been the case with her physician. "She, too, said she hadn't been aware of my depression. She said I often looked angry and anxious but that she hadn't identified the reason."

It's up to the professional to elicit information and make a diagnosis; this is no less true of depression than of other illnesses. Eileen was fortunate in being able to arrive at a proper analysis of her own situation, but she felt awkward having to negotiate treatment for herself. "It was with great difficulty that I told my therapist, 'I want to try an antidepressant.' She wasn't against it, but she wasn't all that knowledgeable, either."

Approaching her doctor also took courage. "My first contact with this woman had been as another professional dealing with one of my own clients. Having to admit that I myself was having this severe problem with depression was a blow to my ego. But I did it. The doctor put me on Tofranil, and within two weeks I was feeling significantly better. As the depression went, so did my anxiety. In three weeks I was better than I'd ever been in my life."

According to the large epidemiological studies recently conducted by the NIMH, half of women alcoholics are seriously depressed, and two thirds of them are depressed before they begin abusing alcohol.[36] Years can go by, with women relapsing and relapsing, mainly because their depression continues untreated.

Or, like Eileen, they manage to remain sober but are so mood impaired that life doesn't amount to much more than the day-to-day victory over addiction. It wasn't until Eileen treated her depression that things in her life really got going. She developed a thriving therapy practice and, at forty-five, entered divinity school. Unfortunately, that was fifteen years after she joined AA!

When Sobriety Isn't Enough

Medication and Other Drugs, an AA pamphlet written by a group of recovering physicians, attempts to inform members that some alcoholics need medication if they're going to recover fully. Depressed patients "have been told by AAs to throw away the pills, only to have depression return with all its difficulties, sometimes resulting in suicide," the doctors report.

The doctors tell of Fran, a seriously depressed woman who finally joined AA, only to be challenged by her group. "I was totally shocked at my first meeting," she said, "when one of the first questions I was asked was 'Are you taking any pills?'" From the outset "there was constant harassment to 'stop using a crutch,' to 'get honest' with myself, and to 'get away from the shrink—AA is all you need.'" Fran wavered back and forth and eventually stopped taking her medication. Before long, she says, "I was on a trip I wasn't sure I would ever return from—a trip of hallucinations, paranoia, and obsessions."

Though hospitalized several times, she continued to feel torn between what the doctors were telling her and "all the 'medical advice' I was receiving from other AAs." Two vying treatment models were trying to claim her, and she felt she had to pick one over the other. Time after time, she says, "I chose AA. Each time I stopped taking my medication my symptoms got worse and my suicidal depression came back."

Not until a psychiatrist diagnosed Fran as manic-depressive did she begin seeing her situation in another light. Sobriety was not enough. "Today I have an entirely different attitude toward taking medication. I am aware that some people still talk about my being 'on something,' but that's okay. I have only one judge, my higher power. It really doesn't matter who knows that I take lithium for my disease."

The battle some twelve-step groups wage against medicine for psychiatric disorders creates a serious problem, as the AA pamphlet points out. Its authors conclude, unambiguously: "Just as it is wrong to enable or support any alcoholic to become readdicted to any drug, it's equally wrong to deprive any alcoholic of medication which can alleviate or control other disabling and/or emotional problems."

Yet the pamphlet implies that only those with severe psychiatric disorders—ones involving paranoia, hallucinations, and suicidal depression—need medical treatment. People like Eileen, whose depressions are more moderate, should expect sobriety alone to do the job. Here is where AA needs to better educate its members. While it's true that alcoholism creates depressed states, people with addictions often have mood disorders that exist separately. Sobriety doesn't treat clinical mood disorders. When it is expected to, tragedy is often the result.

A Desperate Woman

Kitty Dukakis is a dramatic example of someone with a serious psychiatric illness who received inadequate help for many years because she was treated mainly for addiction.

When the story of Mrs. Dukakis's drinking rubbing alcohol broke in the press only months before her memoir, *Now You Know*, was published, everyone was shocked. We had heard first about her diet-pill addiction, treated at Hazeldon, in 1982. Some years later, directly after Governor Dukakis lost the presidential election, she went to Edgehill in Newport, Rhode Island, for treatment of alcohol addiction. However, until the rubbing alcohol incident, depression had only been hinted at. There was the briefest allusion to a mood problem in a *People* article the fall following the election that described Kitty's uplifting experience on an Outward Bound program. Autumns were often "not good times" for her, the piece said, and she had entered the physically demanding program in the hope of heading off a season that for her was usually bleak.

At the point at which *People* turned its cameras on Kitty, the strategy seemed to have worked. The *People* pictures were striking. She had put on a few pounds, and her face had a soft, lively expression, not the taut, brilliant smile we'd come to expect from her campaign photos. But then, months later, in the depths of her winter depression, Mrs. Dukakis made the desperate gesture with the rubbing alcohol. "I had no plan to kill myself," she told hospital doctors later when pressed about suicidal intent. "I only wanted to sleep for a while. I wanted relief from the pain of being awake."

The pain she described was the particular, all-encompassing pain of severe depression. That's clear now. The question is, why hadn't it been clear to the people who'd been treating her all these years? What had gone wrong?

Kitty Dukakis's treatment had been managed primarily by a handful of addiction programs. She was being treated not as someone with a painful psychiatric disorder but solely as an addict. And the depression, which has probably been with her since her adolescence, when she first began taking her mother's energizing diet pills, was somehow not being *seen* by those in a position to help.

Ironically, the fact that she was the governor's wife may have contributed to the poor handling of Kitty Dukakis's medical problems. While she would put herself into treatment for her addictions, she would also get herself out—and quickly. Apparently, she didn't like staying in these programs a moment longer than she felt she needed to. Yet she had little help on the outside. Over the years she met with a psychiatrist only occasionally. She writes that she didn't believe talk therapy could help. She did, during several periods, use an antidepressant medication, and while it helped her, she always stopped taking it rather quickly. Instead, as she describes in her book, she used alcohol—with extreme caution and control—to alter her mood, to boost the flow of neurotransmitters that would keep her functioning.

When Michael's campaign for the presidency began, Kitty started taking an antidepressant. Side effects troubled her, she says, and she again stopped the medication. In hindsight, she believes the extraordinary pace of the campaign kept her from plunging. Also, it was summer, her usual "up" season. But with fall and the foreboding sense of Michael's incipient defeat, Kitty entered another serious depression. A psychopharmacologist prescribed Prozac, but by then she was drinking "uncontrollably." Knowing that medication combined with alcohol was dangerous, she stopped the Prozac. As can happen with women, Kitty's drinking got bad very quickly. She entered Edgehill, in Newport. At about this time, she again took Prozac. It made her feel not euphoric, she writes, but "normal," balanced. But soon after achieving this state, she decided, "there was no need to stay on medication."

Where were the doctors, one wonders, when reading accounts of Mrs. Dukakis's illness? Was no one telling her that people with severe depressions need medication for longer than a few months?

After Edgehill, Mrs. Dukakis stopped even the occasional visits to the psychiatrist. AA meetings were her only sustenance. Whether or not her particular group discouraged her from taking medication, Kitty doesn't say, but it seems unlikely that it encouraged her. No one, apparently, was encouraging her to stick with the treatment of her depression—in spite of the crippling severity of her episodes.

Hers was a tragic situation, and in no way unique. Most people who are both depressed and addicted don't get help for their depression.

The Twelve-Step Deterrent

Addiction treatment in this country is rigidly institutionalized. Most people with substance-abuse problems end up in treatment centers where psychiatric illnesses aren't dealt with. They aren't even diagnosed.

This is true even of the most prestigious places, like Hazeldon and the Betty Ford Center, which make it plain from the first phone call that no matter what other problems may coexist in a given individual—bulimia, depression, panic disorder, or whatever—they will deal *only* with the addiction.

"I won't send anyone to Betty Ford who has to be on medication because they take them off," Virginia Hamilton, a therapist and certified addiction counselor in New York, told me. "So does Hazeldon." She names a handful of treatment centers in the Northeast that *do* treat people with dual diagnoses: Four Winds in Katonah, New York; New York–Cornell Hospital's Westchester Division in White Plains; Silver Hill Foundation in Connecticut. (A list of centers around the country that treat both substance abuse and psychiatric disorders can be found in appendix F.)

"Some of these places, though not all, are terribly expensive," she says. And some of the expensive, private hospital programs for drug abuse, while psychiatrically oriented, are not sufficiently up on substance abuse.

"It seems as if most programs tend to lean too heavily on one side or the other," I say.

"That, or they totally ignore the other side and miss the boat. But statistically, most rehab programs err by having no medical orientation whatsoever. They're based on the traditional 'Hazeldon model' for recovery, which ignores the psychiatric side of the picture and won't allow medication of any sort."

In the last two decades, "recovery" has developed into a huge international movement and business, with 30,000 recovery groups in 70 countries. As recovery has gained in power, the numbers and types of people it holds itself forth as being able to treat has grown enormously. People with serious mood disorders who join a twelve-step group for help with addiction may find themselves swept up in a system that is not equipped to deal with the medical problems that may even have caused the addiction.

How did such a situation come to pass? Nonmedical treatment for substance abuse gained its foothold in part because medicine didn't want to get involved. "You have to remember that in the beginning psychiatrists didn't want to *touch* addiction," psychiatrist Oscar Bukstein says. "Addicts were stigmatized, and no one was helping them."

The self-help movement sprang up in a treatment void. The

first treatment centers were in Minnesota. Hazeldon is one of the best known today. "Believe it or not, it came out of some experiments tried in state mental hospitals. They had shoestring budgets, so they started using self-support groups with former patients as adjunct therapists. That was the beginning of the recovery model. It was based on the theory that patients relate best to former addicts. They saved a lot of money that way. Often these people weren't trained at all, or were poorly trained. You didn't have to pay for someone with a Ph.D. level of training, or a master's, or even a bachelor's. It was extremely cheap."

The "Hazeldon model," or the "Minnesota model," as it came to be known, has been duplicated with varying degrees of integrity and success by profit-making and non-profit-making organizations all over the country. People pop in and out of these twenty-eight-day programs like cars going through a car wash. The length of stay has nothing to do with the severity of a given illness and quite a bit to do with what insurance policies will cover.

Kitty Dukakis attended five or six rehab programs before finally getting a psychiatric workup that determined she was bipolar. The sole focus of her treatment for eight years was her addiction. The emotional desperation underlying her rush to the medicine chest for rubbing alcohol, hair spray, and nail polish remover was apparently missed—or misunderstood. The behavior was seen as part of an addictive syndrome rather than as symptomatic of a psychiatric disorder. She was a desperately ill woman, and no one was getting the picture.

Addiction experts, many of whom are recovering addicts, tend to see depression only as loss of the drug, the "high." They discourage what they call self-pity. When they advise that mood disorders will disappear by themselves after sobriety, they may be crossing over into the province of medicine.

Oscar Bukstein, who heads a treatment program for adolescents with both addictions and psychiatric disorders, is concerned about what he sees as another twelve-step Catch-22. "These programs can create the feeling that if you don't fit the paradigm, it's your fault. If the patient isn't doing well, he's 'in denial.' In this way the patient, not the program, gets blamed when treatment fails."

An individual's capacity to resist twelve-step dogma depends on how developed he or she is to begin with. Young people who go to meetings four or five times a week may be vulnerable to a brainwashing effect. "Adolescents don't have the cognitive development to see the grays," says Virginia Hamilton. "They want everything to be black or white. They can go from polyabusing garbage heads who stick every conceivable drug into every conceivable orifice to recovering addicts who are loath to take an aspirin for a 104-degree fever."

Sometimes adolescent drug abusers are desperately in need of medication. Bukstein thinks *most* adolescents with drug and drinking problems have unidentified mood disorders. But parents may be pressured to adopt the antimedicine philosophy of traditional rehab centers. "We are recovering addicts, and we know the way" is a statement that frightened relatives who don't know a thing about addiction can find powerfully persuasive. Fear for the child (and in some cases, fear for their own well-being) can put parents into a state in which they're readily intimidated. They want to believe that *someone* has the answers. The recovering addicts say, "*We* have them," and worried parents succumb. They may never question whether the child has an illness that led him or her to become a substance abuser in the first place. They are appalled, then, as the child continues to relapse, his behavior becoming more and more erratic. Mistakenly believing that addiction is "mental," parents lie awake nights wondering what it is they did or didn't do, wondering where they went wrong. Eager to expiate their guilt, they may be ripe for ideological seduction.

Phillip's Story

Robert and Eleanor adopted Phillip when he was three months old. It had been one of those marvelous matches. As he grew older, he looked so much like both of them that people were surprised to learn he wasn't their biological son.

As he grew older, Phillip developed Eleanor's wit and Robert's seriousness. Everyone liked him. He was lanky and hip and good on the electric bass, which he started teaching himself when he was ten. When, at eleven, Phillip began getting bored at school,

Robert and Eleanor talked to the teachers and guidance counselors and decided that he needed more stimulation. They would find him a better school. "Nip it in the bud," as Robert said.

Eleanor said, "Structure." She thought that maybe they hadn't given Phillip enough of that. Like many parents who'd come of age in the sixties, they'd encouraged their son's creative side, perhaps at the expense of discipline. They decided on a boarding school with a small student-faculty ratio that focused on developing responsibility. Phillip seemed pleased enough. He would come home weekends to see his friends, and he would escape the hayseed local school where he was always getting into arguments with his teachers.

The director of the new school warned Phillip and his parents about drugs and alcohol. "We do random urinalyses," he said. That surprised Eleanor. "We're sort of casual about pot ourselves," she said. "*We* take it very seriously," said the director. "We don't want our students using it, period."

At twelve, Phillip was already involved with pot, and he liked having a few beers. He'd have to limit his consumption to weekends now. He guessed it would be worth it as long as the kids at the new school were cool.

One Monday in October, the school summoned the seventh-graders for the first urinalysis of the year. Later that week, Phillip's parents were called. "He had marijuana in his urine," the director told Eleanor.

"But he was home for the weekend," she said.

"We don't expect them to use at home, either. I think I made that clear."

That was it. Phillip was out. As it developed, he wasn't unhappy about coming home, and Robert and Eleanor weren't, either. They thought it wasn't the right school, and anyway, they missed him. Phillip begged to be allowed to return to his old school, swearing he'd do better. They agreed. For a while, Robert helped him with his homework, and Phillip's grades improved, but by spring they discovered their son was coming home high on nights when he went out with his friends. He had just turned thirteen.

Robert and Eleanor made rules. They discussed "the problem" endlessly. Sometimes they even grounded their son. All his friends did it, Phillip would say, and they suspected he was telling the truth. Still, they didn't want *him* getting high. It seemed abnormal. In their day, kids were seventeen or eighteen before beginning their weekend beer parties. Now they were *thirteen*? It didn't bode well. Obviously, booze and pot were too hard for kids this age to handle. "Why would they even *want* to get high when they're so young?" Eleanor wondered. She had always thought of adolescent drinking as a way of easing the anxiety of becoming sexual.

"Maybe they *are* becoming sexual," said Robert.

"At thirteen?" said Eleanor.

Not long after his fourteenth birthday, Phillip was shipped off to rehab. He had been found drinking during the school day and had been abusive to his teachers. He'd even struck one of them. Robert and Eleanor felt terrible, but they also felt relieved. They knew that Phillip had been getting out of control but they hadn't known what to do. An addiction program was their only recourse. Maybe the fact that they were getting this thing so soon . . .

New Winds, recommended by a man at Robert's office whose son had been through the program, was only an hour away. Robert and Eleanor quickly became involved, as was required by New Winds. They attended family group sessions every Saturday and once a month went for the whole weekend. They were amazed by how quickly Phillip made gains. "He's actually *talking* about his feelings now," Robert said proudly. "He stood up in group and said he was sorry for the pain he'd caused us," Eleanor said. "He's trying so hard."

The family groups forced them to confront their laxity in dealing with Phillip, their inability to set limits, their own need to be loved by their son at whatever cost. They cried. Robert talked about his relationship with his own father. They learned to be more open with Phillip. Phillip couldn't con them anymore. They had seen the family patterns, had really *gotten* it.

After three months, Phillip "graduated" and returned home. He was going to attend AA every day. Since the school year was ending, he would find a part-time job. And he would be a fully participating member of the family—present and communicating at meals—with regular chores to perform, and curfews. There'd be no going out at night for six months. He could see his friends several times a week during the day. His schedule would have to be very tight, they had said at New Winds. This was a serious problem, and the whole family had to press for change. Robert and Eleanor felt that the situation, though still tenuous, was at last under control.

Before long, Phillip was skipping AA meetings to get high in the parking lot behind the Grand Union. Robert and Eleanor had no idea what was going on until the police brought him home in the back of their car, wrecked out of his mind and laughing like a maniac. He had tried taking money from the newsstand cash register when the owner had his back turned. The guy was pressing charges.

Robert and Eleanor felt betrayed. Everyone had really pulled together to deal with Phillip's addiction. They had seen it as a family problem. The kid was only fourteen years old, for God's sake, a model boy, a lovable boy. What had happened to their son?

Two Camps: "Recovery" Versus Medicine

There was, of course, the question of the boy's family history. When Robert and Eleanor had gotten Phillip, it had been the policy of adoption agencies to provide little information on the biological family. They knew nothing other than that the child had been born medically sound. Their inclination was to look within, to search among the fragments of Phillip's early childhood experiences with them, to face down their own ambivalent feelings as parents. Everything they had ever heard about addiction came from psychology. Still, it was difficult to come up with something traumatic enough to account for what was happening to Phillip. He'd been a happy kid. There had been the usual childhood problems—nightmares for a while, when he was three or four, fear of the dark. When he was five, he would sometimes wake up thinking someone was in his room. Eleanor had even taken Phillip to a shrink. After a few sessions, the doctor had said it was separation anxiety and Phillip would outgrow it. *Had everyone been wrong*, Robert and Eleanor wondered now. *Had everyone been crazy!*

By the time he turned seventeen, Phillip had been in five rehab centers. Somehow he'd managed to get a high school certificate, the triumph of the last center, which had insisted on keeping him six months and pushing him through a certification course. Now Phillip was living in a halfway house in North Carolina. He wasn't feeling very well. He was straight—at least for now—but he was low. Robert did wonder if Phillip was depressed, but the halfway house was adamant: *no antidepressants.*

Several years earlier, Robert had taken Phillip to a psychiatrist who'd said he was depressed and needed medication. Phillip had tried the antidepressant for a couple of months, but side effects annoyed him, and his therapist, a twelve-step person who didn't approve of medication, gave him little encouragement to stick with it. She had said she'd talk with the psychiatrist, but she never did. Any improvement in Phillip's mood she attributed to his "commitment to change." Soon the boy was off his medication and getting high again.

None of the rehab centers he'd been to had suggested a psychiatric evaluation. That was not their business. Addiction was their business.

Today, scientists believe that adolescents become depressed or troubled by some other psychiatric disturbance before the addiction sets in. "People don't become substance abusers when they feel good in the first place," says Bukstein.

But a drunk is still a drunk, AA would counter. This may be true, but the question remains, what is proper treatment when a mood disorder has laid the groundwork for an addiction—when the mood disorder is the "primary" illness? Psychiatrists and psychopharmacologists—and even, these days, some addiction counselors—recognize that people with two illnesses require treatment for both. They cannot simply be treated as addicts. When they are, like Kitty Dukakis, they get sicker.

Fear of Medicine

"A lot of people in the membership aren't exactly the epitome of AA ideals," says Eileen Fitzpatrick. "When I first went into AA, in the mid-seventies, most people were against *any* kind of mental health treatment. AA was supposed to be all things to all recovering alcoholics. Over the years, there's been increasing openness to using psychotherapy as an adjunct to AA, but there continues to be rigidity and ignorance among AA memberships about the use of medications."

"Some persistently depressed alcoholics may, paradoxically, find AA discouraging," says Roger Weiss, "because they may feel alienated from other AA members when they fail to experience the dramatic improvement in the quality of their lives other AA members describe as a result of sobriety." They may feel further alienated when others in the group chastise them for feeling sorry for themselves—in AA parlance, the 'poor me's' or 'sitting on the pity pot.' Says Weiss, "Some AA members may even blame the patient's depression on concurrent antidepressant treatment, on psychotherapy, or on seeing a psychiatrist in general."[37]

"AA needs education about psychiatric disorders," says a woman whose husband is both manic-depressive and a recovering alcoholic. Fear of letting his group know he's on lithium makes his recovery unnecessarily difficult, and it worries her. "They wouldn't tell someone with cancer not to have chemotherapy." She thinks if her husband's AA group found out he was on lithium, "they'd tell him to go off it, and he'd be hospitalized in two days."

Many in the membership are confused about mood disorders and their medications. "They equate these medications with street drugs," said a woman who hides from her group the fact that she takes Nardil. Some AA members imagine that antidepressants produce a "cocktail effect," a discernible change in mood soon after a pill is taken. It's understandable that such a medication might undermine sobriety, but lithium and antidepressants don't have a cocktail effect. The rebalancing of brain chemicals that they accomplish takes weeks, and is steadily maintained.

Fear of medicine is perpetuated as well in books and magazine articles written about addiction. In *The Invisible Alcoholics*, Marian Sandmaier warns that women are more likely to be diagnosed with an emotional disturbance than with alcoholism and to be plied with "mood-changing" drugs. These drugs, she says, "may be welcomed or even requested by the alcoholic woman herself. For a tranquilizer or antidepressant not only provides her with another chemical escape valve, [but] as a respectable 'woman's drug,' it can be taken openly and without guilt."

Not only does such a statement betray ignorance of the distinction between tranquilizers and antidepressants; it reveals a serious bias against women. Such writing implies that women who seek medical help for depression are looking for the easy way. It impugns antidepressants as copout drugs for weak-willed females.

Eileen Fitzpatrick thinks the peculiar narrowness of some AA groups stems from precisely the same black-and-white thinking that is characteristic of alcoholism. As one comes under the domination of a drug, the drug ends up being the choice over any other way of coping. Caught in an increasingly narrow response to life, the drinker becomes inflexible. Information that contradicts the defense on which he has come to rely is simply rejected.

The same rigidity can characterize the thinking of the recovering drinker. "The old attitudes don't vanish the moment a person puts down a drink," says Eileen. Defensiveness gets reinforced day after day, in meeting after meeting. "You learn what to say and what not to say. AA's is a powerful bias, and it can be pretty effective in enforcing compliance in most people. To risk censure is to risk serious ostracism."

In this way, treatment communities can perpetuate the very dysfunctionalism they set out to correct. Nonthinking alcoholics may risk becoming nonthinking recovering alcoholics. Taking on a new set of beliefs to replace the old, they rely on the AA tenets for interpreting reality the way a child clings to pages of a catechism. This is not an emotionally healthy way of operating. Models for reality are always changing, always evolving, and the secure individual is able to adapt accordingly. To the degree that one is unable to, one remains handicapped.

Lost Between Treatment Models

Bias exists as well on the medical side of the addiction fence. Bias in psychiatry is especially disturbing, since people whose emotional problems are complicated by addiction often get turned away. "My colleagues don't like to treat substance abusers," says Bukstein. "They feel uncomfortable with it. 'I don't envy you having to work with "that population," ' they say. But they work with patients, schizophrenics and such, who are every bit as frustrating."

179

Treatment of the addicted is fraught with polarized thinking. Patients, as a result, end up falling between two stools. Too often, both psychiatry and AA offer an overly narrow treatment model. If the individual doesn't fit it, he's in trouble. "When the patient is resistant, the recovery people say he's 'in denial,'" observes Bukstein.

Psychologically oriented therapists are ruled by their own prejudices. They like patients who are pretty well put together to begin with. Says Bukstein, wryly, "The worried well make the best patients because they're not sick."

Roger Weiss, like most medical experts in addiction, recognizes the supportive benefits of twelve-step groups and advises his colleagues to learn to understand them better—and to work *with*, not against, them. The therapists, he says, "should frequently ask their patients about attendance at AA meetings, the patient's attitudes toward AA, whether the patient has obtained a sponsor, and whether he or she speaks at meetings."

In the last analysis, both treatment models hold destructive biases, and both hold responsible the nonresponding patients. "I think we have to stop indulging in patient blame," says Bukstein. "We need to devise treatments that hit different kinds of situations, different kinds of people."

Coming Off the Pink Cloud

One of the biggest treatment controversies today revolves around the issue of how long to wait after sobriety before considering medication. How much of postabstinence mood disturbance is the result of what AA calls "coming off the pink cloud"—the bumping down to reality that occurs after the initial high of achieving sobriety has waned?

Initially, there's exhilaration in being able to get a decent night's sleep and face the bright sun of morning without a hangover. In the wake of daily floods of alcohol, the newly sober feel restored to a measure of health, a measure of sanity. But within weeks, if there's an underlying psychiatric disorder, it will soon be recognized that all is not well. The recovering alcoholic doesn't feel so hot after all. In fact, she feels lousy. "In thirty days, I was on antidepressants," said a woman from San Luis Obispo, in California, whom I met after a lecture. A physician's wife, she was one of the lucky ones to begin treatment for depression soon after achieving sobriety. "I was sober, but my neurotransmitters just weren't doing the job," she recalled. Medication took care of her faulty neurotransmitter function in a matter of weeks, and she felt better and better, until her normal mood and energy level were restored.

Katie Evans and J. Michael Sullivan, specialists in addiction and drug counseling in Portland, Oregon, report that among young people with psychiatric disorders, chemical abuse rates exceed 50 percent.[38] Virginia Hamilton says 70 to 80 percent of her clients— mostly middle-class and upper-middle-class outpatients—are evaluated with psychiatric disorders that require medication. Most often, the diagnosis is unipolar or biopolar depression.

Having two disorders creates a problem that is "greater than the sum of its parts," Evans and Sullivan point out in *Dual Diagnosis*. When he abuses a substance, "the confused person becomes more confused, the hostile person more threatening and assaultive, and the suicidal person more likely to engage in harmful activities."

Until recently, clinicians waited months, even a year, before suggesting a psychiatric evaluation to mood-disordered recovering addicts. Today, drug counselors like Evans and Sullivan think it's foolish to wait so long. "Our medical lab consultants tell us that even the psychoactive ingredient of THC in marijuana, notorious for staying in the body for several weeks because of its affinity for storage in fat tissues, is no longer detectable in the urine of most chronic daily pot smokers after thirty days," they say. "Second, the results of electroencephalography (EEG) exams and dexamethasone suppression tests (a measure of neuroendocrine function) return to normal after thirty days' abstinence."[39] Finally, research data and clinical experience show that many of the psychiatric symptoms caused by the abuse itself subside in under a month. "This is true even in withdrawal from benzodiazepines, notorious for being a drawn-out process."

Some think offering medication to a recovering addict is dangerous because of the possibility of its luring him back to the illicit drug. Any substance—controlled or not—that makes a patient feel better is thus seen as potentially readdicting. Today this sort of thinking is undergoing a change. The newest programs integrate what science has learned about the connection among brain chemicals, mood, and addiction. Clinicians administering the new programs treat mood disorders from the outset. Some even question how important it is to know whether depression is the result of substance abuse or its cause. "After the patient's been clean a few weeks, you begin to say to yourself, 'Hey, what are the risk factors here?'" says Oscar Bukstein. "What is the cost/benefit of *not* treating this person regardless of whether I think the depression might be pharmacologically induced?"

No matter what causes depression, suicide is a risk, Bukstein observes. There is also the social and occupational cost. "You can't afford to leave a person off medication for two years to see if he'll still be depressed. If the patient doesn't get better after several weeks of abstinence, antidepressant treatment should be seriously considered."[40] In Bukstein's experience, anywhere from 65 to 85 percent of depressed recovering addicts respond to antidepressants.

Some therapists and drug counselors are cautious about prescribing antidepressants for adolescent drug abusers. "In general, we find most adolescents can benefit from social-behavior interventions," Evans and Sullivan write; therapy, in other words. But psychiatrists who are comfortable prescribing medication to adults will often try it—with success—in children and adolescents. Bukstein is among them. Of his program in Pittsburgh he says, "We evaluate them, and if they're depressed, we'll say, 'I'm not going to wait until this kid relapses to find out whether his depression is "primary" or "secondary." The benefit of prescribing antidepressants is certainly worth any small risk."

So far, there aren't many dual-diagnosis programs in the country, although, Bukstein says, "I think you'll rapidly see this becoming a buzz word in the addiction field." Already, some treatment centers claim to treat adolescents with both psychiatric and addiction disorders when they haven't really got the programs to do it. "They'll say, 'We have psychiatrists, and we take kids on medication,'" says Bukstein, "but this isn't good enough." To be effective, he says, a dual-diagnosis program has to place a major emphasis on mental health care. "At ADAPT [Adolescent Drug Abuse and Psychiatric Treatment], we have a very loose twelve-step structure, and we think support groups are valuable. But we're looking *all the time* at psychiatric pathology, family history, the kid's history. We're seriously looking."

New Hope for the Addicted

Helen, a friend of mine who lives in New York, had a problem that any parent would find terrifying. Two years ago she discovered that her twenty-two-year-old daughter was addicted to heroin. Fortunately, she was able to find a treatment program for Margaret that seemed to her more humane and more therapeutic than twenty-eight days of "tough love."

Many are extremely young when drugs become compelling. Margaret had started doing angel dust and black beauties when she was thirteen. She dropped out of school in ninth grade. After that, nothing much ever developed in her life. A bright, extremely likable girl, she couldn't hold a job for more than a month or two, couldn't settle down enough even to study for a high school certificate. In her free time, which was virtually all the time, she took to the streets and the downtown clubs, dressed in tatoos and black leather. Helen hoped it was a phase.

As Margaret approached womanhood, her moods became increasingly erratic, with strange outbursts of aggression and hostility. She was twenty-one before her mother found out about her heroin problem, twenty-two before anyone could think what to do about it. Increasingly frustrated by her daughter's relapses (at that point, Margaret had sporadically been attending NA meetings for two years), Helen finally called her old psychiatrist. He suggested a drug counselor who understood the importance of biological factors in drug abuse.

Helen went to see the counselor and felt encouraged. When Helen spoke of her concern about Margaret's lack of education and inability to hold a job, the counselor told her, "Don't even *think* about the job. First, your daughter has to get well."

Margaret was expected to see the counselor seven days a week for the first three weeks. Then she would attend group three times a week and have private sessions twice a week. The counselor explained to Helen, "At six months I drop them down to two groups a week and one individual session, and at about a year they drop down to one group a week and one individual session a week. I have people who are two years sober and who still come once a week."

In the beginning, Margaret dug in her heels. She participated, but she was angry. She went every day and peed in a cup and listened to her counselor babble for an hour. After a week she told her mother, "Virginia's full of shit." Helen said, "Just keep going." Margaret kept going. After a while, it began to be something, having this woman to go to and talk to seven days a week. In a few weeks, Margaret had to begin groups, and she hated them. She told her mother that everyone in the group was full of shit. Helen said, "Just keep going." Margaret kept going.

Anyone with an addiction should be evaluated for a possible psychiatric disorder, (this is especially true of those who become addicted in childhood or adolescence), and Margaret was sent to a psychopharmacologist for an evaluation. He assessed her as clinically depressed. In taking her history, however, he learned of seizures she'd had in infancy and early childhood. He decided to treat her depression with valproic acid, an antiseizure medicine.

In about three weeks, Margaret began to feel substantially better. Her mood was stable; she was neither depressed, nor anxious and agitated. She called her mother and said, "I'm taking charge of my therapy. I'm telling Virginia we have to cut out this twinky shit. I want to dig deeper."

Treating depression helps prevent relapse in those recovering from an addiction. Margaret has been clean for two years. She is also happier and more focused than she's been since early childhood. Her irritable hostility had been caused by her depression. So had her trouble studying and staying in school. So, in all likelihood, had her addiction.

A Better Quality of Recovery

"It used to be thought that these heroin people were so sociopathic you had to knock down their whole ego structure, completely destroy it to rebuild it," one drug counselor told me. "My feeling is that if addicts ever *were* like that, they're not like that now."

"What I'm after," said another counselor, "is a better quality of recovery. Medication often contributes."

Getting Help

With proper treatment, 80 or 90 percent of those suffering from mood disorders get well. But finding the appropriate treatment isn't always easy.

Getting help begins with recognizing that depression and anxiety need—and deserve—to be treated. "It can be hard admitting to the pain," a young neighbor said to me recently. She was having difficulty telling the psychiatrist who'd prescribed her medication that it wasn't working. He'd given her such a low dosage that she was barely getting any relief. Yet having the pills "not work" made her question *not* whether the psychiatrist had prescribed properly but whether her depression was severe enough to warrant treatment in the first place.

It can be hard screwing up the courage to say, "It still hurts." We continue to associate this type of pain with moral weakness. Doctors don't help when they are themselves ambivalent about mood disorders. My neighbor's psychiatrist had explained that he was putting her on a low dose because he wasn't sure how "bad" her depression was. This is a classic prescribing mistake, according to Dr. Michael Gitlin. "There's no such thing as 'a low dose for a little depression,'" he writes in *The Psychotherapist's Guide to Psychopharmacology*.[1] Any depression requiring antidepressants needs a therapeutic-level dose, one that puts enough medicine into the bloodstream to do the job. Yet the NIMH found in a recent study that nine out of ten doctors prescribe antidepressants in doses too low to do any good.

Physicians' reasons for underprescribing vary. Some are concerned about side effects and hope that lower doses will result in fewer complaints from patients. Some are hazy on whether antidepressant medications develop tolerance and dependence. (So many earlier psychotropic drugs were addictive that antidepressants sometimes get sullied by association.) Some aren't set up to do close monitoring for signs of toxicity. These are powerful and complicated medications that require great expertise in administering.

Prescribing safely and effectively requires eliciting a careful and detailed psychiatric history from patients, as well as knowing a lot about the different types of medication that are available and what sorts of symptoms they're best for. Most general practitioners aren't comfortable in this realm simply because they haven't had the training. Overall, it's probably safe to say that lack of knowledge is what prevents doctors from identifying depression—and treating it properly. On some level, doctors who prescribe antidepressants *know* they don't know enough, and so they tiptoe along on the path of least resistance. Unfortunately, prescribing the wrong medication, or the right one in a dosage that is too low to be effective, can push the already hopeless-feeling patient to despair. "I've been given medication, and I still feel miserable! Nothing else can be done."

No physician should leave a depressed patient with the feeling that nothing further can be done. If an adequate response isn't achieved the first time out, the dosage should be increased or a different medication offered. With what's been achieved in psychopharmacology in the last decade, help is available to almost everyone. However, as with other areas of medicine, there are doctors who are expert and those who are more or less muddling through. Never assume that your doctor has the last word on anything. If you're not getting better with him or her, find someone else.

Treatment is complicated by people's reluctance to own up to the symptoms of mood disorders. The depressed often resist the idea of medication, viewing it as confirmation that they're sick, out of control, or possibly even crazy. Acute feelings of guilt or remorse—the very symptoms of their depression!—may result in their blaming themselves for their illness and believing they should "deal with" their depressive feelings alone. Such feelings are the result of the stigma we attach to "mental illness."

The NIMH found that *most* people who become depressed are afraid of losing their jobs if they seek out treatment. Men are visibly uncomfortable even discussing depression and attach a great deal of stigma to the illness. Those in the NIMH study said that if it ever happened to them, they probably wouldn't even try to get help.

Women are more comfortable with depression, consider it treatable, and said that they would definitely try to get help if they became depressed. But they, too, feared that it would be damaging to their careers if word of their illness got out.[2]

Some people don't even like to bring up mood problems with their therapists. They believe that if they worked hard enough at their therapy, they wouldn't be feeling depressed or extremely anxious or still be binging and purging. Admitting the problem, then, is like admitting the therapy is a failure. Eileen Fitzpatrick told us she found it humiliating to divulge her state of mind to her longtime therapist. "To admit to her that I was having this severe problem with depression was kind of a blow to my ego."

Many people think of taking medication as "the easy way out," a quick fix that may relieve symptoms but which sidesteps the deep, inner conflicts popularly thought to be the cause of depression. We've been taught to think we should be able to pull ourselves up out of despair—through the exercise of will or intellect—even if it means suffering for years. To struggle, and even to suffer, is somehow thought nobler than taking "the magic pill" offered by medicine.

We also fear that medication that causes changes in the brain might turn us into someone else.

"I believe this medication can help me, but I'm afraid it will change me," Gabrielle told her therapist, Dr. Monica Salerno, when she began treatment on Nardil, an MAO inhibitor (MAOI).

"It *will* change you," Dr. Salerno replied. "You'll be you again."

Gabrielle's anxiety and her therapist's clear response point up the common concern that antidepressants will alter us, taking away, perhaps, that which makes us unique. Dr. Salerno explained that antidepressants don't change the personality; they *restore* it. They do this by relieving the symptoms of major depression—the abnormal feelings, thoughts, and physical aches and pains—and returning *mood* to its normal state.

The results can be dramatic. Gabrielle recalls, "I woke up from a dream one night—it was four o'clock in the morning—and I felt overwhelmed. The dream had been intensely visual, almost like an abstract painting, and it made me realize that I hadn't had this sort of spontaneous, creative experience in years—that that whole part of me had been shut off."

Gabrielle's dream was the first sign that her depression of ten years was finally lifting—five weeks after she had begun on antidepressants. "It was like the lights switching back on."

Antidepressants aren't "happy pills." They don't produce the euphoric "high" of illicit drugs, and they're not addictive. "A person taking an antidepressant who does not suffer from major depression will experience no change in mood whatsoever," Dr. Francis Mondimore writes in *Depression: The Mood Disease.*[3] For the person who *is* depressed, however, the shift in mood that results when an antidepressant starts to work can be exhilarating. This was the case with Mia, a woman Gabrielle interviewed in New York who had to try three medications before getting one that works.

Mia was forty before she learned that what had been bothering her for so long was depression. "At its worst, it was like continuously being unhappy," Mia told me. "You know that feeling when you wake up in the morning and something's awfully wrong but you don't know what it is? When I finally was given an antidepressant that worked, it was as if a weight had been lifted from my shoulders. I felt this surge of happiness."

That surge of happiness is not a "high." It is the feeling of contentment and self-satisfaction people normally experience when they're healthy—when their mood-regulating neurochemicals are working as they should. And it can make all the difference in the quality of one's life. Those who are happy can do more, feel more, have richer experiences. "I feel I can take chances now," Mia says. "I can do things that are hard for me, things I thought I could never do. At work, I've grown tremendously in the past five years. I've taken on all kinds of new responsibilities, and I've become successful!"

It's not always easy to recognize the degree to which depression is interfering with one's life or even to identify the problem as depression. We tend to fight the illness, to deny its impact on our lives, which is really tragic, for depression is not something that has to be endured. When properly treated, it has an almost 90 percent chance of being relieved.[4]

Treatment with Antidepressants

Currently there are about sixteen antidepressants in use in the United States. They belong to three major groups. The tricyclic antidepressants, or TCAs, include such drugs as imipramine (Tofranil) and desipramine (Norpramin). The monoamine oxidase inhibitors, or MAOIs, include phenelzine (Nardil) and tranylcypromine (Parnate). The third group, called "second-generation" antidepressants, includes fluoxetine (Prozac) and trazodone (Desyrel), among others. Although the mechanisms by which they work differ somewhat, all of these drugs alter the metabolism of the mood-regulating neurotransmitters in the brain.

Antidepressants are, for the most part, equally effective in treating depression, although some people have better results from one than from another. It isn't possible to be sure in advance which antidepressant will work for any given individual. However, the different subtypes of depression respond better to certain *types* of antidepressants. MAOIs are especially effective in treating atypical depression—the type that is marked by anxiety, oversleeping, and overeating. People with bulimia often respond well to an MAOI or to fluoxetine—drugs that not only relieve the depression but often halt, or significantly reduce, the binge/purge cycle.[5] People who vacillate between euphoria and depression often require lithium.

Following are important considerations that guide psychopharmacologists in their treatment strategies.

• If a particular drug has worked in the past either for the patient or a relative, it is usually the drug of first choice. Unfortunately, this sort of information isn't always available. People sometimes forget which medications they've been given before. They may not be aware that a relative was once treated for depression and which medication was effective.

• Because depression creates feelings of hopelessness, it's possible to forget even a medication one took oneself that alleviated the same symptoms currently being experienced. "How come ten months ago you were so enthusiastic about fluoxetine helping your binging," I asked a woman I interviewed in California, "and now you sound less keen on it?" "Because this is a bad time," she replied. "I don't feel very optimistic about anything now."

• Psychiatrists should provide their patients with written records of their drug treatment for future use.

• Whether the probable side effects of a given medication might be intolerable to a particular patient is relevant. For example, some antidepressants, because of their blood pressure–lowering properties, pose potential problems in the elderly.

• The prescribing physician must evaluate whether the patient is likely to comply with any restrictions. For example, certain foods and medications *must* be avoided when taking an MAOI. Some people might not be sufficiently stable emotionally to stick to the restrictions.

Psychopharmacological treatment of mood disorders isn't simply a matter of getting a prescription, having it filled at the pharmacy, and then waiting a few hours for the medication to kick in. Typically, it takes two to four weeks for significant improvement to occur. Sometimes it can take as long as six to eight weeks. Depending on the type of medication prescribed, the starting dosage may be very low and be increased gradually to reduce side effects.

If, after a few weeks, there hasn't been a significant response, the psychopharmacologist will probably try increasing the dosage, not because tolerance to the medication has developed or even because the depression is more severe, but because there are individual differences in metabolism. Two people may have the same type of depression and be on the same medication but require quite different dosages to get relief. The point is that the dosage should be high enough to reach a therapeutic blood level. With certain antidepressants, blood levels can be measured.

If symptoms persist once the maximum dosage level is reached, the psychopharmacologist may try switching to a different class of antidepressants—from fluoxetine to imipramine, say, or from a tricyclic to an MAOI. Or he may supplement the current medication with another antidepressant or a potentiating agent, such as lithium or thyroid hormone. If this doesn't work, the psychopharmacologist may try a new, experimental drug, or if the depression is very severe, electroconvulsive therapy (ECT). ECT produces a seizure in the brain under safe, medically controlled conditions. It is more effective than any other treatment for severe depression and has been vastly refined in recent years. It is no longer the frankly terrifying procedure portrayed in films and novels of the past.

With the variations in efficacy and side effects, antidepressant treatment clearly is not a question of one pill for everything and everyone. Some trial and error is often involved. It takes a specialist—that is, a *psychopharmacologist*—to prescribe properly. Running to your GP for a quick Prozac fix isn't a good idea. Most GPs don't know enough about either the diagnosis or treatment of depression, for they have had no special training or experience in psychiatric illness. As Dr. Jack Gorman notes, "What seems like simple stress to a general practitioner may actually be symptoms of serious depression. Overexcitement may be an early sign of mania."[6]

All too frequently, according to the NIMH Epidemiological Catchment Study, GPs prescribe drugs in doses too low to be effective.[7] Even psychiatrists may not be up to date on the proper use of medication. Too often people who are being dragged down by depression say, "I tried antidepressants, and they didn't work for me." Chances are they were never given a high enough dose. Or if one medication didn't work, their doctor didn't switch them to another.

Sometimes, of course, the patient contributes to treatment failure by not taking the medicine as prescribed. Writing down your doctor's instructions helps. Make sure you know:

- What to do if you miss a scheduled dose, or even a day, of your medication.
- What other medications might interfere with the efficacy of your antidepressant or cause a dangerous synergistic reaction.
- What side effects may occur, how to manage them if they do, and which side effects are serious enough that you should notify your psychopharmacologist immediately.
- What the signs are that the medication is beginning to do its work and how long it will take for the drug's benefits to appear.

If you have any questions or doubts about your ability to take the medication as directed (e.g., if you're bulimic and fear you may purge the medication), discuss them openly with your psychopharmacologist. These specialists aren't interested in casting blame; their interest is in *treating*. They understand the symptoms of the different illnesses we've discussed in this book. The more they know about your particular case, the better able they'll be to develop a successful treatment program.

Prozac: The Controversy

Fluoxetine (Prozac) was approved by the Food and Drug Administration (FDA) for the treatment of depression in 1987. Since then, over 3 million people have been treated with it. It's prescribed often in the treatment of atypical depression, depression accompanied by either panic attacks or obsessive-compulsive disorder (OCD), and bulimia. It may also be the first choice for someone with heart disease (who therefore cannot safely take a tricyclic antidepressant) or for a patient who can't afford to gain any weight.[8]

Although fluoxetine has been widely reported *not* to cause side effects (and, in fact, does not cause the anticholinergic effects commonly seen with TCAs), it *frequently* causes nausea, headache, nervousness, insomnia, and delayed orgasm.[9] Usually these side effects pass once the individual has adjusted to the medication.

The media have stressed that fluoxetine causes weight loss rather than weight gain. While a small amount of weight loss *is* fairly frequent, a few patients who take fluoxetine gain weight, and those given fluoxetine to reverse weight gain caused by other antidepressants are frequently disappointed.[10]

Agitation and impulsivity—a syndrome known as *akathisia*—may also occur after a few days to a few weeks of fluoxetine therapy. A woman I know asked an osteopath for a prescription for Prozac and was given it without a careful medical history being taken. Within days, she said, "I felt like I wanted to jump out of my skin." A skilled psychopharmacologist would have quickly recognized this syndrome as akathisia and could have prescribed a medication to counteract it, Harrison Pope says.

More troubling are recent reports of suicidal thoughts developing in patients who were given fluoxetine. In 1989, a man in Louisville, Kentucky, was reported to have gone on a shooting rampage, killing eight people and wounding a dozen before killing himself. An autopsy revealed that he had been taking Prozac. In February 1990, the *American Journal of Psychiatry*[11] published a report by Martin Teicher of Harvard Medical School claiming that "6 depressed patients free of recent suicidal ideation developed intense, violent, suicidal preoccupation after 2–7 weeks of fluoxetine treatment."

Teicher reported that his patients suffered from various illnesses, including depression. His report raised the question of whether these developments were the direct result of treatment with Prozac. He believes the profound influence of Prozac on serotonin may be a factor. "We're only starting to understand the role that serotin plays in depression, aggression, and suicide," he said. "It's possible that by prolonging the effects of serotonin in patients who are especially sensitive to it, you can tip the balance in the wrong direction, toward violence and aggression."

Once this paper was picked up by the media, Prozac's manufacturer, Eli Lilly & Co., was hit with dozens of lawsuits demanding payments in the millions. Generally, the suits charged that the company had failed to inform doctors about a link between Prozac and suicidal or violent behavior and also charged that the drug was unsafe. Since then, Lilly has made no public comments except to say that Prozac is safe. In May 1990, however, it added "suicide attempt" to the list of possible adverse reactions.

The Teicher paper received an extraordinary flood of publicity. *Nightline,* for example, referred to it as "a major study." As psychiatrist Jeffrey M. Jonas, M.D., has written,[12] "The Harvard report was neither major nor a study." It was, instead, a report on six patients who suffered from a variety of psychiatric disorders and had experienced suicidal ideation after taking Prozac. Jonas notes that the usual procedure when such "preliminary information" has been gathered is to report it to a journal in the form of a letter to the editor. "In this case, however, the report appeared as a full blown article in a highly respected professional journal. The title of the article was, 'Emergence of Intense Suicidal Preoccupation During Fluoxetine Treatment.' Such a title is somewhat misleading, because it does nothing to indicate that the report is merely a series of patient anecdotes and not a formal scientific study."

Another serious problem with the Teicher study was the report that the patients had been free of *recent* suicidal thoughts. "Delving into the details of the cases, however, you'd get a different picture entirely," Dr. Jonas observes. For example, "the authors state that 'Ms. A' had a seventeen-year history of depression, among the symptoms of which were 'occasional passive suicidal thoughts.' 'Mr. B.' and 'Ms. C' both had passive suicidal thoughts a mere *two weeks* before starting Prozac; Ms. C even had a 'history of mild suicidal gestures.' During the preceding eight years 'Ms. D' had become enraged and had made at least three serious suicide attempts by taking drug overdoses. Two years before taking Prozac, 'Ms. E' had reported having persistent suicidal thoughts. 'Ms. F' had made 'three significant suicidal gestures' in the past thirteen years, and for the past five years had experienced 'intermittent suicidal thoughts.'

"Thus, strangely, the researchers apparently define 'recent' to mean occurring only within the last two weeks," Jonas notes. "I believe the compelling evidence showing that the six patients in this report had suicidal tendencies before they began taking Prozac is enough to undermine the credibility of the findings," he concludes.

Certainly, the therapist and psychopharmacologist treating a depressed person must keep a watchful eye for any suicidal thoughts that the patient may express after beginning treatment with fluoxetine or any other antidepressant. Should they occur, the medication should be *discontinued immediately*, since there are indications that, once begun, the suicidal ideation may continue even after the medication is stopped.[13]

Drugs for the Treatment of Bipolar Disorder

People with manic-depressive illness often express the fear that medication will make them lose their energy and their creative edge. In his book *Depression: The Mood Disease*, Mondimore writes, "Lithium is not an emotional 'downer,' nor is it known to affect normal energy or creativity . . . the patient remains free to experience the normal emotions of life, but is protected from destructive or bizarre swings of mood."[14]

Lithium (lithium carbonate) has been used in the treatment of bipolar disorder since the fifties and is still the treatment of choice.[15] Other drugs, such as carbamazepine (Tegretol) and valproate (Depakene), are being used more and more often either as the primary treatment for certain types of bipolar disorder, as adjuncts to lithium, or when someone is unable to take lithium.

Lithium is effective 70 to 80 percent of the time. Twenty percent of patients will experience a complete remission of symptoms, and the rest will have substantial, though not complete, relief, meaning that they'll experience fewer episodes of mania and those they do have will be both shorter and less severe. They will also enjoy a more stable mood state in the time between episodes.

Lithium works only when it reaches a certain level in the body. In contrast to antidepressants, the level is roughly the same for all patients. Plasma levels, rather than dosage, determine the appropriate amount of medication, and regular blood tests are necessary to ensure that the lithium level is being maintained in the therapeutic range. Not only are these tests critical in determining whether the patient is getting *enough* medication; they also ensure that he or she is not getting *too much*, since the therapeutic level of lithium is not far below the toxic level.

Once the therapeutic dosage has been determined, regular blood tests are still necessary, since the lithium level can be effected by changes in body weight, medications, and other factors. Dr. Mondimore explains that the timing of the tests is very important. "A blood test taken too long or short a time after the last dose will give inaccurate information, and erroneous changes in dosage may be made."[16] For lithium, the general rule is that blood levels should be checked twelve hours after the last dose.

People with bipolar disorder usually require medication on a long-term basis, since it's rare to have just one episode of mania. Rather, cycles tend to be frequent (every several years, yearly, or even—in the more severe cases—several times a year). Since the effects of a manic episode can be very destructive to relationships, jobs, and bank accounts, not to mention self-esteem, preventive (or maintenance) treatment is generally necessary.

There is some debate over when maintenance treatment

should be initiated. Some clinicians feel this should begin as soon as a diagnosis of bipolar disorder is made. Others do not discuss long-term treatment until the second episode occurs.[17] At that time, the patient can be reasonably sure that the first episode was not just a "fluke," and the cycling frequency—the length of time between the onset of the first and second episodes—can be calculated.[18]

While episodes of mania may be brief and remit spontaneously, in most people they run an inexorable course, with reckless behavior, which may involve physical danger to the patient or others, or disinhibited social behavior.[19] When a manic episode escalates into psychosis, hospitalization is necessary so that the psychosis can be rapidly brought under control.

The treatment of an acute manic episode generally begins with an antipsychotic drug, such as haloperidol (Haldol) or chlorpromazine (Thorazine).[20] Although such drugs have unpleasant and sometimes serious side effects (when used on a long-term basis), it is essential that extreme mania be brought under control quickly. The therapeutic effects of antipsychotic medications are seen within hours, while the effects of lithium do not begin for five to ten days. Because antipsychotics are used only during the "crisis" stage, the risk of serious side effects, such as tardive dyskinesia, is unlikely.[21] While dystonia (mild to severe muscle cramps) is a frequent side effect, often occurring within the first 24 to 48 hours of treatment, it can be rapidly reversed by the administration of anticholinergic medication.[22]

Usually, lithium is gradually introduced 2 to 3 days after treatment has begun, and once therapeutic levels have been reached, the antipsychotic drug is tapered off. According to Dr. Gordon Johnson, "three weeks of treatment are required to obtain marked improvement and/or remission in the majority of patients with mania."[23]

Once the acute episode of mania has been treated, lithium levels of about 0.8 mmole/L. are recommended for the maintenance of most patients, although some require slightly higher levels (1.0–1.2) and others, especially the elderly, may show a good response at levels of 0.4. Once the appropriate maintenance level has been established, it must be followed consistently.[24]

Some studies have shown that people with more severe or rapid-cycling mania, or those who do not have a family history of

197

bipolar disorder, are less likely to respond well to lithium. For those who don't respond completely to lithium alone, carbamazepine (an anticonvulsant) may be used instead of, or in addition to, lithium. It can also be effective for those who can't tolerate side effects caused by lithium. Of the alternatives to lithium, carbamazepine has been the best studied, and its current clinical use is widespread.

Drugs for the Treatment of Anxiety and Panic Disorders

The NIMH's Epidemiological Catchment Study surprised many by showing that anxiety disorders are the most common psychiatric illnesses today. In any given six-month period, at least one out of twenty Americans will suffer from an anxiety disorder severe enough to be treated by a mental health professional. "In many instances," says Jack Gorman, "medication is the best and safest way to treat those anxiety disorders."[25] Anyone who is abusing alcohol, tranquilizers, or any drug in an attempt to calm down should seek a psychiatric consultation. Anxiety disorders can cause alcohol and drug abuse.

As discussed in chapter 3, there is normal anxiety, related to real-life events; there is excessive anxiety, which grows out of proportion to any real threat; and there are anxiety disorders. These last are categorized as generalized anxiety disorder (GAD), a form of chronic anxiety that lasts at least six months; panic disorder, which almost always requires treatment; and phobia, an extreme or irrational fear of a thing or situation. Finally, there is also OCD, an illness that compels the individual to almost constantly wash or count or check things.

Generalized anxiety disorder (GAD) is often treated with benzodiazepines, and a relatively new drug called buspirone (BuSpar). It's important to note that certain forms of depression are accompanied by anxiety and, when this is the case, should be treated with antidepressants, not antianxiety agents. (Unfortunately, antianxiety agents are the drugs most frequently prescribed for depression. In a large 1982 study conducted by the NIMH, "more than half the depressed patients encountered had been treated with anxiolytics instead of antidepressants," reports the *American Journal of Psychiatry*.)[26]

People with GAD are almost always worried, tense, and anxious. "In panic disorder, the main problem is the sudden, episodic bursts of anxiety and physical symptoms (like palpitations, dizziness, and difficulty in breathing) that generally lasts 10–30 minutes," notes Gorman.[27]

Antidepressants are used to treat panic disorder. Gorman says "the tried and true" drug for panic is the antidepressant imipramine. He usually begins with about 10 mg per day—much lower than would be given for depressed patients. Then the dosage is raised to that which is given to depressed patients. Panic attacks are usually blocked completely in four weeks. In the meantime, anxiety can be treated with one of the benzodiazepines.

Some clinicians treat with Xanax, which is effective in blocking panic but more difficult to stop than imipramine because of the withdrawal problems that are described later in this chapter.

The most powerful drug for panic is an MAOI. Drugs like phenelzine (Nardil) and tranylcypromine (Parnate) work for almost everyone with a panic disorder. Because of the diet restrictions, however, most psychiatrists will try imipramine or Xanax first. Prozac is also beneficial in panic attacks, and because it has few side effects and isn't habit forming, Gorman thinks it may be "the ideal antipanic drug." He says panic-disorder patients tend to be more sensitive to Prozac than depressed patients, so that one-fourth to one-half capsule a day should be taken the first week. The dosage should be gradually increased to a whole 20 milligram capsule—which is usually enough to block panic attacks.

Some drugs used to treat heart conditions and high blood pressure have also been tried for panic. Beta blockers, for example, are often prescribed because they block the effect of adrenaline and reduce heart rate; however, these drugs usually do not block panic attacks.

Special therapy is also offered for panic control and can take up to three months. Patients learn how to breathe correctly, how to relax, how to stop exaggerating every palpitation and tingle. They may also practice breathing without hyperventilating. The outlook for this type of therapy is promising, although it has not yet been demonstrated whether it works as well as antipanic drugs.

Some think that patients who receive special panic-control

therapy will stay free from attacks after the therapy is completed for a longer time that those who take antipanic drugs and then discontinue them. "This hypothesis is far from proven," says Gorman. He also raises an important warning. Many therapists, psychologists, and psychiatrists claim to know how to carry out these treatments, "but in fact they adapt more traditional forms of psychotherapy and wind up seeing the patient on a regular basis for months or years." Some psychiatric problems require such lengthy psychotherapy, but Gorman says the specific therapy aimed at controlling panic should *not* take longer than three months.

Until the mid-eighties, psychiatrists barely paid attention to *social phobia.* Now it is recognized as being quite common and sometimes a serious problem. Some clinicians think subconscious forces make people tremble and blush in social situations and recommend long-term psychotherapy and even psychoanalysis. Others may recommend short-term behavior and cognitive psychotherapy; they think the social phobia stems from passivity and poor social skills.

Pharmacology has such effective treatments for social phobia that many clinicians today would recommend combining medication and short-term psychotherapy. Two kinds of drugs are being used: beta-adrenergetic blockers and MAOIs. The most effective medications to date are propranolol (Inderal) for occasional problems—anxiety before a lecture or performance, say—and atenolol (Tenormin) and phenelzine (Nardil) for more chronic problems. Prozac may also work with social phobia. Performance anxiety can be relieved significantly by taking a single dose of Inderal about an hour before the performance. Many musicians do this to combat stage fright. The drug usually controls rapid heart beat, trembling, sweating, and blushing for several hours. Taken in this way, the drug produces few side effects.

About 70 percent of patients with social phobia respond to MAOIs. "After four weeks, they find their social fears almost totally eliminated," says Gorman. While Nardil usually works, anyone who takes it must maintain a special diet that is outlined in appendix D. People taking this drug will usually find themselves entering social situations more and more frequently. After a while, they may be able to stop the drug and still feel confident.

Gorman notes that some patients taking MAOIs for social phobia are overstimulated and become high. They then become too sociable, talking, laughing, boasting, and taking too many social risks. If this happens, the dose is lowered.

In January 1990, the drug clomipramine (Anafranil), a cyclic antidepressant, was finally granted approval for marketing in the United States. This drug is a breakthrough in the treatment of one of the most difficult psychiatric conditions—*obsessive-compulsive disorder* (OCD). Although more research is needed, Prozac also appears to be useful in the treatment of OCD. There have been many psychological theories about what causes this distressing illness, but biopsychiatrists think it is one of the most biological of all mental disorders. People with OCD usually appear perfectly normal to the observer, but they are obsessed with repetitive thoughts and meaningless rituals. Interestingly, people with OCD don't actually believe their hands need incessant washing or that they really need to check whether the stove is lit ten times before they leave their home. Something forces them to do this—possibly, scientists think, some abnormality in the brain.

People with OCD almost invariably need behavioral psychotherapy which restricts the amount of time they are able to engage in rituals. Some clinicians have found that they are able to treat compulsions behaviorally even without drugs. But the combination appears to be superior.

Doctors need to explain to OCD patients that their thoughts and actions are not their fault. "Although we encourage patients to exercise as much control as possible over the symptoms, we want them to understand that they are not to blame and will not be condemned," Gorman says.

Why Psychotherapy?

One might wonder, If mood disorders are biological in origin, why is psychotherapy necessary at all?

Mood disorders are complex illnesses that have very real effects on people's lives. Relationships with friends, family, and co-workers may be damaged, especially when someone has been ill for a long time.

Frederick Goodwin, M.D., of the NIMH, notes that while biology is at their core, these illnesses manifest in ways that "are behavioral and psychological, with profound changes in perception, attitudes, personality, mood, and cognition. Therapy can be of unique value to persons undergoing such devastating changes in the way they perceive themselves and are perceived by others."

It can also help with other life problems that may be playing a role in the mood disorder. Marion, a woman whose depression was complicated by alcoholism, believed her drinking had caused the depression and that once she'd been sober for a while, it would lift. But it didn't. Two years after she had begun recovery, she was still depressed. At that point, her therapist suggested that something other than the drinking was causing the depression and recommended that she try medication. Although several types of medication were prescribed before one was found that worked, Marion felt the results were worth the wait. Not only did she no longer feel depressed; she felt the antidepressants helped her take advantage of therapy. "You can work better at it when you're not in such terrible pain all the time."

Therapy will help resolve the residual effects of a mood disorder. "A combination of antidepressants and psychotherapy worked very well for me," Marion said, "because the depression had psychological, emotional and social ramifications that were every bit as significant as those caused by the alcohol. Once I was feeling better, I found I had a lot of problems to clean up that were generated by the depression."

When mood disorders arise in childhood, adolescence, or early adulthood, they interfere with the developmental tasks that normally occur during these periods. As Fred Goodwin notes, "Separation from parents and family, development of close personal relationships, romantic involvements, hurts and rejections, childbearing and child-rearing, and career development—are impaired or halted." So, again, psychotherapy can play a vitally important role. These developmental "tasks" are important in becoming a whole person. They also develop aspects of the personality that can help prevent mood disorders from recurring in the future. Studies have shown that relapse is less likely to occur in people who are treated with therapy as well as medication.

How Therapy Works

In general, what people with mood disorders need from therapy is not confrontation but affirmation. "Encouragement, support, and education," should be the focus of therapy, says Mondimore, "not getting them to understand themselves better."[28]

Therapy for mood disorders, while bolstering self-esteem and self-confidence, addresses the realistic problems, such as side effects and fear of recurrence, caused by the illness. It will help a person accept the losses that have occurred—in relationships, creativity, career advancement—due to the illness.

Psychotherapy, on the other hand, is centered around a confiding relationship between the therapist and patient. The goal of treatment is to allow the patient to better understand his or her emotions and behavior and to use this knowledge to function more successfully.

While there are almost as many types of therapy as there are therapists, two types have been found to be particularly helpful in treating depression: *cognitive therapy* and *interpersonal therapy*. Both of them are short-term, lasting months rather than years, and both are oriented to the "here and now." Therapists may combine one or both of these approaches, tailoring the techniques they use to the individual patient.

Cognitive therapy, founded by Dr. Aaron Beck, views depression as the result of negative attitudes and distorted perceptions of the world. The aim of this type of therapy has been to get the patient to recognize the connection between negativity and depression and to correct distorted perceptions. Interestingly, some practitioners of cognitive therapy have acknowledged the biological basis of depression and now use their techniques to challenge the patient's resistance to accepting that their depression can be successfully treated with medication.

Interpersonal therapy helps the patient identify current problems in relationships that may have contributed to (or be the result of) the depressed mood and learn to work them out. Interpersonal therapy is not open-ended. In common with other brief psychotherapies, it focuses on one or two problem areas, which are agreed upon by the patient and the psychotherapist after the initial evaluation session. Because relationships are often thrown into disarray when a person becomes depressed, this form of therapy may be especially useful when used in conjunction with medication.[29]

Classic, psychoanalytically oriented psychotherapy, on the other hand, views mood disorders as mainly psychological, rooted in unconscious memories of the past. The goal of this type of therapy—which typically takes years—is to learn to recognize and eventually resolve conflicts arising from past experiences. While it may be useful in treating other types of problems, psychoanalytic therapy is not appropriate for the treatment of mood disorders. In fact, it may even exacerbate them. As Mondimore observes, "Traditional, long-term psychotherapy with the goal of helping patients change their approach to life can even make things worse by putting too much responsibility for getting well on the patient."[30]

How Therapists Can Support Medical Treatment

It's extremely important that your therapist and psychopharmacologist be able to work *together*. We were surprised by how many people we interviewed who felt torn apart because they had a therapist who clung to the view that their depression was strictly psychological and a psychopharmacologist whose view was solely biological. The ideal is to have a therapist and a psychopharmacologist who recognize—and value—one another's contributions and who work together. This is how Rima Greenberg, a psychotherapist in Manhattan, approaches medical treatment with her depressed patients:

"I always recommend that the patient have a thorough physical to rule out any underlying illness. Then I ask him or her to see a psychopharmacologist for an assessment. The psychopharmacologist is an expert, someone who can really tailor treatment to the individual. In general, I try to use someone who's geared toward research, because that person's going to be up to date on what's new in the field."

Ms. Greenberg says it's critical that she be able to work closely with the psychopharmacologist. "If any decision is to be made about changing dosage or types of medication, it should come out of an open dialogue among the patient, the psychopharmacologist, and me. I feel that what's going on in the therapy is an important factor in any decisions about the medication."

A strong patient/therapist/psychopharmacologist relationship is crucial to successful treatment. Greenberg told the story of a young woman, whom she called Donna, whose earlier treatment strategy had not been effective. "Donna came to me when she was in her mid-twenties. She'd suffered from cyclical depression since she was about sixteen and had a family history of serious depression, both bipolar and unipolar. Every year and a half, Donna would go into a year-and-a-half-long episode of depression. After I reviewed her history, I felt her previous psychiatrist hadn't been doing an adequate job. Each time he took her off medication, she'd relapse into a new episode."

Ms. Greenberg had Donna see a psychopharmacologist, who identified a low thyroid condition that was contributing to Donna's depression and prescribed thyroid medication. Then they all decided on something new. "We made a joint decision to try a double cycle of antidepressant medication—three years without a stop—to give her a chance to get a hold on the therapy. But as soon as we withdrew her from medication, at the end of three years, we saw immediately that she was becoming depressed again. So we put her back on for another double cycle, making it a total of six years on medication. This time, when we withdrew the medication, she didn't relapse. In fact, she's been off medication for a year, and she terminated therapy six months ago. She's doing extremely well."

Greenberg feels that the particular psychopharmacologist she sent Donna to was an important part of her treatment. "Donna is a very bright woman, and he treated her as a peer. When she expressed interest in certain aspects of her illness, he gave her a lot of literature to read. With her previous doctor, it had been more like 'You're the patient, I'm the doctor, and this is what you do.' "

People with major depressions sometimes need follow-up help even after their formal treatment period has ended. When Donna decided to become pregnant, for example, she and her psychopharmacologist discussed the situation thoroughly. Greenberg says, "Although Donna has concluded her treatment, both her psychopharmacologist and I will follow her when the child is

205

born. She's going to have the baby at the hospital to which he's attached just to absolutely cover any possibilities."

Women with major depression have a higher probability of a post-partum depression. Quick intervention is important to keep things from escalating. With the help of her two therapists, Donna has her bases covered.

As discussed in chapter 2, there continues to be a rift in the profession between those who feel medication is usually appropriate in the treatment of mood disorders and those who feel therapy alone is better.

Some therapists mistakenly believe that the medication will work *against* the therapy, and they dissuade their patients from trying it. Research shows that quite the opposite is true: Not only will psychotherapy make it more likely for someone to stay on their medication, but medication will make it more likely that they stay in psychotherapy.

Even when therapists don't actively discourage patients from pursuing medical treatment, reservations they may have can filter through to their patient. Thus, the therapist's own ambivalence may undermine the patient's faith in the medical approach as well as his or her ability to stay on the medication.

What happened in the case of Ariel shows what can happen when a therapist isn't supportive. At age twenty-nine, Ariel had spent several years in therapy and had successfully resolved many of her interpersonal problems. However, despite the therapy, she continued to be depressed. Eventually, the illness became so much worse that she had to take a leave of absence from work and stop attending classes at the local university. Effectively, her life was on hold.

Ariel had always thought that if she just kept working hard in therapy, her depression would eventually lift. This idea was reinforced by her therapist, Steve. But the severity of her most recent episode made her begin to doubt whether therapy alone would ever be enough to help her.

"Finally, I told Steve I wanted to try antidepressants. He was afraid I'd lose the motivation to deal with the issues we'd been working on in therapy. But I was miserable—I couldn't work, I was crying all day—so I persisted. Reluctantly, he referred me to a psychiatrist, who prescribed imipramine for me."

Unfortunately, the psychiatrist Ariel consulted was not knowledgeable in the use of antidepressants. He prescribed a very low dose of medication for Ariel, and when she reported feeling better the first week after she began treatment, he decided that that was all she needed. So he sent her on her way, with a follow-up visit scheduled in *six weeks.*

Ariel's good feelings didn't last long. As mentioned earlier, it takes four to six weeks for the full effects of an antidepressant to be seen. Feeling good so shortly after beginning treatment was a result of Ariel's hopefulness about trying a new approach. Her depression soon returned in full measure, and before long she began to have thoughts of suicide.

Ariel's psychiatrist had not only prescribed too low a dose of antidepressant; because he wasn't monitoring her closely, he couldn't see that what he'd prescribed wasn't working. She was then left on her own, and when her depression worsened, she was in no shape to evaluate her situation clearly. She wanted to give up the medication entirely. Fortunately, a friend recommended another psychopharmacologist who knew how to treat Ariel's depression properly.

Learning What "Well" Is

Fear of relapse or recurrence is common in people recovering from mood disorders. While these are genuine concerns, some people become preoccupied with such fears and become hyperalert for signs of an impeding episode. "I think a person who's had a history of depression always fears that the bottom's going to fall out and they're going to get depressed again," Marion told me. People may also fear that their families and friends will be less supportive if an episode recurs.

Like Marion, Gabrielle says that at first she, too, did not trust that her recovery would last. "In the beginning I felt guarded. It took a while to drop that." Her anxiety worsened when she returned to work. "I was very worried that I wouldn't be able to get up in the morning," she recalled. "I was feeling much better, but I was afraid that the same old pattern would evolve—that I'd somehow manage to get myself to the office the first few days, then I'd start coming in late, and eventually I wouldn't be able to go in at all."

Gabrielle's therapist reassured her that this was unlikely, reaffirming the changes she'd experienced as a result of the anti-depressants. "To my great relief," Gabrielle said, "the old pattern did not reemerge. In fact, I found I really enjoyed getting up early, and frequently I was one of the first people in the office! In six months, I was only late once. . . . Everyone oversleeps once in a while."

Mood disorders in general and bipolar disorder in particular can take "a severe toll on other relationships, professional activities, and the individual's ability to handle the emotional stress of the affective episodes," notes Dr. Goodwin. The personal toll can be great as well. As Joshua Logan wrote in his autobiography, "I was only forty-five years old, but I felt exhausted by this last experience, hollowed out, as though I were a live fish disembow-eled."[31]

The process of learning to make the distinction between normal and abnormal moods and states, is another area where psychotherapy can play an important role. "Normal" mood is, of course, variable. We all experience periods of grief, anger, ela-tion, and joy. But for someone who's suffered from a mood dis-order, it can be difficult to distinguish the normal variations from signs of impending illness. If they are angry or irritable or a little down or even feeling especially good, they may justifi-ably worry that these feelings are not part of the normal range of human emotion but early symptoms of depression or hypo-mania.

Dr. Goodwin notes, "These overlapping emotions can be con-fusing and arouse anxiety in many patients, who may then ques-tion their own judgment and become unduly concerned about recurrences of their affective illness." Therapy can help with "learning to unravel what is normal personality from what the illness has superimposed upon it—turbulence, impulsiveness, lack of predictability, and depression."

"No pill can help me deal with the problem of not wanting to take pills; likewise, no amount of analysis alone can prevent my manias and depressions. I need both," said one of Dr. Goodwin's patients.[32]

Even when they are helped by medication, people may continue to believe they should have been able to handle things without medication. The people I spoke with who *weren't* in therapy when they started medication—and they were certainly in the minority—had the most difficulty in contending with side effects *and* with accepting that their illness was biologically based. They continued to feel that had they tried a little harder or had they done this thing or that differently, they would not have become ill. Even when the medication was clearly working, they kept believing they should go off it. When faced with disagreement in their choice of treatment by their friends or family, their struggle was all the more difficult because they didn't have a therapist to support them.

In the minds of some, the stigma of suffering from a "mental illness" is replaced by the stigma of having to take a pill to be well. Or, paradoxically, they may feel that by taking the medical approach (which Goodwin says is *"the major real control a person can exert over his illness")* they have given up control or that they had absolutely no involvement in their becoming well. A therapist can help to resolve these conflicts.

The more severe the illness, the more important therapy is. It is almost always indicated for the treatment of bipolar disorder, for example. Bipolar disorder can be particularly disruptive to a person's relationships, self-esteem, and self-image. Manic episodes are especially distressing and often result in social embarrassment. "Medications can control the symptoms, but psychotherapy is necessary to understand the stresses of the illness, to work out the problems created by the disorder, and to re-establish the relationships and healthy self-image that have been shaken by the illness," Fred Goodwin explains in *Manic Depressive Illness*, a new and extremely readable textbook.[33]

Bipolar disorder reduces self-esteem, disrupts relationships, and may lead to secondary alcoholism and drug abuse, economic chaos, hospitalizations, and lost jobs. "Contending with such a reality understandably rouses people to anger," Goodwin explains. "The anger can lead people to reject an effective treatment irrationally."

Here one of Dr. Goodwin's patients describes his feelings about his illness: "People expect that you will welcome being 'normal,' be appreciative of lithium, doctors, and modern science, and take in stride having normal energy and sleep. But if you are used to sleeping only five hours a night and now sleep eight, are used to staying up all night for days and weeks in a row and now cannot, it is a very real adjustment to blend into a three-piece-suit schedule which, while comfortable for many, is new, restrictive, seemingly less productive, and for sure less fun. People say, when I complain of being less lively, less energetic, 'Well, now you're just like the rest of us,' meaning, among other things, to be reassuring. What they don't realize is that I compare myself with my former self, not with others. Not only that, I always compare myself with the best I have been, which is when I have been hypomanic. When I am my present 'normal' self, I am far removed from when I have been my liveliest, most productive, most intense, most outgoing and effervescent. In short, for myself, I am a hard act to follow."[34]

It becomes clear that people with bipolar disorder have special needs for psychotherapy. The illness is by no means easy to manage: It tends to begin when people are young, and the degree of its disruptiveness is frightening. It is easy, after the first manic episode, to want to deny the illness. Young people, especially, find it difficult to accept that they may have to stay on medication, maintain a regular sleep schedule, and avoid drugs and alcohol. Once the episode is treated and they return to a normal state, they want to believe it's over. Things that remind them of their illness become annoying. They don't want to be sick; they want to be well. Well people don't take medicine every day. And yet, if someone who's had a manic episode stops taking medication, there's a very high risk of becoming ill again—and far sooner and more seriously than if they were taking the drug.

There is also the issue of control. No one particularly *likes* the feeling of having to be on medication and even then not being able to be positive one will stay well. Young people are likely to feel helpless with an episodic illness. Rather than learning to accept the reality of their bipolar disorder, they may have a great need to deny. Parents and friends, wanting to be on their side, may unwittingly support them in their denial. For various reasons, psychotherapy can play a valuable role. In fact, most experts on bipolar disorder would rather not see patients try to make it on medication alone. As Fred Goodwin of the NIMH notes in his book *Manic Depressive Illness*, "Formal psychotherapy is extremely beneficial to many manic-depressive people and unquestionably essential for many others, especially those who are suicidal or unwilling to take medication in the manner prescribed."

Again, younger patients are more likely to try taking their medication in some self-devised fashion. Some don't like having to take their pills in the presence of others and so may avoid doses prescribed at mealtimes. Steven would do this when he was at college. As you'll recall from chapter 6, he would stop taking his lithium for a day or two before a weekend date, thinking he could in this way make it less risky to drink alcohol. Soon he was down to taking his medication several days a week. The issues Steven was struggling with would have been easier to deal with had he had the help of a therapist. He wanted to avoid therapy, however, because he felt it would be a constant reminder of his illness. "I'm trying to put this behind me," he said. His mother did her best to encourage him, but she also sympathized with his wish to be "normal." She probably had that same wish for him herself.

Stress is a precipitant of both mania and depression. The better an individual is able to handle, or avoid, stress, the greater his chance of leading a relatively stable life. Therapy teaches people to handle stress. It also helps them explore the meaning the illness has for them. Both patients and their families benefit by ongoing education about the natural course of the illness and discussions of the risks and benefits of the medication. As one patient explained, "Lithium prevents my seductive but disastrous highs, diminishes my depressions, clears out the wool and webbing from my disordered thinking, slows me down, gentles me out, keeps me from ruining my career and relationships, keeps me out of a hospital, alive, and makes psychotherapy possible. But psychotherapy *heals*. It makes some sense of the confusion, reins in the terrifying thoughts and feelings, returns some control and hope and possibility of learning from it all."[35]

Also, the early signs of a manic episode can be so subtle—slight agitation or grandiosity or difficulty in sleeping—it may take an expert to recognize them. Once these signs occur, symptoms often progress rapidly into a full-blown manic episode. If the patient is seeing a therapist regularly, the chances are best for quick intervention.

Experts Who Can Help

Even psychiatrists rarely keep up to date on pharmacology, which is a highly specialized field. If possible, it's best to find a psycho-pharmacologist, which is a psychiatrist specializing in treatment with drugs. Medical schools are a good source for referrals. Friends, family, and your physician may be able to provide you with information as well.

Once you've located a psychopharmacologist, you'll need to determine whether he or she is willing to explain and justify the suggested treatment approach. It's your right to be fully informed about your treatment. As Jack Gorman points out, "A good psychiatrist knows how to simplify things sufficiently—without being condescending—so that a patient can understand how the various drugs recommended work."[36] The doctor should also be able and willing to explain all the possible alternatives to drug treatment and why they were not chosen.

The doctor should schedule regular office visits to follow up on the medication and make himself or an associate available on a twenty-four-hour, year-round basis in case of emergency. It's a terrible feeling to experience an unexpected or frightening side effect and find that you can't reach your doctor immediately. But this isn't something you should *have* to experience: As Gorman succinctly states, "If your doctor is hard to get hold of, switch to a different doctor."[37]

Finding a Therapist

There are three types of licensed therapists: psychiatrists, psychologists, and social workers. Psychiatrists are medical doctors. Among the various types of health practitioners that treat mood disorders, only psychiatrists are licensed—and qualified—to prescribe medication.

Psychologists do graduate work in clinical psychology after college and usually complete a one-year internship in which they evaluate and treat patients. They are often qualified to make diagnoses and conduct psychotherapy.

Social workers have masters of social work degrees (M.S.W.), which usually requires two years of training and working with patients. Many do extra training in psychotherapy after getting the M.S.W. degree.

Unfortunately, there is no legal definition of "psychotherapist" in most states. Anyone who chooses to can call himself a psychotherapist regardless of whether or not he's completed any training in the area. It's probably best to avoid a therapist who is not a psychiatrist, psychologist, or M.S.W., as there is no way to tell whether he is experienced and good at what he does. Credentials, of course, don't guarantee effectiveness, but at least they tell you the person's been trained.

Finding a therapist who is familiar with the biological aspects of mood disorders and with whom one will feel comfortable can be difficult. Friends, family members, and/or your doctor may be able to provide referrals. Almost every community in the country has a community mental health center. They are mandated by the state, county, or other municipalities to provide high-quality mental health care to anyone regardless of ability to pay. Community health centers usually have lists of private-practice psychiatrists as well and will be glad to make a referral. Another resource is the National Depressive and Manic Depressive Association, whom you can contact in writing. (Their address is listed in appendix F at the end of the book.)

If you'd prefer a therapist who is male or female, don't be afraid to specify. Many therapists also identify themselves as serving blacks, Hispanics, and other ethnic groups and as being affirmative of gay and lesbian orientation.

Don't be reluctant to interview more than one therapist or psychopharmacologist until you find someone you're comfortable with. You may be surprised at how easily you can select one over the others, and it's important to work with someone you trust. After going through all available channels to get the best possible referrals, consult with as many specialists as you have to—and trust your instincts.[38]

Coping with Side Effects

Like most other medications, antidepressants can have annoying side effects. Some produce some weight gain; some, difficulties with dry mouth or constipation; and some have sedating effects.

Since many of these side effects are also *symptoms* of depression, it can be difficult to tell whether they're caused by the medication or by the illness. Only a physician experienced in administering psychotropic medications will be able to distinguish symptoms from side effects.

It isn't possible to know in advance whether a particular drug will produce intolerable side effects in a particular patient or if it will cause no side effects at all. This can be very frustrating to both patient and doctor.

Fortunately, side effects are not often so severe that switching to another drug becomes necessary. "The worst problem I had was dry mouth, which caused the corners of my mouth to crack," Eileen Fitzpatrick told us. "Since I use my voice in psychotherapy and teaching, it was a problem for me." But Eileen felt that the benefits she gains from antidepressants are greater than the nuisance of side effects or having to take pills every day. "I have too much to lose by going into a slump," she says.

What the question comes down to is this: Is the therapeutic effect of a particular medication worth putting up with its side effects? Usually, the answer is yes.[39] Also, it's important to remember that those side effects that do occur generally diminish in intensity over time.

Weight gain is a common side effect of many antidepressants. It's not clear why they have this effect, nor can it be predicted who is more likely to gain weight. Not everyone gains when they take these medications, however, although people who are already overweight when they begin treatment tend to gain more than those who are not. What is clear, though, is that the gain is usually caused by the medication, *not* by overeating. As Jack Gorman points out, "Many psychiatric drugs produce weight gain, *even if the patient does not eat a lot*"[40] (emphasis mine).

While those who've lost too much weight as a result of depression may appreciate the addition of a few pounds, most people find weight gain one of the more troubling side effects of antidepressants. If the possibility of gaining weight concerns you, keep in mind that if you do gain weight, the amount may be negligible. Both exercise and careful restriction of your diet can help, as they do for anyone who needs to lose weight. Also, when your treatment ends, you'll lose any weight you may have gained as a result of the antidepressants.

214

The weight gain may simply be the natural result of the lifting of depression—and, consequently, the return of normal appetite. Or it might be caused by water retention, changes in metabolism, and/or reduced thyroid function.[41] MAOIs can cause edema (swelling due to water retention) of the legs and ankles, contributing to the weight gain. Sometimes diuretics may be prescribed for this, although Drs. Jonathan O. Cole and J. Alexander Bodkin of McLean Hospital report they are not likely to be helpful.[42]

Those with bulimia may dread the thought of gaining even a little weight. If you feel this way, try to keep in mind that the extreme fear of gaining weight is part of the illness. When treatment is successful, the fear disappears along with the urge to binge.

Weight that's gained due to antidepressant treatment can be lost only through diet and exercise. Exercise is a good idea anyway, since it increases natural endorphins and helps to relieve depression. (If you aren't already on an exercise program, it's probably a good idea to start one—even if you don't have a weight problem.) If you do need to diet, avoid extreme methods, such as liquid diets, as they may affect the way your body metabolizes the antidepressant and they lower serotonin levels.

Should weight gain become a serious problem, it's possible to try changing medications. However, there is *no guarantee* that a different antidepressant will be effective. If your current antidepressant is relieving your depression, you'll have to give careful consideration to whether the possibility of losing the excess weight is worth the very real risk that changing to another medication may cause the depression to return.

Most tricyclic antidepressants partially block the reuptake of the mood-regulating neurotransmitter acetylcholine. This effect is called *anticholinergic*. However, because acetylcholine is also involved in various functions of the body (such as the digestive system and the focusing of the eyes), the anticholinergic action often results in some unwanted side effects. However, when they do occur, they tend to get better with time, as the body gradually adjusts to the medication.

Constipation and dry mouth are the most common of these side effects. Sugarless gum or sour candies stimulate the flow of saliva and can be taken to relieve the dry mouth. Constipation

215

can usually be relieved by taking a bulk laxative, such as Metamucil or psyllium fiber (available in health food stores), and drinking plenty of fluids.[43]

In some people, tricyclic antidepressants cause a variety of urinary problems, including, in extreme cases, complete urinary retention.[44] They usually occur in older men with prostate problems. A man who has trouble emptying his bladder after starting on an antidepressant should stop taking the medication and immediately call his doctor. In this case, it will probably be necessary to switch to a different medication.[45]

MAOIs generally have fewer anticholinergic effects, but some patients treated with these agents develop dry mouth, constipation, and even difficulties in urinating. However, these particular side effects are substantially less common with MAOIs than with the TCAs.[46]

Sedation may occur with certain cyclic antidepressants and MAOIs as well as some of the newer antidepressants. When depression causes insomnia, this side effect can actually be helpful. While tolerance to sedating effects usually develops, it can take quite a while. Unwanted sedation may be reduced by taking the full dose of medication at bedtime, but if it is both persistent and severe, it may be necessary to change medications.[47] Interestingly, trazodone (Desyrel), a rather poor antidepressant but very effective sedative, may be prescribed when insomnia is a problem.

Other antidepressants are somewhat stimulating, which may be helpful to those who feel lethargic and/or sleep too much.[48] Of course, this wouldn't be desirable for someone suffering from insomnia. In this case, trazodone might be prescribed, or another antidepressant might be tried. When deciding which medication to prescribe, the psychopharmacologist should take the patient's sleep patterns into account.

All antidepressants may occasionally cause such *sexual problems* as decreased libido, inhibited or painful ejaculation, or erectile impotence. Delayed orgasm is the most common of these side effects and seems to be more likely with MAOIs and Prozac than with other antidepressants.

Certain medications may be helpful in relieving sexual dysfunction, but the problem may disappear spontaneously over time.[49] Mark H. Pollack, M.D., and Jerrold F. Rosenbaum, M.D., report that some of their patients who had experienced delayed orgasm "for over a year eventually achieved normal sexual response with no medical intervention or loss of therapeutic benefit."[50] The best method of managing these problems may be "to reassure the patient that these effects are medically benign and to wait for them to resolve with time."[51]

MAOIs frequently cause episodes of faintness or dizziness, called *orthostatic* or *postural hypotension,* which are caused by a drop in blood pressure upon standing. This is one of the most frequent side effects of MAOIs. It may lead to fainting, giddiness, muscular weakness, and tachycardia as well as nausea, perspiration, hyperventilation, and possibly confusion. Rarely, and then usually in the elderly, fractures can occur from falling. These symptoms are potentially worse on awakening, when blood pressure is normally at its lowest.[52]

As do most other antidepressant side effects, postural hypotension usually improves over time. It can be reduced by taking care when standing up, being especially careful to get out of bed slowly in the morning, and sitting on the edge of the bed for a few moments before rising.[53] You can also try exercise to strengthen calf muscles, which may prevent pooling of blood in the legs, or you might try wearing supportive (i.e., firm and snugly fitting) hosiery that goes over the calf. Keeping hydrated by drinking plenty of fluids also helps.

If feelings of faintness do occur, they can be relieved promptly by immediately sitting or lying down.

If hypotension continues to be a problem, the following strategies may be helpful (although, of course, you should check with your psychopharmacologist first):

- Divide the total dose into several administrations throughout the day.
- Take doses after meals.
- Take salt tablets.

Also, your psychopharmacologist may prescribe medication to raise your blood pressure for a few weeks or months, until the hypotension remits.

Virtually all the antidepressants can, on rare occasions, cause *mania* or *hypomania* (a milder form of mania) even in patients not previously known to have bipolar illness. Why this happens is not certain, though it's now suspected that the problem only occurs in patients who are actually suffering from bipolar disorder but who have not yet experienced a manic episode.

Antidepressants readily cross the placenta and should be avoided in *pregnancy*, at least during the first trimester. In those patients for whom treatment through pregnancy can't be avoided, it is prudent to discontinue the drug well before conception is anticipated and resume after the first trimester.

The most troublesome aspect of MAOI therapy is the so called cheese reaction, or *hypertensive crisis*. If you're taking MAOIs, foods high in tyramine can cause a hypertensive crisis—a sharp elevation of blood pressure. The effect can also be caused by a wide variety of medications. Although it's rare, it can be a frightening experience.

However, MAOIs are basically safe, since the foods and medications that might cause a problem are well known (see Appendix D for a list of restricted foods and medications). When you begin treatment on an MAOI, your doctor will provide you with a list of what you need to avoid—be sure to adhere to it strictly! He or she should also provide you with medication, Procardia, to carry with you in the event that you accidentally ingest something that causes a hypertensive reaction. (For a more complete discussion of MAOIs and this side effect, see appendix C.)

Discontinuing MAOIs abruptly may result in a *withdrawal syndrome* virtually indistinguishable from relapse of depression. In extreme cases, it can result in severe anxiety, agitation, pressured speech, sleeplessness or drowsiness, hallucinations, delirium, and paranoid psychosis.[54] Therefore, it's essential that the dosage be tapered off slowly.[55] *Never* decide on your own to stop taking your medication!

Benzodiazepines (such as Xanax, Valium, Librium, and Ativan) are by far the drugs most often prescribed to treat anxiety problems. They provoke heated debate, with some clinicians believing they are relatively harmless and others considering them potentially addictive.

In fact, *tolerance* to benzodiazepines (tolerance involves the need to increase the dosage to maintain the effect) is uncommon, according to Jack Gorman.[56] However, a definite withdrawal syndrome does occur. In a sense, says Gorman, "patients get 'hooked' on benzodiazepines." He feels the term *addiction* doesn't apply, though, since addiction usually refers to a strong, totally consuming compulsion to take the drug. Medically, it's correct to say that benzodiazepines produce both physical and psychological *dependence*. "Once you take them, it is important to try to keep the dose low, and stop as quickly as possible," says Gorman. The higher the dose, *and* the longer a person has taken benzodiazepines, the worse will be the withdrawal once the drug is stopped. Very potent benzodiazepines (Klonopin, Xanax, and Ativan) are likely to cause more severe withdrawal.

People who abuse other drugs, especially alcohol, have a harder time stopping benzodiazepines than people who don't abuse drugs.

Withdrawal symptoms will be more severe if the medications are stopped abruptly. Extremely rapid heart beat, insomnia, nausea, depressed mood, and, in rare cases, severe depression or psychosis are among the possibilities. Therefore, it's extremely important that medication be tapered slowly. As Michael Gitlin states, "There is virtually no clinical reason to abruptly stop a benzodiazepine."[57] Depending on the dosage and duration of treatment, it can take as long as four to six months to slowly taper the medication.

"*Lithium* is closely related to sodium (salt), and the body handles it much the same way," Mondimore explains.[58] Like sodium, lithium is excreted through the kidneys, and many of its side effects are similar to those that would occur if you upped your salt intake: increased thirst, urination, and water retention (edema). However, the body often adjusts to the new "salt/water balance," and the symptoms subside. Diuretics should *not* be taken unless under your doctor's supervision, as they can increase the concentration of lithium in the blood, potentially causing lithium toxicity.

Lithium can irritate the stomach and digestive system, and some patients experience nausea and/or diarrhea. These symptoms can be avoided, or at least reduced, by taking the medication immediately before or after meals. If the problem persists, it may be possible to switch to a slow-releasing form of lithium, which tends to be less irritating.

Lithium may also cause a fine tremor, usually of the hands, which can be exacerbated by anxiety or nervousness. In fact, Mondimore reports that many of his patients only notice this problem at such times. Usually the side effect is not a significant problem, but when it is, other medications can be prescribed to lessen it.

Some patients experience slight changes in memory and their ability to concentrate. Fortunately, such effects seem to be dosage related and will often improve if the dose of lithium is lowered.

Lithium is *not safe* to take during pregnancy, particularly during the first trimester, when major fetal development takes place. Studies have shown that lithium taken during pregnancy significantly increases the chances of birth defects. If lithium is administered postpartum (a high-risk period for the development of mania), breast-feeding is contraindicated, as lithium is excreted in breast milk. If medication is necessary during pregnancy, carbamazepine may be a better choice, as it appears less likely to cause birth defects. Preliminary data show it to be "a relatively benign drug with little systematic evidence of consistent fetal malformations when administered throughout pregnancy."[59] There is also no evidence that antipsychotic drugs cause birth defects, so if a manic episode occurs during pregnancy, they may be used with relative safety.

LITHIUM TOXICITY

The most serious side effects of lithium treatment is toxicity. Dehydration, in particular, can cause lithium to become too concentrated in the bloodstream. For this reason, those taking it should drink plenty of water to avoid becoming dehydrated, particularly in hot weather. Patients need to be familiar with the signs of toxicity so that they can seek immediate treatment should it occur. These symptoms include fatigue and lethargy, clouded thinking and impaired concentration, severe nausea and vomiting, dizziness, muscle weakness, slurred speech, and unsteady gait.[60]

Physicians should tell their patients about lithium's side effects and signs of toxicity.

Family and Friends Can Help

There's a lot of information to take in while discussing treatment strategy with your psychopharmacologist. When you're depressed, it can be difficult to digest it all. It may even be confusing or a little frightening. It helps to have a close friend or family member present for reassurance and to take note of what's discussed. That way, he or she can remind you if you've forgotten anything later on.

Also, the symptoms of depression (such as unrealistic hopelessness or withdrawal from communication) may make it impossible for you to be receptive to the information your doctor gives you. Friends or relatives can ask any questions you might overlook. And they can be more supportive of your recovery when they've heard the details of your treatment firsthand.

Once treatment with antidepressants begins, sleep and appetite may improve before changes in mood occur. When someone is depressed, he or she may not notice such changes. Family members can be very helpful in identifying, to both the patient and the treating psychiatrist or psychopharmacologist, early signs that the antidepressant is working. "Without hearing from this family member, the patient and the doctor might miss the early evidence of a positive drug effect and prematurely discontinue medication," explains Jack Gorman, M.D., author of *The Essential Guide to Psychiatric Drugs.*[61]

Family members may also be able to report side effects to the doctor, if they occur, since if the patient is feeling bad to begin with she may not consider a rash or nausea significant.

According to Bob Hausman, the director of a therapy center in upstate New York that provides treatment for the family members of people suffering from depression and other disorders, "Given the right tools, the family can help enormously. Actually, the family is part of the same team as the psychiatrist and whomever else may be working with the patient."

On the other hand, when *not* well informed about your treatment and your illness in general, family members can be counterproductive, unintentionally hindering your recovery. So it's important that they know as much as possible about your illness.

Someone who's depressed not only has to deal with her own worries about medication; she often faces negative, dissuading comments from her friends, family, and even relative strangers. While well intentioned, their concerns are often misguided and even potentially harmful to the person who's trying to get well. If you learned you had cancer, you'd hardly expect a friend to question whether you really needed to have chemotherapy or radiation treatment. Or to suggest your "negative outlook" had caused the cancer so what you really need is to see a therapist!

Yet when it comes to depression, people often give just this sort of advice. "Have you tried changing your diet?" they may suggest, or, "Maybe you should switch therapists." They may even go so far as to say, "Well, when I've felt depressed, I just get myself out of the house and take a long walk, and that usually takes care of it." Such comments can lead someone suffering from true depression to believe that their illness isn't serious enough to require medical intervention.

As Dr. Priscilla Slagle notes, "When you pressure a depressed person to 'think positive,' it's almost as if you're insisting he speak to you in Latin, and he becomes even more guilt-ridden and helpless. 'I can't think any of the positive thoughts other people are talking about. Something terrible is wrong with me. I am bad. I am hopeless.' And the cycle continues."[62]

By beginning antidepressant treatment, one is taking steps to be *in control* of the illness. Once that decision's been made, it's important to elicit support from people and to either challenge or dismiss those who react negatively. Once treatment has begun, try to keep in mind that you've made a medical decision about your health and that when it comes to the best treatment *for you*, the final decision is yours.

When It Happens to Someone You Love

Little is more disconcerting than the peculiar twilight zone of a conversation with someone who's depressed. It can be like dangling expectantly at the top of a seesaw while the other person sits at the bottom, refusing to budge. You call out, you wave your arms and jump up and down, but there he sits, grim-faced and noncommunicative. *Why is he angry?* You wonder if you've done something wrong, but there's also something infuriating about the situation.

"Whenever we talked, I would get the feeling that I was disappointing John," said a woman we interviewed, describing her experience with her husband before she learned of his depression. "There would be these gaps. I would try to fill them. I thought, Is it me? What's going on here?"

Having not the least idea what was going on, Ellen felt guilty. *She* became anxious as she tried pumping up their flat discussions with her own energy. What bothered her most was the creepy feeling that John *knew* what was going on—knew and took gratification from it. "I found myself feeling paranoid, as if he were manipulating this whole thing and as if I had no real leverage."

It is easy to feel victimized by a loved one who's depressed. In fact, John had little real sense of what Ellen was going through. He was too overwhelmed by his own state to be able to have much sensitivity toward hers.

We've been taught to equate feeling sad with depression and believe that we could easily muster up some empathy for a friend or spouse who was feeling sad. But this is not the effect depressed people tend to have on us. They rarely seem sad. What they seem is down or dark or flat and feelingless. And we sometimes find ourselves feeling quite annoyed—as if they were *doing* something to us.

Depression, psychiatrists recognize, is more akin to emotional limbo, as if all feelings were on hold. Even people who cry a lot will say they don't feel sad. What they feel is empty. And this empty state is baffling to others, who wonder why *they* are beginning to feel so empty.

What becomes very apparent in someone who's depressed is lack of interest. There is no curiosity. Nothing excites. The person doesn't seem to be taking in much from the world around him or her. This bland insularity can come across as criticalness. A friend who recently was visiting us for the weekend seemed strangely aloof. She seemed not to be initiating conversations but only responding, and not with much enthusiasm. "What's wrong?" I said. "Oh, nothing," she replied. She said she was going to get some sun, but she continued to sit in the shade, thumbing listlessly through a newspaper. I suggested going to a play, but she demurred, commenting that she didn't like the playwright. A group of African musicians playing at a local club seemed to spark a little interest, but when we arrived, something about the place "turned her off," and she wanted to leave. I found myself growing desperate to produce something that would excite her when it occurred to me suddenly: "She's depressed!" I'd spent three days on the up end of the seesaw waiting for some movement on her part before figuring out what the problem was.

No matter how much you know about depression, it can still be difficult to identify in a friend or a loved one. The most reliable clues can come from observing our own reactions. Depression, in someone we're close to, pushes all our buttons. We feel criticized and become annoyed. In conversation, it is we who have to do all the work. And there's that maddening lack of facial expression— *"le masque,"* the French call it, and it seems precisely right. That immobile face seems to take some dark delight from refusing us a response.

It's easy to feel manipulated by someone who's depressed. A psychoanalyst wrote a long and quite brilliant paper putting forth his theory that the essence of "the depressive position," as he called it, is its aggression. He argued that the whole point of depression is to force others to respond, to pay attention, to pay over the love and approval that have been withheld for so long. He described their "demandingness" as hostile and exploitative. Rather than filling up the empty hole within themselves, they were always aggressively trying to get it filled by someone else.

When I first read this paper ten years ago, I found fascinating its idea that the depressed are being quite pushy with us. I'd certainly had that feeling. (Haven't we all?) The next time someone tried to pull it on me, I wouldn't buckle under.

Today I'd say that no matter how exquisitely argued, that paper missed the boat. The mood-disordered person isn't trying to push anyone's buttons. He's closed up and incommunicative because of his brain chemistry. When we feel upset by him, it may be because of our own needs. Instead of accepting that our depressed friend is incapable of good conversation, we scurry and perform, trying to get the response that makes *us* feel comfortable. When that doesn't happen, we feel disregarded, even abused.

It's best, while this illness prevails, not to expect too much from the suffering individual. Others may need to assume responsibility. Depression is an illness that can leave its victim unable to seek help. When this is the case, others must take over. Later, when the patient is feeling better, he or she can begin to take responsibility.

Stepping In

Perhaps the most important thing family and friends can do is encourage the depressed person to get treatment. The very nature of depression—its feelings of hopelessness and worthlessness—can make those it afflicts too immobilized to take the steps required to get better. Which makes them feel even worse.

When symptoms linger—even if there seems to be an event that triggered them—help is needed, and the caring friend or relative should seek out a professional. I used to think this would be intrusive and unappreciated until my experience with Gabrielle. Since then, I've offered to get referrals and make appointments for others. With one friend, I went along to the doctor and waited in the waiting room. Those who are depressed, I've found, are grateful for an offer of help. On some level, they know they need it.

Depression destroys self-esteem and confidence, and family and friends can help the depressed person feel worthwhile by providing love, support, and encouragement. It isn't always easy to know the best way to do this, however. The NIMH has set forth some guidelines that I've found helpful.[63]

The first thing is to try to maintain as normal a relationship as possible. It's important to spend time with the person and not to accede to his or her wish to withdraw. Telephone frequently and don't be satisfied with leaving a message on the answering machine. The idea is to get the person to engage with you, not just to let him or her know that you're concerned.

It's helpful to acknowledge that your friend or loved one is suffering and in pain. It isn't necessary to say, "I know just how you feel." You may not know how the person feels, especially if you haven't been there yourself. On the other hand, you may say, "I know depression is an illness that makes people feel really terrible. I'm so sorry this is happening to you, but there's treatment available that can make you feel better again." Communicating your conviction that help is available and that the person *will* feel better is extremely important. The self-doubt that is symptomatic of depression spills over into pessimism about things ever being any different. You have to push through that pessimism. Of course, optimism can't be faked. If you need reassurance, speak, yourself, to the psychiatrist or therapist you're thinking of recommending to your loved one. When I called the psychiatrist in New York to make an appointment for Gabrielle, I had a lengthy conversation with a knowledgeable assistant who was so firm in her own conviction that Gabrielle could be helped I called Gabrielle immediately and said, "They say they can help you, and I'm sure that they can."

There is no time like now for kind words and compliments, even if they seem to fall on deaf ears. Remember, this is an illness that diminishes people's ability to *respond.* So don't expect the usual reactions; just keep offering encouragement and kindness and ignore the feeling that you're dropping your pennies into a bottomless barrel. Your caring is getting through.

Again, and this may seem obvious, express your affection openly. Show that you value and respect the depressed person. This is something that needs to be verbalized because the illness is preventing them from feeling good about themselves. The idea, then, is not "How could you feel so low when you've tallied up so many accomplishments in your life?" That may be the very question he's asking himself. The point is, he *does* feel low. He needs you to remind him that this horrible mood is *separate* from who he is, his accomplishments, his character, his goodness. Feeling rotten about himself is a symptom that will go away, like a fever in the night, once he gets treatment.

Here are some important caveats. Blaming the depressed person for his or her condition is harmful. As by now you must have gathered, people do not cause their mood disorders. In the same vein, it's important not to do anything that will exacerbate your friend's poor self-image. Refrain from criticizing or voicing disapproval. Believe me, you may be tempted, particularly if it's a spouse or child who's ill. Messy disorder and even personal slovenliness are a hallmark of this illness. Curtail any desire you may have to say, "Darling, your hair is filthy." Or, "Can't you do something about that room?" You may, however, say, "Let's the two of us go to the hairdresser together," or, "How would you like it if I gave you a massage and a shampoo?" or, "I know you haven't had the energy to clean. I'd like to clean for you."

The bottom line is to do whatever you can to help your friend or loved one feel better, and to be firm in your conviction that the illness can be treated.

Epilogue

....

Is There Life After Medication?

Perhaps it is some peculiar part of our Puritan heritage that we struggle to make do, to grin and bear it, although I am more inclined to think that it is within the nature of the illnesses discussed in this book that we are made too lethargic by them to want to fight for a better life. Ill, we focus on the good days and deny the bad. Ill, we insist on getting A's, and if we can't get them will avoid school, not understanding that that A-need is symptomatic of a mood disorder, one that will keep us living a narrow, underachieving life if we don't get help. Ill, we can't think straight—are too anxious and/or depressed—to study, to read, to write. The struggle to do these things is so painful that we avoid them. It makes us feel stupid to be told constantly how bright we are when we are unable to do the things people expect of us. What is wrong? We try to think about the good times and dismiss the bad. We hope to fall in love. We eat excessively; we drink. We live promiscuously, in desperation. We rock-climb, overspend, work fourteen hours a day, and do cocaine in the bathroom in order to keep going. In short, we suffer, and the worst part is, we *expect* to suffer; we have come to think it is our due.

Some of the people whose stories have been told here are fortunate. For various reasons, they have gotten the help they needed, and their lives have been fundamentally changed as a result. Margaret continues to be drug-free and is supporting herself for the first time. She is living in her own apartment in Berlin and working as a gaffer and lighting assistant on rock concert productions. She still talks to her therapist on the telephone from time to time and to her mother, who says Margaret has never sounded so grounded and happy.

Nikka, whose experience with depression first prompted me to seek medical treatment for Gabrielle, has recently moved to a studio apartment in New York. She is interested in doing comedy and has been accepted as a student at the American Academy of Dramatic Arts.

Gabrielle does research and writing on health care and has a computer consulting business. Recently, she heard from Jim Dailey, whom she interviewed for this book, and whose depression-related cognitive problems are described in chapter 3. He wrote, "I had a real breakthrough six weeks ago. All my life, since early grade school, I've had to struggle with certain kinds of tasks, principally writing, that people said should be easy for me. It's been torture, and my success has been rather limited. I've been depressed most of my life, and on antidepressants for most of the last ten years. I'm forty-three." Several months ago, Jim decided to consult a new psychiatrist. This doctor "followed a hunch" and worked him up to a fairly high dose of Nardil, 90 mg/day. "Even at 75 mg/day," Jim writes, "there was no effect, but at 90, my problem with writing vanished! I can sit down at the keyboard and work productively from the start, instead of being stuck and baffled for hours on end. My mood has lifted considerably with the easing of the struggle to force thoughts out of my head. It's as if my right brain has been on standby all along and now it's come on-line." Jim says that while he's been treated by some good psychiatrists, "only this man, an older physician about to retire, had this particular experience and insight. I'm extremely fortunate to have found him. To fellow sufferers, I'd say: Don't give up, and don't assume your present doctor knows all there is to know. If he's not getting results after a reasonable time, consider trying someone else."

Steven finished up his school year in Canada and decided to go to Israel to complete his undergraduate education. He is happy and productive, but is taking his lithium only several times a week and is seeing neither a therapist nor a doctor. Home for a visit at midyear, Steven went to see his New York psychopharmacologist at his mother's prodding. She was worried that he wasn't taking enough medication. The doctor said that while he wouldn't advise Steven to take lithium on a less than a daily basis, over the years he had had several patients who had managed to do what Steven was doing and had not become manic again. Esther told the doctor that since he'd gone to Israel, Steven had stopped having his lithium levels tested. The doctor said there was no point in having his blood tested, since he wasn't taking enough lithium to keep the proper amount in his blood anyway. Somehow, both Steven and Esther left this consultation feeling they'd gotten tacit permission for Steven to continue underdosing himself.

Statistically, *most* people who've had one manic episode will have another at some point in the future, and this is far more likely to occur in people who aren't taking adequate medication. Psychopharmacologists need to offer psychological support as well as to educate their patients about the nature and course of their illnesses. Gabrielle and I worry about Steven. We remember the day when, sitting in my studio by the stream, he told us of his harrowing experiences with mania and depression. We remember his terror, his visions of God, his description of being straitjacketed. In remembering, we wonder what possibly could have been going on in that psychopharmacologist's mind to have suggested that *some* people with manic depression have gotten by, at least for a while, without taking any medication. Did he forget the narcissism of the typical adolescent, who finds it virtually impossible to believe that he will not transcend? Or had the doctor, in reporting to Steven and his mother the "facts" of his practice, lost touch with his heart?

Lest any reader take this book to be a one-sided push for pills (I would hope the previous chapter would disabuse anyone of that notion), let Steven's story make it finally clear that therapy and psychoeducation are important handmaidens of pharmacology. Mood, anxiety, and addiction disorders are serious illnesses, with the potential to destroy lives. That is the reason biopsychiatry is exciting; it offers hope and happiness to those who otherwise would not have had them. But, essential as medicine is for many with these disorders, it is only part of the therapeutic picture. People who have been psychiatrically ill need help in putting their lives together. They need to understand the nature of their illnesses and, perhaps, how other members of their families were—or are—ill in the same way. They need to be helped to see how their thinking has been distorted—*by the illness itself.* They need to be shown that the illness may have cognitive effects, producing tremendous negativity and fearfulness, but that their illness is not their personality: *It is not them.*

Accomplishing this requires therapy, not simply medication. But it requires therapy from someone who understands the biological nature of the illnesses. The practice of therapy, fortunately, is changing as the results of biopsychiatric research are becoming more widely known. Gabrielle and I hope the day will not be far off when therapists would *never* withhold medication from someone with a mood, an anxiety, or an addiction disorder.

By the same token, we hope the day is also not far off when a biopsychiatrist would *never* send a young man who's had a manic episode out into the world without therapy and a mandate to stay on his medication.

Finally, the excitement of biopsychiatry does not reside in the intellectual triumph of recognizing patterns, symptom clusters, lines of related mood disorders stretching back for generations in a single family. The excitement of biopsychiatry has its locus in the ability to improve lives, to provide, as Virginia Hamilton put it (although she was specifically referring to addictions), "a better quality of recovery." What the NIMH study of psychiatric disorders uncovered is that many people are living their lives on the edge from day to day, without knowing that there is more—a better quality of life—to be had. They slog through life, "hanging in," as the saying goes, but barely getting by. And it is not because of poverty per se, or child abuse per se, or misogyny per se, that many find their lives so difficult, but because their neurotransmitters aren't functioning properly—a problem that is correctable with adequate treatment.

Properly functioning neurotransmitters, in rendering us more energetic, can help us to *fight* poverty, child abuse, and misogyny. Biopsychiatry's discoveries may help to improve not only individual lives, but also the society in which we live. By medically correcting faulty neurotransmission, we may end up being able to take a giant step beyond the poverty, violence, and disease that have been endlessly repeated, through the generations. But if this is to happen, the gifts of this scientific revolution must first be recognized.

They then must be administered with wise minds and loving hearts.

Signs of Depression in Children

....

School phobia: complains of feeling unwell, tries to stay home
Not interested in eating (or eating all the time)
Low mood, or "bad" feeling
Avoids or isn't interested in playing with others
Sleep disturbances: napping after school; unable to wake up in
    the morning; or waking and staying awake in the middle of
    the night
Psychomotor retardation: slow speech, slow movements, slow
    thinking, difficulty remembering
Agitation, irritability, anger
Mood volatility (now up, now down)
Hypomania: grandiose, overly confident, delusions of grandeur ("I
    can do anything")
In infants: fretfulness, sleeplessness, failure to thrive

Hudson and Pope's Treatment of Bulimia

In most cases we suggest starting with the antidepressant fluoxetine (Prozac), raising the dose to 60 mg per day by the end of the first week. Although some patients will respond to doses of less than 60 mg per day, bulimic patients are generally young, and capable of metabolizing antidepressants rapidly; hence, it may be wise to use a full 60 mg, except in cases in which patients show difficulty tolerating this dose. Fluoxetine may be given all at once, morning or evening, since the drug has a half-life of several days. Side effects are usually modest with fluoxetine (gastrointestinal upset, sedation, or stimulation being most common) but in a small percentage of patients allergic rash may develop, necessitating discontinuation of the drug and substitution of another medication.

Although controlled data with fluoxetine in bulimia are not available at the time of this writing, the authors' experience suggests that at least 50% of patients will experience a remission or at least a major improvement (greater than 75% reduction in frequency of eating binges) after 21 to 28 days of treatment. For those who show no improvement, or inadequate improvement, lithium carbonate, starting at 300 mg 3 times per day, may be added to fluoxetine and the lithium dose raised to achieve a blood level (measured 12 hours after the previous dose of lithium has

Excerpted from "Pharmacological Treatment of Bulimia Nervosa: Research Findings and Practical Suggestions," by Harrison G. Pope, Jr., M.D., and James I. Hudson, M.D., *Psychiatric Annals* 19 (1989): 483–87.

been administered) of about 1.0 mEq per liter. For patients who still show no improvement after about two weeks of lithium plus fluoxetine treatment, another antidepressant is usually required.

In such cases, fluoxetine and lithium may be stopped abruptly without adverse effects, since both drugs in effect "taper themselves" as they are slowly removed from the central nervous system. A tricyclic antidepressant with a low incidence of side effects, such as desipramine (Norpramin) or nortriptyline (Aventyl), may then be begun immediately and raised to full doses within a week. Since bulimic patients are generally young and metabolize tricyclics rapidly, larger-than-average doses of these drugs may be required: at least 3.5 mg per kg of body weight for desipramine and 1.5 mg per kg for nortriptyline. Because of wide differences in individual metabolism of these drugs, it is important to measure plasma levels after 5 to 7 days of full doses. Desipramine dose should then be adjusted to achieve plasma levels of at least 200 ng per ml; nortriptyline levels should be adjusted to be between 50 and 140 ng per ml. If plasma levels are not determined, a fair number of patients will not receive an adequate trial of tricyclics. . . .

In patients who fail both fluoxetine and a tricyclic trial, a monoamine oxidase inhibitor such as tranylcypromine (Parnate), may succeed where previous drugs have failed. Although manufacturers of MAO inhibitors generally recommend a 14-day washout period between the discontinuation of tricyclics and the MAO inhibitors, many authorities feel that this is not necessary and will administer the later drug within only a few days or even immediately upon discontinuing the tricyclics. However, an MAO inhibitor should not be given until five days after discontinuation of fluoxetine. . . .

As in the case of fluoxetine and tricyclics, young bulimic patients frequently require and tolerate surprisingly large doses of MAO inhibitors, such as 40 to 80 mg per day* of tranylcypromine (Parnate) or 75 to 105 mg per day* of phenelzine (Nardil). Typically, these drugs are started at modest doses (say 10 mg twice daily of tranylcypromine or 15 mg twice daily of phenelzine), with the dose raised every couple of days until the patient notices some lightheadedness. At this point, the dose

*Exceeds the maximum dosage recommended by the manufacturer.

can usually be raised no further, or disabling postural hypotension ensues.

Severe insomnia may occur with tranylcypromine, and to a lesser extent with phenelzine. This can often be treated with trazodone, usually 100 to 400 mg at bedtime. Trazodone sedative rarely causes a "hangover" in the morning, and has clear antidepressant effects of its own. Thus, it may act synergistically with monoamine oxidase inhibitors in the treatment of bulimia. . . .

A substantial majority of bulimic patients will respond to one of the above three sequential antidepressant strategies with either a remission or marked reduction of bulimic symptoms. Another small group of bulimic patients . . . display symptoms of concomitant bipolar disorder and may respond to lithium, carbamazepine, or valproate. Finally, occasional patients refractory to standard medication may respond to anorexigenic drugs, such as fenfluramine (Pondamin). . . .

Groups for women with eating disorders, often organized by local self-help organizations, are available in many areas. These are often inexpensive and offer powerful support and reassurance, particularly to women who have not had a chance to share their experience with fellow sufferers.

MAO Inhibitors and Hypertensive Crises

....

Tyramine is found in a variety of foods, the majority of which are aged proteins. *Anyone*—on MAOIs or not—will experience a rise in blood pressure if enough tyramine is absorbed in the bloodstream. When a person who isn't on MAOIs ingests a tyramine-containing food, the enzyme monoamine oxidase (MAO), which exists in the lining of the intestinal tract and in the liver, metabolizes the tyramine so that very little gets into the bloodstream. But someone on an MAOI, which breaks down the MAO, naturally absorbs more tyramine. Once tyramine is absorbed, it is taken up into the cells, where it releases norepinephrine, and this, in turn, raises the blood pressure. Since MAO metabolizes norepinephrine within the cells, patients on an MAOI have greater stores of norepinephrine to be released, thereby raising the blood pressure even more. These two mechanisms—*the increased absorption of tyramine and the increased release of norepinephrine*—explain why patients on MAOIs can have hypertensive reactions when they ingest foods high in tyramine.

A hypertensive crisis can be prevented by adhering strictly to the prescribed diet. However, if the patient develops a severe headache (on one side of the head), or experiences the sudden onset of rapid heartbeat, it's possible he or she has accidentally eaten food rich in tyramine. If this happens, the patient should immediately ingest the capsule of Procardia provided by his or her physician for just such an emergency.

Characterized by the sudden onset of a severe throbbing headache, the hypertensive crisis is often described by patients as the worst headache they have ever experienced. Other symptoms include flushing and/or profuse perspiration, blurred vision, stiff neck, nausea, and vomiting. The duration and severity of hypertensive reactions vary greatly. Generally, they last less than twenty-four hours, and the symptoms range from mild headache to (extremely rarely) death from intracranial hemorrhage. The symptoms occur between ten minutes and two hours after the ingestion of the tyramine-rich foods.[1]

Gabrielle says her first psychopharmacologist imprudently played down the dietary restrictions when he prescribed an MAOI (Nardil) for her: "He told me, 'Yes, there are a few dietary restrictions. You don't like pickled herring, do you? Most people don't find that a problem. And wine, particularly Chianti. And cheese.' I balked at the mention of cheese. Not only did I love cheese, it was the staple protein of my diet. But, I decided, if it meant not being depressed, I could give it up."

After the doctor's summary of restrictions, Gabrielle was surprised by the list of contraindicated foods and medications given to her by the nurse. Beyond what the doctor had mentioned, there were many more restrictions, including summer sausage, chicken liver, fava beans, ripe figs, sour cream, avocados, soy sauce, bananas, raisins, and chocolate. When she asked the nurse for further information, she was given a technical report that broke down the restricted items into categories: "Foods to Be Avoided," "Foods That Are Questionable: Unlikely to Cause Problems Unless Consumed in Large Quantities," and "Foods Which May Be Used: Evidence Insufficient to Support Exclusion."

What Gabrielle wanted, and should have been given, was a *discussion* of the whole subject, as we're giving it to you here. Unfortunately, patients' justifiable concern about what they may or may not safely eat is sometimes treated as if it's childish or neurotic. A New York psychoanalyst interpreted as "provocative" her patient's wish to know what was meant by an "over-ripe" banana. This, in fact, is a perfectly legitimate concern for someone on an MAOI who wants to avoid a hypertensive crisis: How ripe *is* overripe?

One reason there is so much confusion about which foods are safe and which aren't, according to *The Psychotherapist's Guide to Psychopharmacology*, is that many lists enumerate *all* foods that have ever been reported to cause a reaction. The lists do not distinguish between foods that may have caused a reaction in one individual on one occasion and those likely to cause reactions frequently. Unfortunately, a great number of the foods proscribed have not been extensively analyzed chemically. The major offenders, however, are almost always the same. With only rare exceptions (e.g., broad [fava] bean pods, which contain dopamine), these forbidden foods are *aged proteins*. This is because tyramine is formed as protein ages or ferments.

The list provided in appendix D is a reliable guide to those foods that must be avoided or not consumed in excess (e.g., eating half an avocado *could* be safe, while consuming four avocados is quite likely to provoke a hypertensive reaction). Keep in mind, however, that the effects of those foods that are safe in "moderate" consumption is additive. It would be inadvisable to drink two beers and then eat an avocado with sour cream and a bowl of canned soup!

There are two important things to remember regarding dietary restrictions. One, a food that causes no reaction the first ten times it is eaten can provoke a reaction the eleventh time. With cheese, for example, this happens because every wheel of cheese contains a different amount of tyramine. Also, the amount of tyramine varies greatly, depending on whether the particular slice comes from the rind or the center of the wheel. Thus, there is no way of knowing that any cheese (other than cottage cheese, cream cheese, or fresh ricotta) is safe no matter how many times you may have eaten it in the past without having problems. The best advice, with cheese, is to stay off the stuff if it's aged.

The second thing to remember is that *the quantity of tyramine ingested* is what's important. Four glasses of Chianti (a red wine), for instance, are more likely to provoke a hypertensive reaction than are two ounces. The foods and beverages listed under "to be used in moderation" generally contain a small amount of tyramine. If a lot of these foods are eaten, however, a hypertensive reaction is possible.

There is also a group of medications listed in appendix D that can provoke hypertensive episodes in patients taking MAOIs. With the exception of the two opiates, meperidine (Demerol) and dextromethorphan (found in many cold/cough medicines and usually labeled DM), these medications are all stimulants and provoke hypertension by the increased release of norepinephrine (as explained earlier). Tyramine is not a factor with the medication-induced reactions.

The most dangerous drugs are cold medications, which are often sold over the counter. There are a few safe cold tablets that are *pure antihistamines*, but most cold preparations (such as Dristan and Contac) contain decongestants, which can easily provoke a hypertensive episode.

Sometimes one formulation of a certain medication will be safe, but another will contain added ingredients that are not. For example, I recently took Benadryl Plus, thinking it was just a stronger version of regular Benadryl. After a sleepless night, I discovered it contained pseudoephedrine, a decongestant, in addition to the diphenhydramine found in regular Benadryl. For me, the result was just a lack of sleep, but had Gabrielle made this simple mistake, she would very likely have had a hypertensive crisis. A good general rule is: *Call your psychopharmacologist before taking any new medication* and be sure to read the list of ingredients on the package.

Food Restrictions for Patients on MAO Inhibitors

....

FOODS AND BEVERAGES TO AVOID COMPLETELY

Cheese (except cottage, cream, and American cheeses)
Smoked or pickled fish such as lox, pickled herring, anchovies
Aged meats such as summer sausage, pepperoni, salami
Beef liver or chicken liver
Concentrated yeast/protein extracts—i.e., Marmite and Bovril
Beer, vermouth, brandy, and red wine—especially Chianti (white wine and champagne are okay)
Fava or broad bean pods (Italian green beans)—string beans are okay
Overripe figs or overripe bananas—young bananas are okay
NOTE: Many doctors emphasize that food must be fresh. This is because even slightly spoiled foods can cause a reaction. This problem is mostly limited to restaurants, where preparation may mask spoilage. This doesn't mean you shouldn't eat in restaurants. Just be sure they're reputable, and avoid fast, "street" food, where the quality may be questionable.

FOOD AND BEVERAGES TO BE USED IN MODERATION

Yogurt
Sour cream
Imported chocolate (Dutch-processed chocolate is okay)

MEDICATIONS

In case of emergency, it's important to carry a card or wear a medical alert tag indicating that you're taking an MAO inhibitor so that health care providers will be alert to any contraindications before administering medication, especially anesthesia. Your doctor or pharmacist should be able to provide you with such a card.

NOTE: All antibiotics are safe, as are aspirin, plain Tylenol, or Motrin. *Check with your psychiatrist before taking any other medicines.* Be sure to tell your doctors and dentist that you are taking an MAOI.

MEDICATIONS WITH STIMULANT PROPERTIES

Virtually all cold, cough, or sinus medications (except pure antihistamines such as Benadryl, Chlor-Trimeton, or Seldane) *Check labels to be sure no decongestants have been added.*

Weight-reducing or pep pills

Asthma inhalants (except for steroid sprays or Intal)

Local anesthesia containing epinephrine, such as is used in dental work. (Local anesthesia that does not contain epinephrine is safe.)

Cocaine

Amphetamines (speed)

Other illicit drugs, such as LSD and psilocybin mushrooms

Other antidepressants (except in special circumstances)

OTHER OPIATE NARCOTICS

Demerol (meperidine)

Dextromethorphan—found in many cold and cough preparations and usually labeled DM

NOTE: The instructions in this appendix must be followed for two weeks after stopping an MAOI.

Binge-Eating Quiz

	FRE-QUENTLY	OCCA-SIONALLY	RARELY OR NEVER
1. Do you experience eating binges in which you consume large quantities of calorie-rich foods, usually in the space of less than 2 hours? [If you answer "rarely or never," skip to question 7; score questions 2 to 6 as zero.]	☐	☐	☐
2. Do you tend to binge on high-calorie, easily ingested foods that require no preparation, such as candy, ice cream, etc.?	☐	☐	☐
3. Do you try to be inconspicuous during binges so that others will not notice your eating?	☐	☐	☐
4. Do the eating binges ever go on without stopping until your stomach hurts too much to eat anymore?	☐	☐	☐
5. Do you ever feel depressed or down on yourself after an eating binge?	☐	☐	☐
6. Have you ever had suicidal thoughts after an eating binge?	☐	☐	☐
7. Do you ever feel that you've lost control and cannot stop once you've started eating?	☐	☐	☐

	FRE-QUENTLY	OCCA-SIONALLY	RARELY OR NEVER
8. Do you ever eat foods without preparing them in the usual way—such as eating dough without baking it or eating canned frosting or maple syrup directly from the container—because you cannot delay the satisfaction of eating them?	☐	☐	☐
9. Have you ever felt that your eating pattern was abnormal?	☐	☐	☐
10. Do you find yourself thinking continuously about food the entire day?	☐	☐	☐
11. Do you find yourself continuously preoccupied with your weight throughout the day?	☐	☐	☐
12. Have you ever experienced rapid weight fluctuations of greater than 10 pounds as a result of alternating binge eating and fasting?	☐	☐	☐
13. Have you ever used pills such as diet pills or diuretics (water pills) in an attempt to control your weight?	☐	☐	☐
14 Have you ever used large amounts of laxatives to lose weight after eating?	☐	☐	☐
15. Have you ever deliberately made yourself vomit after eating in order to lose weight?	☐	☐	☐

Scoring

Allow 2 points for each response of "frequently," 1 point for each response of "occasionally," and 0 for a response of "rarely or never."

Score of 0–7: The odds are low that you have a serious eating disorder. Your behavior is probably within the normal range for Americans.

8–15: Your eating patterns are probably abnormal, and there is a definite possibility that you have bulimia. You should read chapter 5 in detail in order to decide whether you should consult a psychiatrist or try the type of treatment described in appendix B.

16–23: Your eating patterns are definitely abnormal, and you probably have bulimia. There is a good chance that your eating symptoms can be successfully treated with antidepressant medications by a psychiatrist as described in appendix B.

24–30: You almost unquestionably suffer from bulimia. You should definitely consult a psychiatrist and seriously consider treatment with one of the medications described in chapter 5 and appendix B.

Adapted from Harrison G. Pope, Jr., M.D., and James I. Hudson, M.D., "Sally's Story," in *New Hope for Binge Eaters* (New York: Harper & Row, 1984).

Facilities with Combined Treatment Programs for Substance Abuse and Mood Disorders

....

Bethany Center
RR #5, Box 170
Honesdale, PA 18431
800-544-1861

McLean Hospital
Alcohol and Drug Abuse
    Treatment Center at
    Appleton House
115 Mill Street
Belmont, MA 02178
617-855-2781
Director: Roger Weiss,
    M.D.

The Meadows
P.O. Box 97
Wickenburg, AZ 85358
800-621-4062

New York Hospital
Westchester Division
21 Bloomingdale Road
White Plains, NY 10605
914-682-9100

Palm Beach Institute
1014 N. Olive Avenue
West Palm Beach, FL
    33401
407-833-7553

Payne Whitney Psychiatric
    Clinic
528 East 68th Street
New York, NY 10021
212-746-3912

Sierra Tucson
P.O. Box 8307
16500 N. Lagodeloro
    Parkway
Tucson, AZ 85738
800-624-9001

Silver Hill Foundation
P.O. Box 1177
New Canaan, CT 06840
203-966-3561

A P P E N D I X   G

For Further Information on Mood Disorders

....

National Depression and Manic Depression Association
730 N. Franklin, Suite 501
Chicago, IL 60610
312-642-0049

National Alliance for the Mentally Ill
201 Wilson, Suite 302
Arlington, VA 22201
703-524-7600

The National Depressive and Manic Depressive Association
P.O. Box 1939
Chicago, IL 60690

It conducts a nationwide network of support groups that are extremely useful. Call (312) 642-0049.

National Foundation for Depressive Illness (NAFDI)
(800) 245-4344

A recorded announcement about the symptoms and treatment of depression advises callers on how to send for a complete information packet, including a referral list (by state) of doctors who specialize in treating depression and a list of local support groups.

CHAPTER ONE:

"I Wish There Were a Pill"

1. Darrel A. Regier, M.D., M.P.H., Robert M.A. Hirschfeld, M.D., Frederick K. Goodwin, M.D., Jack D. Burke, Jr., M.D. M.P.H., Joyce B. Lazar, M.A., and Lewis L. Judd, M.D., "The NIMH Depression Awareness, Recognition, and Treatment Program: Structure, Aims, and Scientific Basis," *American Journal of Psychiatry* 145 (November 1988): 11.

2. Lee N. Robins, Ph.D., and Darrel A. Regier, M.D., M.P.H., eds. *Psychiatric Disorders in America* (New York: Free Press, 1991).

3. Kenneth B. Wells et al., "The Function and Well-Being of Depressed Patients," *Journal of the American Medical Association* 7 (August 18, 1989).

4. Regier et al., "NIMH Program."

5. James I. Hudson, M.D., and Harrison G. Pope, Jr., M.D., "Affective Spectrum Disorder: Does Antidepressant Response Identify a Family of Disorders with a Common Pathophysiology?" *American Journal of Psychiatry* 147 (May 1990): 552–64.

6. Susan L. McElroy, M.D., James I. Hudson, M.D., Harrison G. Pope, Jr., M.D., and Paul E. Keck, Jr., M.D., "Kleptomania: Clinical Characteristics and Associated Psychopathology," *Psychological Medicine* 21 (1991): 93–108.

CHAPTER TWO:

The Serotonin Connection

1. James M. Ellison, M.D., ed., *The Psychotherapist's Guide to Pharmacotherapy* (Chicago: Yearbook Medical Publishers Inc., 1989).

2. David Gelman, "Drugs vs. the Couch," *Newsweek*, 26 March 1990.

3. The NIMH Consensus Development Panel, whose report came out in 1986, was made up of experts in the fields of psychology, psychiatry, psychopharmacology, and internal medicine.

4. Presented at the Consensus Development Conference sponsored by the National Institute of Mental Health and the Office of Medical Applications for Research, National Institutes of Health, April 24–26, 1985. Published in *American Journal of Psychiatry* 142 (April 1986), under the title "Mood Disorders: Pharmacologic Prevention of Recurrences." The chairman of the panel was David J. Kupfer, M.D., Pittsburgh, Pennsylvania.

5. Laura M. Markowitz, "Better Therapy Through Chemistry?" *The Family Therapy Networker* (May/June 1991).

6. Ibid.

7. Gelman, "Drugs vs. the Couch."

8. Martin E. P. Seligman, *Learned Optimism* (New York: Alfred A. Knopf, 1990).

9. Laura M. Markowitz, "Better Therapy."

10. Ibid.

11. Ibid.

12. Ibid.

13. Ibid.

14. Ibid.

15. G. L. Klerman, "The Psychiatric Patient's Right to Effective Treatment: Implications of *Osheroff* v. *Chestnut Lodge*," *American Journal of Psychiatry* 147 (4 April 1990): 409–18.

16. Ibid.

17. It's an interesting aside that although the patient's final diagnosis on discharge from Silver Hill was manic-depressive illness, depressed type, the testimony of the treating physician at Silver Hill revealed that of the two DSM-II diagnoses that would subsume a depressive illness as severe as Dr.

Osheroff's (manic-depressive illness, depressed type, and psychotic depressive reaction), the diagnosis of manic-depressive illness, depressed type, was selected because of the potential future complications regarding child custody that could arise from a diagnostic label including the term "psychotic."

18. Klerman, *"Osheroff v. Chestnut Lodge."*

19. Ellison, *Guide to Pharmacotherapy.*

20. Laura M. Markowitz, "Better Therapy."

21. Nathan Kline, M.D., *From Sad to Glad* (New York: Ballantine Books, 1974.)

22. Kline, *Sad to Glad.*

23. However, he was advised to stay on a small maintenance dose of lithium. Kline writes, "In six months, Dr. Cade was disappointed to get back his 'dirty little man,' now as agitated as before, but the reason proved reassuring." Feeling utterly cured, the man had stopped taking the lithium. Once he started again, the attack subsided.

24. Kline, *Sad to Glad.*

25. Ellison, *Guide to Pharmacotherapy.*

26. C. B. Pert and S. H. Snyder, "Opiate Receptors: Demonstration in Nervous Tissue," *Science* 179 (1973).

27. Kenneth Blum, Ph.D., and James E. Payne, *Alcohol and the Addictive Brain* (New York: Free Press, 1990).

28. Jon Franklin, *Molecules of the Mind* (New York: Dell, 1987).

29. Henn was quoted by Jon Franklin in *Molecules of the Mind.*

30. Ibid.

31. Ibid.

32. Daniel Goleman, "Brain Structure Differences Linked to Schizophrenia in Study of Twins," *New York Times*, 22 March 1990, p. B15.

33. Ibid.

34. This brief history of research in the biology of suicide was provided by Dr. J. John Mann, director of the Laboratories of

Neuropharmacology and of the Suicide Clinical Research Center at Western Psychiatric Institute and Clinic in Pittsburgh. The scientists who did the early work establishing low 5HIAA levels in depressed patients were Asburg and Traskman-Benz. Mann's report was printed in a newsletter from Western Psychiatric Institute, *Star-Center Link*, May 1990.

35. "Other research groups, including our own, have found a relationship between low 5HIAA levels and suicidal behavior," reports Dr. J. John Mann, director of the Suicide Clinical Research Center at Pittsburgh's Western Psychiatric Institute and Clinic.

36. The Suicide Clinical Research Center is part of Western Psychiatric Institute and Clinic, located in Pittsburgh.

37. Ronald R. Fieve, M.D., *Moodswing* (New York: William Morrow and Company, Inc., 1989), p. 219.

38. What about "separation anxiety"—the type that seems to occur because of loss—or fear of loss—of a loved one? In the new theory, panic is still considered a type of separation anxiety, but one in which certain brain mechanisms have miscarried, pushing people into intense anxiety states *that no longer have anything to do with inner or outer psychic events*. Biologically induced panic, in other words; panic that is the result of malfunction in the central nervous system.

39. Cooper cites Donald Klein of Columbia Psychiatric on the use of imipramine in treating panic disorder.

40. Cooper's talk at the Babcock Symposium at Pittsburgh Psychoanalytic Institute in 1984 was published in *American Journal of Psychiatry* in December 1985, p. 1395, under the title "Will Neurobiology Influence Psychoanalysis?"

41. "Prescribing medication earlier might have permitted a much clearer focus on her content-related psychodynamic problems."

42. Cooper, "Will Neurobiology . . . ?"

43. Shepard J. Kantor, M.D. "Transference and the Beta-

adrenergic Receptor: A Case Presentation," *Psychiatry* 52 (February 1989).

44. Eric Marcus, "Integrating Psychopharmacotherapy, Psychotherapy, and Mental Structure in the Treatment of Patients with Personality Disorders and Depression," *Psychiatric Clinics of North America* 3, no. 2 (June 1990).

CHAPTER THREE:
What's Happening to Me?

1. Personal communication.

2. Jack M. Gorman, M.D., *The Essential Guide to Psychiatric Drugs* (New York: St. Martin's Press, 1990).

3. Ibid.

4. J. Raymond DePaulo, Jr., M.D., and Keith Russell Ablow, M.D., *How to Cope with Depression* (Baltimore: Johns Hopkins University Press, 1989).

5. Max Hamilton, M.D., "Mood Disorders: Clinical Features," in *Comprehensive Textbook of Psychiatry*, vol. 1, 5th ed., eds. Harold I. Kaplan, M.D., and Benjamin J. Sadock, M.D. (Baltimore: Williams and Wilkins, 1989).

6. Ibid. Re phases of depression, Hamilton notes additionally, "Treatment seems to reduce the amplitude of the phases, but probably not their length. Lithium, however, appears to reduce the length as well as the amplitude."

7. Francis M. Mondimore, M.D., "The Treatment of Major Depression," in *Depression: The Mood Disease* (Baltimore: Johns Hopkins University Press, 1990).

8. Ibid.

9. Ibid.

10. Ibid.

11. Hamilton, "Mood Disorders."

12. Harold A. Sackheim, Ph.D., and Barbara L. Steif, M.A., "Neuropsychology of Depression and Mania," in *Depression and*

Mania, eds. Anastasios Georgotas, M.D., and Robert Cancro, M.D. (New York: Elsevier Science Publishing, 1988).

13. Mondimore, "Major Depression."

14. Ibid.

15. DePaulo and Ablow, *How to Cope with Depression.*

CHAPTER FOUR:

Biology and Women's Depression

1. David Inwood, M.D., "Postpartum Psychotic Disorders," in *Comprehensive Textbook of Psychiatry,* vol. 1, 5th ed., Harold I. Kaplan, M.D., and Benjamin J. Sadock, M.D. (Baltimore: Williams and Wilkins, 1989).

2. Myrna Weissman, Ph.D., and Gerald Klerman, M.D., "Gender and Depression," in *Women and Depression: A Lifespan Perspective,* eds. Ruth Formanek, Ph.D., and Anita Gurian, Ph.D. (New York: Springer Publishing Co., 1987).

3. Susan Nolen-Hoeksema, Ph.D., *Sex Differences in Depression* (Palo Alto, Calif.: Stanford University Press, 1990).

4. The scale used was the Beck Depression Inventory. Nolen-Hoeksema notes that the study was small; sixty-three subjects were used.

5. J. H. Kashani et al., "Psychiatric Disorders in a Community Sample of Adolescents," *American Journal of Psychiatry* 144 (1987): 584–89.

6. Nolen-Hoeksema, *Sex Differences.*

7. D. E. H. Russell, *Sexual Exploitation* (Beverly Hills, Calif.: Sage Library of Social Research, 1984).

8. Ellen McGrath et al., *Women and Depression: Risk Factors and Treatment Issues* (Washington, D.C.: American Psychological Association, 1990).

9. Ibid.

10. D. L. Taylor et al., "Serotonin Levels and Platelet Uptake During Premenstrual Tension," *Neuropsychobiology* 12

(1984): 16–18; C. R. Ashby, Jr., et al., "Alteration of Platelet Serotonergic Mechanisms and Monoamine Oxidase Activity in Premenstrual Syndrome," *Biological Psychiatry* 24 (1988): 225–33.

11. Sally K. Severino, M.D., and Margaret L. Moline, Ph.D., *Premenstrual Syndrome* (New York: The Guilford Press, 1989).

12. The story of Ellen is based on a case history reported in *Premenstrual Syndrome.*

13. Severino and Moline, *Premenstrual Syndrome.*

14. Other studies have shown that B_6 only alleviates depression in women who are deficient in B_6 to begin with. Drs. Severino and Moline warn that high doses of B_6 can cause toxicity and neurological symptoms, such as bone pain, nervous twitches, muscle weakness, and numbness. These physicians take a cautionary view of B_6. "Even 100 mg daily is 25–50 times the recommended daily dose," they note. The neurological symptoms reported in some studies of B_6 seem reason enough for caution. "One cannot prescribe a treatment regimen whose outcome may be worse than the initial symptoms."

15. W. M. Harrison, J. Endicott, and J. Nee, "Treatment of Premenstrual Depression with Nortriptyline: A Pilot Study," *Journal of Clinical Psychiatry* 50 (1989): 136–39.

16. Severino and Moline, *Premenstrual Syndrome.*

17. Study reported in the *New York Times*, 8 January 1991.

18. Postpartum weeping has been explored cross-culturally with the same reported incidence of 50–70 percent.

19. These studies have been controlled for social stress factors.

20. Inwood, "Postpartum Psychotic Disorders."

21. A five year-study in the psychiatric Mother and Baby Unit in Sheffield, England, supports the position that postpartum psychosis differs from other psychoses in that symptoms become acute and develop more rapidly than in other psychiatric illnesses, in most instances with no forewarning and no prior history.

22. Ruth Nemtzow, Ph.D., "Childbirth: Happiness, Blues, or Depression?" in *Women and Depression: A Lifespan Perspective.*

23. Weissman and Klerman, "Gender and Depression," in *Women and Depression: A Lifespan Perspective.*

24. Ruth Nemtzow offers no follow-up information on her depressed new mothers, so we have no way of knowing if and when their depressions ever went away. And if they went away, whether they stayed away.

25. Ruth Formanek, Ph.D., "Depression and Menopause: A Socially Constructed Link," in *Women and Depression: A Lifespan Perspective.*

26. Weissman and Klerman, "Gender and Depression," in *Women and Depression: A Lifespan Perspective.*

27. C. B. Ballinger, M.C. Browning, and A. H. Smith, "Hormone Profiles and Psychological Symptoms in Peri-Menopausal Women," *Maturitas* (November 1987).

28. Randy S. Milden, "Episodic Mood Disorders in Women," in *Women and Depression: A Lifespan Perspective.*

29. Ellen McGrath et al., *Women and Depression: Risk Factors and Treatment Issues* (Washington, D.C.: American Psychological Association 1990).

CHAPTER FIVE:

Compulsive Eating: A Disturbance in the Brain

1. Harrison G. Pope, Jr., M.D. and James I. Hudson, M.D., *New Hope for Binge Eaters* (New York: Harper & Row, 1984).

2. D. B. Herzog et al., "Frequency of Bulimic Behaviors and Associated Social Maladjustment in Female Graduate Students," *Journal of Psychiatric Research* 20, no. 4 (1986): 355–61.

3. D. M. Kagan, and R. L. Squires, "Eating Disorders Among Adolescents: Patterns and Prevalence," *Adolescence* 19, no. 73 (Spring 1984): 15–29.

4. Katherine A. Halmi, J. R. Falk, and E. Schwartz, "Binge-Eating and Vomiting: A Survey of a College Population," *Psychological Medicine* 11 (1981): 697-706.

5. Hudson and Pope corrected this figure for certain statistical anomalies.

6. Pope and Hudson, *Binge Eaters*.

7. In a study at Duke, 31 percent of obese subjects reported binges. At the University of Maryland, 55 percent of obese subjects reported moderate binge eating, and an additional 23 percent reported severe problems with binge eating. Hudson and Pope found that bulimia exists in a sizable but little recognized group of obese women.

8. Diane Duston, "Diets—Teens," Associated Press release, 24 September 1990.

9. J. E. Mitchell, R. L. Pyle, and E. D. Eckert, "Frequency and Duration of Binge-Eating Episodes in Patients with Bulimia," *American Journal of Psychiatry* 138 (1981): 835–36.

10. Pope and Hudson, *Binge Eaters*.

11. Ibid.

12. Ibid.

13. Ibid.

14. Ibid.

15. Jeffrey Jonas, "Do Substance Abuse, Including Alcoholism, and Bulimia Covary?" in *Opioids, Bulimia, and Alcohol Abuse and Alcoholism*, ed. Larry D. Reid (New York: Springer-Verlag, 1990).

16. McElroy Susan, M.D., et al., "Pharmacological Treatment of Kleptomania and Bulimia Nervosa," *Journal of Clinical Psychopharmacology* 9, no. 5 (October 1989).

17. Pope and Hudson, *Binge Eaters*.

18. Ibid.

19. All sorts of psychosocial theories have been put forth as to

why this is happening to women now—at a time when they have more social support and, presumably, more to look forward to in their lives than ever before. On closer inspection, however, young females in this society don't have as much support as we would like to think. They feel enormous pressure to succeed as well as psychological conflict over their roles as females. When I was interviewing college women and women in their twenties and thirties for *Perfect Women*, I found many to be confused and anxious and quite unsure about what the future held in store. They felt their mothers had given them mixed messages about their ability to succeed as women, and many had big problems with self-esteem.

20. Marlene Boskind-White and William C. White, Jr., *Bulimarexia: The Binge/Purge Cycle*, 2nd ed. (New York: W. W. Norton, 1987).

21. Ibid.

22. Pope and Hudson, *Binge Eaters*.

23. Ibid.

24. B. T. Walsh et al., "Treatment of Bulimia with Monoamine Oxidase Inhibitors," *American Journal of Psychiatry* 139: 1629–30.

25. P. L. Hughes, L. A. Wells, and C. J. Cunningham, "Controlled Trial Using Desipramine for Bulimia," presented at the Annual Meeting, American Psychiatric Association, Los Angeles (May 9, 1984).

26. J. E. Mitchell et al., "A Comparison Study of Antidepressants and Structured Intensive Group Psychotherapy in the Treatment of Bulimia Nervosa," *Archives of General Psychiatry* 47, no. 2 (February 1990): 149–57.

27. Often the comparative studies of antidepressant medication and psychotherapy only cover a period of four weeks, which doesn't allow enough time to see if the antidepressant is going to be effective or not.

    Another design flaw in Michell's study had to do with the nature of the therapy program. During the first week, patients spent three hours, five nights a week, in the program, which included eating dinner every evening in a group along with the psychotherapists. The frequency of meetings then tapered down over the next four weeks to meeting only twice a week. During the treatment phase, the patients were in an environment where it would be difficult, if not impossible, to binge and experienced constant reinforcement to suppress the urge to binge while not at the program. Once treatment ended and the patients returned to their ordinary environments, would they return to their previous levels of binging? Though the program was effective in the short term, no long-term results of this study were reported. On average, other studies of behaviorally oriented psychotherapeutic treatment for bulimia have reported that only 35 percent of patients for whom treatment was initially successful remain abstinent one year after therapy is terminated.

28. James E. Mitchell, M.D., Richard L. Pyle, M.D., Elke D. Eckert, M.D., Dorothy Hatsukami, Ph.D., Claire Pomeroy, M.D., and Robert Zimmerman, Ph.D., "Response to Alternative Antidepressants in Imipramine Nonresponders with Bulimia Nervosa," *Journal of Clinical Psychopharmacology* 9, no. 4 (August 1989).

29. J. I. Hudson, H. G. Pope, Jr., and J. M. Jonas, "Treatment of Bulimia with Antidepressants: Theoretical Considerations and Clinical Findings," *Research Publications of the Association for Research in Nervous and Mental Disease* (Baltimore) 62 (1984): 259–73.

30. Pope and Hudson, *Binge Eaters*. "However, this figure may be an underestimate of efficacy since the group was using almost exclusively 'first generation' antidepressants (primarily tricyclics and monoamine oxidase inhibitors) and did not have available second generation drugs. With the addition of fluoxetine to the therapeutic armamentarium, we have achieved marked improvement or remission in a majority of those patients who were refractory to trials of 'first-generation' agents."

31. Michael Gitlin, M.D., *The Psychotherapist's Guide to Psychopharmacology* (New York: Macmillan, 1990).

32. Dr. Maurizio Fava, *American Journal of Psychiatry* (August 1990).

CHAPTER SIX:

Children in Pain

1. Frederick K. Goodwin, M.D., and Kay Redfield Jamison, Ph.D., "Psychotherapy," in *Manic Depressive Illness* (New York: Oxford University Press, 1990).

2. Maria Kovacs, Ph.D., "The Natural History and Course of Depressive Disorders in Childhood," *Psychiatric Annals* (1985).

3. Goodwin and Jamison, "Psychotherapy."

4. M. Strober and G. Carlson, "Bipolar Illness in Adolescents with Major Depression: Clinical, Genetic, and Psychopharmacologic Predictors in a Three- to Four-Year Prospective Follow-up Investigation," *Archives of General Psychiatry* 39 (1982).

5. Joaquim Puig-Antich, M.D., et al., "Psychosocial Functioning in Prepubertal Major Depressive Disorders," *Archives of General Psychiatry* 42 (1985): 500–73.

6. Anita Gurian, "Early Sorrows and Depressive Disorders," in *Women and Depression: A Lifespan Perspective*, eds. Ruth Formanek, Ph.D., and Anita Gurian, Ph.D. (New York: Springer Publishing Company, 1987).

7. Anita Gurian, "Depression and Young Girls," in *Women and Depression: A Lifespan Perspective*.

8. H. S. Akiskal et al., "Affective Disorders in Referred Children and Younger Siblings of Manic-Depressives: Mode of Onset and Prospective Course," *Archives of General Psychiatry* 42 (1985).

9. Robert DeLong, M.D., "Lithium Treatment and Bipolar Disorders in Childhood," *North Carolina Medical Journal* 5, no. 4 (April 1990).

10. Frederick K. Goodwin, M.D., and Kay Redfield Jamison, Ph.D., "Children and Adolescence," in *Manic Depressive Illness*.

11. Javad H. Kashani et al., "Correlates of Suicidal Ideation in a

Community Sample of Children and Adolescents," *Journal of Child and Adolescent Psychiatry* 28, no. 6 (November 1989).

12. Joaquim Puig-Antich, M.D., and Burt Weston, "The Diagnosis and Treatment of Major Depressive Disorder in Childhood," *Annual Review of Medicine* 34 (1983): 231–45.

13. Tests to ask about are the Diagnostic Interview for Children and Adolescents (DICA), the Kiddie-Schedule for Affective Disorders and Schizophrenia for School-Age Children (K-SADS), the Diagnostic Interview Schedule (DIS), and the Structured Clinical Interview for DSM-III-R (SCID).

14. Lee N. Robins, Ph.D., and Darrel A. Regier, M.D., M.P.H., eds., *Psychiatric Disorders in America* (New York: Free Press, 1991).

15. Ibid.

16. Kerim Munir, "Child and Adolescent Pharmacotherapy Comes of Age," in *The Psychotherapist's Guide to Pharmacotherapy*, ed. James M. Ellison (Chicago: Yearbook Medical Publishers, 1989), p. 191.

CHAPTER SEVEN:

When Sobriety Is Not Enough

1. Daniel Goleman, "Scientists Pinpoint Brain Irregularities in Drug Addicts," *New York Times*, June 26, 1990.

2. Ibid.

3. E. J. Khantzian, "The Self-Medication Hypothesis of Addictive Disorders: Focus on Heroin and Cocaine Dependence," *American Journal of Psychiatry* 142 (1985).

4. Cited in a 1986 report from the Alcohol, Drug Abuse and Mental Health Administration.

5. Michael L. Johnson and James M. Ellison, "Interactions of Alcohol, Street Drugs, and Prescribed Medications," in *The Psychotherapist's Guide to Pharmacotherapy*, ed. James M. Ellison, M.D. (Chicago: Yearbook Medical Publishers, 1987).

6. Ibid.

7. James C. Anthony and John E. Helzer, "Syndromes of Drug Abuse and Dependence," in *Psychiatric Disorders in America*, eds. Lee. N. Robins et al. (New York: Free Press, 1991). The criteria used for "abuse" and "dependence" were those established by the DSM-III.

8. Michael Gitlin, M.D., *The Psychotherapist's Guide to Psychoparmacology* (New York: Macmillan, 1990).

9. Conducted jointly by the University of Pittsburgh and New York State's Research Institute on Alcoholism, the Westinghouse study was reported on the UPI wire on January 28, 1991. It found that the persons at highest risk for depression were separated or divorced women with a family history of depression. Those most likely to suffer alcohol abuse were unmarried men with a family history of alcoholism.

10. Jeffrey Jonas, "Do Substance Abuse, Including Alcoholism, and Bulimia Covary?" in *Opioids, Bulimia, and Alcohol Abuse and Alcoholism*, ed. Larry D. Reid (New York: Springer-Verlag, 1990). Larry Reid, Ph.D., is professor of psychology and neuroscience at Rensselaer Polytechnic Institute, in Troy, New York. The text of this book is the written form of the proceedings of a fascinating satellite symposium associated with the 1988 meeting of the Society for Neuroscience, during which the "opioid processes" involved in additions and eating disorders were explored.

11. Larry Reid. *Opioids, Bulimia, and Alcohol Abuse and Alcoholism*.

12. C. R. Cloninger et al., "Inheritance of Alcohol Abuse," *Archives of General Psychiatry* 38 (1981): 861–68.

13. Goleman, *New York Times*.

14. Goleman, *New York Times*.

15. Kenneth Blum, Ph.D., and James E. Payne, *Alcohol and the Addictive Brain* (New York: Free Press, 1991).

16. Roger D. Weiss, M.D., and Steven M. Mirin, M.D., "Tricyclic Antidepressants in the Treatment of Alcoholism and Drug

Abuse," *Journal of Clinical Psychiatry* 50, suppl. no. 7 (July 1989).

17. J. M. Murphy, W. J. McBride, L. Lumeng, and T. K. Li, "Alcohol Preference in Regional Brain Monoamine Contents of N/NIH Heterogeneous Stock Rats," *Alcohol and Drug Research* 7 (1986).

18. J. M. Murphy, M. B. Waller, G. J. Gatto, W. J. McBride, L. Lumeng, and T. K. Li, "Effects of Fluoxetine on the Intragastric Self-Administration of Ethanol in the Alcohol-Preferring P Line of Rats," *Alcohol* 5 (1988).

19. D. A. Gorelick, "Effect of Fluoxetine on Alcohol Consumption," *Alcoholism: Clinical and Experimental Research* 10 (1986).

20. Weiss and Mirin, "Tricyclic Antidepressants."

21. C. Gianoulakis et al., "Inbred Strains of Mice with Variable Sensitivity to Ethanol Exhibit Differences in the Content and Processing of Beta-Endorphin," *Life Sciences* 39 (1986).

22. C. Gianoulakis et al., "Differences in the Response of the Pituitary Beta Endorphin to an Acute Ethanol Challenge in Individuals With and Without a Family History of Alcoholism," *Alcoholism: Clinical and Experimental Research* 11 (1987).

23. The discovery of opiate receptors in the brain was made independently, and reported in the same year, by Solomon Snyder and Candace Pert of Johns Hopkins University, Eric Simon at New York University, and Lars Terenius in Sweden.

24. At the International Narcotics Research Club Conference in 1975, papers throwing light on opiate receptors and the natural materials that activate them were presented by John Hughes, Lars Terenius, Solomon Snyder, and Avram Goldstein.

25. K. Oka, J. D. Kantrowitz, and S. Spector, "Isolation of Morphine from Toad Skin," *Proceedings of the National Academy of Sciences* 82 (1985).

26. G. J. Cardinale, J. Donnerer, A. D. Finck, J. D. Kantrowitz, K. Oka, and S. Spector, "Morphine and Codeine Are Endogenous Components of Human Cerebrospinal Fluid," *Life Sciences* 40 (1987).

27. Ellen M. Unterwald and R. Suzanne Zukin, "The Endogenous Opioidergic Systems," in *Opioids, Bulimia, and Alcohol Abuse and Alcoholism.*

28. Blum and Payne, *Alcohol and the Addictive Brain.*

29. Ibid.

30. Roger D. Weiss, M.D., Steven M. Mirin, M.D., Margaret L. Griffin, Ph.D., and Jacqueline L. Michael, M.S.W., "Psychopathology in Cocaine Abusers: Changing Trends," *Journal of Nervous and Mental Disease* 176, no. 12 (1988).

31. Gitlin, *Guide to Psychopharmacology.*

32. Weiss et al., "Cocaine Abusers."

33. Karen Klinger, "Mental Disorders Increase Drug and Alcohol Abuse," United Press International release, 21 November 1990.

34. Goleman, *New York Times.*

35. Goleman, *New York Times.*

36. Robins et al., eds., *Psychiatric Disorders in America.*

37. Roger D. Weiss, M.D., and Steven M. Mirin, M.D., "The Dual Diagnosis Alcoholic: Evaluation and Treatment," *Psychiatric Annals* 19 (May 1989): 5.

38. Katie Evans and J. Michael Sullivan, *Dual Diagnosis* (New York: Guilford Press, 1990).

39. Ibid.

40. Bukstein's comments were made in a personal interview conducted for this book.

41. Hamilton's comments were made in a personal interview.

CHAPTER EIGHT:

Getting Help

1. Michael Gitlin, M.D., *The Psychotherapist's Guide to Psychopharmacology* (New York: Macmillan, 1990).

2. Women from blue-collar families did not express as much concern about losing their jobs if they sought treatment for depression.

3. Francis M. Mondimore, M.D., "The Treatment of Major Depression," in *Depression: The Mood Disease* (Baltimore: Johns Hopkins University Press, 1990).

4. Darrel A. Regier, M.D., M.P.H., et al., "The NIMH Depression Awareness, Recognition, and Treatment Program: Structure, Aims, and Scientific Basis," *American Journal of Psychiatry* 145 (November 1988): 11.

5. See appendix B for an extensive discussion of how doctors Hudson and Pope, at Harvard, treat bulimia with antidepressant medication.

6. Jack M. Gorman, M.D., *The Essential Guide to Psychiatric Drugs* (New York: St. Martin's Press, 1990).

7. Lee N. Robins, Ph.D., and Darrel A. Regier, M.D., M.P.H., eds., *Psychiatric Disorders in America* (New York: Free Press, 1991).

8. Gorman, *Psychiatric Drugs.*

9. Jonathan O. Cole, M.D., and J. Alexander Bodkin, M.D., "Antidepressant Drug Side Effects," *Journal of Clinical Psychiatry* 51, suppl. (January 1990): 1.

10. Ibid.

11. Martin H. Teicher, M.D., et al., "Emergence of Intense Suicidal Preoccupation During Fluoxetine Treatment," *American Journal of Psychiatry* (February 1990).

12. Jeffrey M. Jonas, M.D., and Ron Schaumburg, *Everything You Need to Know About Prozac* (New York: Bantam Books, 1991).

13. Teicher, "Suicidal Preoccupation."

14. Mondimore, "Major Depression."

15. See chapter 2 on the history of discovery of lithium.

16. Mondimore, "Major Depression."

17. However, a panel of experts recently concluded " 'the occurrence of a manic episode should always raise the question of preventive therapy' (Consensus Development Panel, 1985). Their rationale is clearly based on the assumption of a second potentially highly destructive episode in the life of a young person whose self-esteem and social reputation are not established and are subject to major disruption" (Gitlin, *Guide to Psychopharmacology*).

18. Gitlin, *Guide to Psychopharmacology*.

19. Gordon F. S. Johnson, "Highlights on the Main Pharmacological Treatments of Mania," in *Depression and Mania*, ed. Anastasios Georgotas, M.D., and Robert Cancro, M.D. (New York: Elsevier Science Publishing, 1988).

20. Recent studies, however, have shown that carbamazepine is equally effective in treating acute manic symptoms. However, because it does not cause "acute parkinsonian and long-term tardive dyskinesia side effects, it would appear that carbamazepine should begin to emerge as an alternative to neuroleptics in the treatment of acute mania, particularly as an adjunct to lithium carbonate." (Robert M. Post, M.D., and Thomas H. Uhde, M.D., "Refractory Manias and Alternatives to Lithium Treatment," in *Depression and Mania.)*

21. While often involuntary facial movements will not disappear when the drug is discontinued, they usually don't occur unless the antipsychotics have been given at high doses over a longer period of time. Also, some antipsychotics, such as chlorpromazine and thioridazine, are less likely to cause this effect than are others, such as haloperidol and fluphenazine.

22. Johnson, "Highlights on the Main Pharmacological Treatments of Mania," in *Depression and Mania*.

23. Ibid.

24. Gitlin, *Guide to Psychopharmacology*.

25. Gorman, *Psychiatric Drugs*.

26. Regier et al., "Depression Awareness."

27. Gorman, *Psychiatric Drugs*.

28. Mondimore, "Major Depression."

29. J. Raymond DePaulo, Jr., M.D., and Keith Russell Ablow, M.D., *How to Cope with Depression* (Baltimore: Johns Hopkins University Press, 1989).

30. Mondimore, "Major Depression."

31. Logan is quoted in Ronald R. Fieve, M.D., *Moodswing* (New York: William Morrow and Company, Inc., 1989), p. 219.

32. Frederick K. Goodwin, M.D., and Kay Redfield Jamison, Ph.D., "Psychotherapy," in *Manic Depressive Illness* (New York: Oxford University Press, 1990), p. 725.

33. Ibid.

34. Ibid.

35. Ibid.

36. Gorman, *Psychiatric Drugs.*

37. Ibid.

38. Harrison G. Pope, Jr., M.D., and James I. Hudson, M.D., *New Hope for Binge Eaters* (New York: Harper & Row, 1984).

39. Mondimore, "Major Depression."

40. Gorman, *Psychiatric Drugs.*

41. Mark H. Pollack, M.D., and Jerrold F. Rosenbaum, M.D., "Management of Antidepressant-Induced Side Effects: A Practical Guide for the Clinician," *Journal of Clinical Psychiatry* 48 (January 1987): 1.

42. Cole and Bodkin, "Antidepressant Drug Side Effects."

43. Mondimore, "Major Depression."

44. Pollack and Rosenbaum, "Antidepressant-Induced Side Effects."

45. Mondimore, "Major Depression."

46. Cole and Bodkin, "Antidepressant Drug Side Effects."

47. Ibid.

48. Mondimore, "Major Depression."

49. Claims have been made that bethanechol will relieve sexual dysfunction in patients taking TCAs if taken one to two hours before intercourse, but Cole and Bodkin report that in their experience this has been only occasionally useful.

50. Pollack and Rosenbaum, "Antidepressant-Induced Side Effects."

51. Cole and Bodkin, "Antidepressant Drug Side Effects."

52. Leslie A. Cockhill, M.D., and Ronald A. Remick, M.D., "Blood Pressure Effects of Monoamine Oxidase Inhibitors— The Highs and Lows," *Canadian Journal of Psychiatry* 32 (December 1987).

53. Mondimore, "Major Depression."

54. S. C. Dilsaver, "Monoamine Oxidase Inhibitor Withdrawal Phenomena: Symptoms and Pathophysiology," *Acta psychiatrica scandinavica* 78 (København) (1988): 1–7.

55. Reid, "Mood Disorders."

56. Gorman, *Psychiatric Drugs.*

57. Gitlin, *Guide to Psychopharmacology.*

58. Mondimore, "Major Depression."

59. Post and Uhde, "Refractory Manias."

60. Mondimore, "Major Depression."

61. Gorman, *Psychiatric Drugs.*

62. Priscilla Slagle, M.D., *The Way Up from Down* (New York: St. Martin's Press, 1987).

63. Marilyn Sargent, *Depressive Illnesses: Treatments Bring New Hope,* Office of Scientific Information, National Institute of Mental Health, DHS Publication No. (ADM) 89-1491, Printed 1986, Revised 1989 (Washington, D.C.: U.S. Government Printing Office).

BIBLIOGRAPHY

Books

Blum, Kenneth, Ph.D., and Payne, James E. *Alcohol and the Addictive Brain.* New York: Free Press, 1990.

Boskind-White, Marlene, and White, William C., Jr. *Bulimarexia: The Binge/Purge Cycle.* 2nd ed. New York: W. W. Norton & Company, 1990.

DePaulo, J. Raymond, Jr., M.D., and Ablow, Keith Russell, M.D. *How to Cope with Depression.* Baltimore: Johns Hopkins University Press, 1989.

Dukakis, Kitty. *Now You Know.* New York: Simon & Schuster, 1990.

Ellison, James M., M.D., ed. *The Psychotherapist's Guide to Pharmacotherapy.* Chicago: Yearbook Medical Publishers, Inc., 1987.

Evans, Katie, and Sullivan, J. Michael. *Dual Diagnosis.* New York: The Guilford Press, 1990.

Fieve, Ronald R., M.D. *Moodswing.* New York: William Morrow and Company, Inc., 1989.

Formanek, Ruth, Ph.D., and Gurian, Anita, Ph.D., eds. *Women and Depression: A Lifespan Perspective.* New York: Springer Publishing Co., 1987.

Franklin, Jon. *Molecules of the Mind.* New York: Dell, 1987.

Georgotas, Anastasios, M.D., and Cancro, Robert, M.D., eds. *Depression and Mania.* New York: Elsevier Science Publishing, 1988.

Gitlin, Michael, M.D. *The Psychotherapist's Guide to Psychopharmacology.* New York: Macmillan, 1990.

Gold, Mark. S., M.D. *The Good News About Depression.* New York: Bantam Books, 1986.

Goodwin, Frederick K., M.D., and Jamison, Kay Redfield, Ph.D. *Manic Depressive Illness.* New York: Oxford University Press, 1990.

Gorman, Jack M., M.D. *The Essential Guide to Psychiatric Drugs.* New York: St. Martin's Press, 1990.

Jonas, Jeffrey M., M.D., and Schaumburg, Ron. *Everything You Need to Know About Prozac.* New York: Bantam Books, 1991.

Kaplan, Harold I., M.D., and Sadock, Benjamin J., M.D., eds. *Comprehensive Textbook of Psychiatry*, vol. 1, 5th edition. Baltimore: Williams and Wilkins, 1989.

Klein, Nathan, M.D. *From Sad to Glad.* New York: Ballantine Books, 1974.

McGrath, Ellen; Keita, Gwendolyn Puryear; Strickland, Bonnie R.; and Russo, Nancy Felipe. *Women and Depression: Risk Factors and Treatment Issues.* Washington, D.C.: American Psychological Association, 1990.

Mondimore, Francis M., M.D. *Depression: The Mood Disease.* Baltimore: Johns Hopkins University Press, 1990.

Nolen-Hoeksema, Susan, Ph.D. *Sex Differences in Depression:* Palo Alto, Calif.: Stanford University Press, 1990.

Pope, Harrison G., Jr., M.D., and Hudson, James I., M.D. *New Hope for Binge Eaters.* New York: Harper & Row, 1984.

Reid, Larry D., ed. *Opioids, Bulimia, and Alcohol Abuse and Alcoholism.* New York: Springer-Verlag, 1990.

Reid, William H., M.D., M.P.H., *The Treatment of Psychiatric Disorders/Revised for the DSM-III-R.* New York: Brunner/Mazel, 1989.

Robins, Lee N., Ph.D.; and Regier, Darrel A., M.D., M.P.H., eds. *Psychiatric Disorders in America.* New York: Free Press, 1991.

Russell, D.E.H., *Sexual Exploitation.* Beverly Hills, Calif.: Sage Library of Social Research, 1984.

Sandmaier, Marian. *The Invisible Alcoholics.* New York: McGraw-Hill Book Co., 1979.

Sargent, Marilyn. *Depressive Illnesses: Treatments Bring New Hope.* Office of Scientific Information, National Institute of Mental Health, DHS Publication No. (ADM) 89-1491. Washington, D.C.: U.S. Government Printing Office, 1986; revised 1989.

Seligman, Martin E. P. *Learned Optimism.* New York: Alfred A. Knopf, 1990.

Severino, Sally K., M.D., and Moline, Margaret L., Ph.D. *Premenstrual Syndrome.* New York: The Guilford Press, 1989.

Slagle, Priscilla, M.D. *The Way Up from Down.* New York: St. Martin's Press, 1987.

Washton, Arnold, and Boundy, Donna. *Willpower's Not Enough.* New York: Harper & Row, 1989.

Zal, H. Michael. *Panic Disorder.* New York: Plenum Press, 1990.

Journals

Akiskal, H.S.; Downs, J.; Jordan, P.; Watson, S.; Daugherty, D.; and Pruitt, D. "Affective Disorders in Referred Children and Younger Siblings of Manic-Depressives: Mode of Onset and Prospective Course." *Archives of General Psychiatry* 42 (1985): 996–1003.

Ashby, C. R., Jr.; Carr, L. A.; Cook, C. L.; Steptoe, M. M.; and Franks, D. D. "Alteration of Platelet Serotonergic Mechanisms and Monoamine Oxidase Activity in Premenstrual Syndrome." *Biological Psychiatry* 4 (1988): 225–33.

Ballinger, C. B.; Browning, M. C.; and Smith, A. H. "Hormone Profiles and Psychological Symptoms in Peri-Menopausal Women." *Maturitas* (November 1987).

Cardinale, G. J.; Donnerer, J.; Finck, A. D.; Kantrowitz, J. D.; Oka, K.; and Spector, S. "Morphine and Codeine Are Endogenous Components of Human Cerebrospinal Fluid." *Life Sciences* 40 (1987).

Cockhill, Leslie A., M.D., and Remick, Ronald A., M.D. "Blood Pressure Effects of Monoamine Oxidase Inhibitors—The Highs and Lows." *Canadian Journal of Psychiatry* 32 (December 1987).

Cole, Jonathan O., M.D., and Bodkin, J. Alexander, M.D. "Antidepressant Drug Side Effects." *Journal of Clinical Psychiatry* 51, suppl. (January 1990): 1.

Cooper, Arnold M. "Will Neurobiology Influence Psychoanalysis?" *American Journal of Psychiatry* (December 1985).

DeLong, Robert, M.D. "Lithium Treatment and Bipolar Disorders in Childhood." *North Carolina Medical Journal* 5, no. 4 (April 1990).

Dilsaver, S. C. "Monoamine Oxidase Inhibitor Withdrawal Phenomena: Symptoms and Pathophysiology." *Acta psychiatrica scandinavica* 78 (København) (1988): 1–7.

Duston, Diane. "Diets—Teens." Associated Press release, September 24, 1990.

Gelman, David. "Drugs vs. the Couch." *Newsweek*, March 26, 1990.

Gianoulakis, C., et al. "Differences in the Response of the Pituitary Beta Endorphin to an Acute Ethanol Challenge in Individuals With and Without a Family History of Alcoholism." *Alcoholism: Clinical and Experimental Research* 1 (1987).

———. "Inbred Strains of Mice with Variable Sensitivity to Ethanol Exhibit Differences in the Content and Processing of Beta-Endorphin." *Life Sciences* 39 (1986).

Goleman, Daniel. "Brain Structure Differences Linked to Schizophrenia in Study of Twins." *New York Times*, March 22, 1990.

———. "Scientists Pinpoint Brain Irregularities in Drug Addicts." *New York Times*, June 26, 1990.

Gorelick, D. A. "Effect of Fluoxetine on Alcohol Consumption." *Alcoholism: Clinical and Experimental Research* 10 (1986).

Harrison, W. M.; Endicott, J; and Nee, J. "Treatment of Premenstrual Depression with Nortriptyline: A Pilot Study." *Journal of Clinical Psychiatry* 50 (1989): 136–39.

Herzog, D. B.; Norman, D.K.; Rigotti, N.A.; and Pepose, M. "Frequency of Bulimic Behaviors and Associated Social Maladjustment in Female Graduate Students." *Journal of Psychiatric Research* 20, no. 4 (1986): 355–61.

Hudson, J. I.; Pope, H. G., Jr.; and Jonas, J. M. "Treatment of Bulimia with Antidepressants: Theoretical Considerations and Clinical Findings." *Research Publications of the Association for Research in Nervous and Mental Disease* 62 (1984): 259–73.

Hudson, James I., M.D., and Pope, Harrison G., Jr., M.D. "Affective Spectrum Disorder: Does Antidepressant Response Identify a Family of Disorders with a Common Pathophysiology?" *American Journal of Psychiatry* 147 (May 1990): 5.

Kagan, D. M., and Squires, R. L. "Eating Disorders Among Adolescents: Patterns and Prevalence." *Adolescence* 19, no. 73 (Spring 1984): 15–29.

Kantor, Shepard J., M.D. "Transference and the Beta-adrenergic Receptor: A Case Presentation." *Psychiatry* 52, February 1989.

Kashani, Javad H., et al. "Correlates of Suicidal Ideation in a Community Sample of Children and Adolescents." *Journal of Child and Adolescent Psychiatry* 28, no. 6 (November 1989).

Kashani, J. H.; Beck, N. C.; Hoeper, E. W.; Fallahi, C.; Corcoran, C. M.; McAllister, J. A.; Rosenberg, T. K.; and Reid, J. C. "Psychiatric Disorders in a Community Sample of Adolescents." *American Journal of Psychiatry* 144 (1987): 584–89.

Khantzian, E. J. "The Self-Medication Hypothesis of Addictive Disorders: Focus on Heroin and Cocaine Dependence." *American Journal of Psychiatry* 142 (1985).

Klerman, G. L. "The Psychiatric Patient's Right to Effective Treatment: Implications of *Osheroff* v. *Chestnut Lodge*." *American Journal of Psychiatry* 147 (4 April 1990): 409–18.

Kovacs, Maria, Ph.D. "The Natural History and Course of Depressive Disorders in Childhood." *Psychiatric Annals* (1985).

Kupfer, David J., M.D. "Mood Disorders: Pharmacologic Prevention of Recurrences." *American Journal of Psychiatry* 142, April 1985.

Marcus, Eric. "Integrating Psychopharmacotherapy, Psychotherapy, and Mental Structure in the Treatment of Patients with Personality Disorders and Depression." *Psychiatric Clinics of North America* 3, no. 2 (June 1990).

Markowitz, Laura M. "Better Therapy through Chemistry?" *The Family Therapist Networker*, May/June 1991.

McElroy, Susan, M.D., et al. "Pharmacological Treatment of Kleptomania and Bulimia Nervosa." *Journal of Clinical Psychopharmacology* 9, no. 5 (October 1989).

McElroy, Susan L., M.D.; Hudson, James I., M.D.; Pope, Harrison G., Jr., M.D.; and Keck, Paul E., Jr., M.D. "Kleptomania: Clinical Characteristics and Associated Psychopathology." *Psychological Medicine* 21 (1991), 93–108.

Mitchell J. E.; Pyle, R. L.; and Eckert, E. D. "Frequency and Duration of Binge-Eating Episodes in Patients with Bulimia." *American Journal of Psychiatry* 138 (1981): 835–36.

Mitchell, J. E.; Pyle, R. L.; Eckert, E. D.; and Hatsukami, D. "A Comparison Study of Antidepressants and Structured Intensive Group Psychotherapy in the Treatment of Bulima Nervosa." *Archives of General Psychiatry* 47, no. 2 (February 1990): 149–57.

Mitchell, James E., M.D.; Pyle, Richard L., M.D.; Eckert, Elke D., M.D.; Hatsukami, Dorothy, Ph.D.; Pomeroy, Claire, M.D.; and Zimmerman, Robert, Ph.D. "Response to Alternative Antidepressants in Imipramine Nonresponders with Bulimia Nervosa." *Journal of Clinical Psychopharmacology* 9, no. 4 (August 1989).

Murphy, J. M.; McBride, W. J.; Lumeng, L.; and Li, T. K. "Alcohol Preference in Regional Brain Monoamine Contents of N/NIH Heterogenous Stock Rats." *Alcohol and Drug Research* 7 (1986).

Murphy, J. M.; Walter, M. B.; Gatto, G. J.; McBride, W. J.; Lumeng, L.; and Li, T. K. "Effects of Fluoxetine on the Intragastric Self-Administration of Ethanol in the Alcohol-Preferring P Line of Rats." *Alcohol* 5 (1988).

Oka, K.; Kantrowitz, J. D.; and Spector, S. "Isolation of Morphine from Toad Skin." *Proceedings of the National Academy of Sciences of the United States of America* 82 (1985).

Pert, C. B., and Snyder, S. H. "Opiate Receptors: Demonstration in Nervous Tissue." *Science* 79 (1973).

Peselow, Eric D., M.D.; Robins, Clive, Ph.D.; Block, Paul, Ph.D.; Barouche, Faouzia, M.D.; and Fieve, Ronald R., M.D. "Dysfunctional Attitudes in Depressed Patients Before and After Clinical Treatment and in Normal Control Subjects." *American Journal of Psychiatry* 147 (April 1990): 4.

Pollack, Mark H., M.D., and Rosenbaum, Jerrold F., M.D. "Management of Antidepressant-Induced Side Effects: A Practical Guide for the Clinician." *Journal of Clinical Psychiatry* 48 (January 1987): 1.

Puig-Antich, Joaquim, M.D., et al. "Psychosocial Functioning in Prepubertal Major Depressive Disorders." *Archives of General Psychiatry* 42 (1985): 500–573.

Regier, Darrel A., M.D., M.P.H.; Hirschfeld, Robert M. A., M.D.; Goodwin, Frederick K., M.D.; Burke, Jack D., Jr., M.D., MPH.; Lazar, Joyce B., M.A.; and Judd, Lewis L., M.D. "The NIMH Depression Awareness, Recognition, and Treatment Program: Structure, Aims, and Scientific Basis." *American Journal of Psychiatry* 145 (November 1988): 11.

Strober, M., and Carlson, G. "Bipolar Illness in Adolescents with Major Depression: Clinical, Genetic, and Psychopharmacologic Predictors in a Three-to-Four-Year Prospective Follow-up Investigation." *Archives of General Psychiatry* 39 (1982).

Taylor, D. L.; Mathew, R. J.; Ho, B. T.; and Weinman, M. L. "Serotonin Levels and Platelet Uptake During Premenstrual Tension." *Neuropsychobiology* 12 (1984): 16–18.

Teicher, Martin H., M.D., et al. "Emergence of Intense Suicidal Preoccupation During Fluoxetine Treatment." *American Journal of Psychiatry*, February 1990.

Weiss, Roger D., M.D.; Mirin, Steven M., M.D.; Griffin, Margaret L., Ph.D.; and Michael, Jacqueline L., M.S.W. "Psychopathology in Cocaine Abusers: Changing Trends." *Journal of Nervous and Mental Disease* 176, no. 12 (1988).

Weiss, Roger D., M.D., and Mirin, Steven M., M.D. "The Dual

Diagnosis Alcoholic: Evaluation and Treatment." *Psychiatric Annals* 9 (May 1989): 5.

———. "Tricyclic Antidepressants in the Treatment of Alcoholism and Drug Abuse." *Journal of Clinical Psychiatry* 50, suppl. no. 7 (July 1989): 4–9; discussion, 9-11.

Wells, Kenneth B., et al. "The Function and Well-Being of Depressed Patients." *Journal of the American Medical Association* 7 (August 18, 1989).

Yapko, Michael D. "A Therapy of Hope." *Family Therapist Networker*, May/June 1991.